BIG SAUSAGE

RICK KRIZMAN

ACME Press

Copyright © 2025 Rick Krizman

The moral right of the author has been asserted.

All rights reserved.
No part of this publication may be reproduced, stored in a retrieval system, or transmitted, in any form or by any means, without the prior permission in writing of the publisher, nor be otherwise circulated in any form of binding or cover other than that in which it is published and without a similar condition including this condition being imposed on the subsequent purchaser.

Published by ACME Press

Typesetting services by BOOKOW.COM

for Debra

Epigraph

I'm not shouting, I'm Croatian
-Anonymous

Part 1

1

On a brisk and bright Sunday morning in 1931, Vlado Novosel strode up Strawberry Hill, looking forward to a plate of fried eggs and pickled anchovies and a few quiet minutes with the morning paper. He pretended not to hear the lamenting voice calling his name, which could only be Stefani. Whatever she wanted, now was not the time. In fact, now was never the time. So now—seeing her layered up like an overdressed snowman and pumping after him faster than he thought possible—he remembered he'd forgotten his gloves, which meant his fingers were cold, and the rest of him as well. He ducked down an alley, then up Eighth Street to the safe harbor of Morty's, thinking about an Irish coffee for his hands, and something a little more for his insides.

Stuck on the Kansas side of Kansas City, Morty's didn't benefit from the "Pendergast dispensation," the political system across the river that guaranteed the free flow of booze, Eighteenth Amendment be damned. No sign advertised the joint, a former dry-goods store that had tanked when everyone ran out of money. Vlado preferred Morty's at night, when you didn't so much notice the peeling wallpaper and grimy linoleum floor. By day, the hazy light meandering along the sagging pine shelves, smeared mirror, and bottles of murky wine and homemade rakija painted a disheartening picture. But Sunday mornings were sacred, as it were, which meant Inky and Bootnose and a rogues gallery of cutters from the plant were perched at the bar, their wives at Mass. Next to a tiny dance floor, Morty hunched over the cathedral radio, turning dials and spitting Croatian curses. *Mali vrag* if he should ever miss his precious tamburitzans, with their plucking and trilling that sounded less like music and more like Dorothy Penny's chicken coop on a hot afternoon.

"Probably a loose tube," Vlado told him.

"You the expert?"

"We'll see." Vlado shook the walnut cabinet, listening for a rattle. He gave it a kick next to its *Majestic* logo, and his foot went right through the flimsy wooden speaker grill. "Well, so what? It doesn't work anyway." He rubbed at a scuff on his new boot.

The front door squeaked, and anything Morty might have said was interrupted by the chilly breeze that blew Stefani into the room. She was panting and glistening with sweat, her cheeks flushed. Vlado steered her into a booth and flashed two fingers at Morty.

"You're looking well, Stef."

"Cut the crap, Vlado. I can't pretend for much longer."

"I have no idea what you mean."

Stefani huffed out a breath and inched her coat open to where Vlado could see her poochy belly straining against the thin threads of her frock.

"I always liked your ma's sarma," Vlado said.

"That's no cabbage roll in there."

Morty appeared with glasses and a bottle, and Stefani closed her wrap.

"You're looking well, Stef," Morty said.

"Oh, for God's sake."

Morty went back to his radio, and Vlado draped an arm around Stefani.

"No kidding, Stef, you really do look nice. And well fed, which is a good thing because then who knows, right? Like Joe's wife. Last time she was, you know, nobody could even tell. Joe about shit himself. He comes home one day and there's this other kid."

When Stefani didn't laugh, he went on. "Seriously, who can tell what's going on under all this?" He repositioned her shawl over her new and improved cleavage.

She pulled his hand inside her coat and laid it on her belly, and Vlado felt the tight melon skin that in no way resembled an excess of cabbage or potatoes. He looked at her face, at how the new fat in her cheeks smoothed over her scolding look, how her thin lips puffed out like a kiss, and thinking that Stefani really was prettier than he usually gave her credit for, he slid his hand upward, happy that at least now they wouldn't have to worry about the timing and whatnot. She slapped him away.

"Vlado, you're a thirty . . . thirty . . . however the hell old you are, and let me just tell you, what am I supposed to do?"

"Okay, not that this is my business at all, I mean, you've got a problem, I can see." But was it his problem? Necessarily? Of course not. Well . . . He leaned in. "I know this guy, Mike Stipovich, you know Stipovich? We play baseball together, and sometimes this other guy, Dmitri, shows up, Russian obviously, who's a doctor with a side business—"

"Get away from me!" Stephanie pounded his shoulder surprisingly hard and elbowed him out of the booth. She looked like she had something more to say . . . but apparently not, and the same chilly breeze that had blown her in sucked her back out the door. Vlado drained his drink and reached for hers. Inky shot him an amused look from his barstool, rubbing the wine-stain birthmark on his neck as one might stroke a beard or twirl a mustache during a moment of deep thought.

"It's the hormones," Inky said, with a knowing tilt of his head. As if his marriage to Tereza Lesac made him the expert. Maybe it did. In fact, Vlado didn't feel so great either, guy hormones maybe. Like most Sunday mornings, he was already dreading the coming week, chopping up steers and pigs and freezing his ass off at the plant. He dragged over to the bar where he laid down a couple bills, buttoned his faded herringbone overcoat, and tightened his scarf. He tapped the radio with his toe and Morty flinched. "Don't worry, I'll fix that for you," Vlado said, then shrugged out the door, afraid of what he might find but hoping for the best.

The bells of St. John's pealed the noon hour. Smoke curled into the gray sky from the clapboard bungalows along Eighth Street, and Vlado could smell the first hints of roast lamb and baking bread drifting out of invisible kitchens, reviving his appetite. He squinted up and down the street. Stefani was nowhere in sight, but still, he wouldn't want to run into Lydia at a time like this.

5

2

At five o'clock the next morning Vlado's back and fingers were already aching as he shivered onto the trolley that crossed the river to the packing house. There, he followed a line of men clad in coveralls into the chilled and cavernous Armour shed. He found his assigned carving station and began stropping his blades, inhaling the metallic stench of blood and guts that discharged from the wooden carving tables and stained floors and unwashed coveralls. After ten years it was almost comforting, a familiar part of him, always there no matter how hard Sophie scrubbed his clothes or how long he lingered in a hot bathtub. The same aroma perfumed Morty's every night and every weekend—a holy trinity of blood, sweat and alcohol.

Vlado's activity for the day would involve pig heads: three quick swipes at the neck with a boning knife, then the next one. A horn blew, the line clanked into motion, and a line of hogs swung toward him, dangling by their back feet. For an accomplished swordsman like Vlado the worst part of the job was the hypnotic repetition, always the same whether he was slitting cattle necks or halving carcasses or cleaving off pigs' heads, but every time he caught himself drifting off, he thought of his friend Lubo, who was missing the two middle fingers of his left hand. Today he struggled to focus, but his eyes kept blurring, his thoughts drifting to Stefani and her swollen belly, which prompted a stab of dread that tightened his grip on the knife.

The following Sunday afternoon, Vlado and his cousin Joe huddled in the back yard of Joe's new house to sample their latest batch of rakija. Joe wanted to duplicate the plum brandy his dad used to make in Zagreb, which would be a dubious achievement, thought Vlado, who recalled their teen years puking it all up into the Sava River. If Vlado had his way, they'd toss in some coriander or dandelion greens, or figs even, all part of a running argument as to who made the best or worst hooch, as if there was any real difference.

In deference to the damp breeze off the Kaw River, they dragged the wrought iron table and chairs close to the garage. Joe's garage. And a house to go with it. Somehow Joe'd come up with all this on the same crap wages they both eked out from those greedy pigstickers at Armour. Joe had tried to explain it, that somehow you didn't have to pay for the whole thing, but Vlado didn't get the point of banks. To him, money was a tangible thing. Every two weeks he cashed his paycheck and kept the roll of bills in his pocket. He paid his rent in cash and doled out the rest regretfully until the roll could be replenished two weeks later.

Joe held a bottle up to the greyed-out sun and peered with one eye at the amber liquor. "Who knows, maybe Stefani did it with somebody else."

"Why would you say that?" The idea stabbed Vlado in the heart. No way had Stefani been cheating on him. It was bad enough that he and Lydia—no, forget Lydia. That had been a mistake, right?

Martina came out the kitchen door with a watering pot and moved, maybe slower than necessary, toward a bed of wilting geraniums. Joe leaned in to Vlado.

"You could tell her dad it's a virgin birth. Maybe that's the new little baby Jesus in there."

Vlado would have laughed, but for the image of Stefani's dad. Ivan the Terrible, they called him, a giant of a guy who was never happy to see Vlado, and the feeling was mutual. Vlado wished he could pretend Stefani was a virgin, but of course he knew better. So, no baby Jesus.

Martina was holding the can over the flowerbed, but no water was coming out and her head was cocked their way. Vlado whispered to Joe, "All right, it could be mine." He waved his arm like a magician. "But who knows? The problem with Stefani is—"

"The problem with Stefani is you." Martina turned and pointed the watering can at him and wagged it like an accusing finger. "Do they have to fix you like a goddam steer?"

She came at Vlado and poked him in the ribs with the spout. "Go on, there's already enough poor souls and I can only say so many goddam rosaries!" She jabbed once more and Vlado scrambled out of his chair, reaching for his glass, but Martina slapped it off the table and into the bed of geraniums.

"I know you'll think of something, Joey," Vlado called behind him.

"What do I know, Vlado? Maybe you should get on a boat again and go to some new place."

Vlado sulked back toward the house on Barnett St. where he rented a room from Martina's sister Sophie, who was also good for a daily supper and some laundry consideration. Had he stuck around to listen to Martina, he would have heard her go on yet again about what a womanizer he was, how he had no regard for the feelings of others, how she didn't want to stand too close to the edge when he was dragged down to hell. He wanted to say she had the wrong idea about him, but then, maybe she had a point. He only wished he was as much of a player as apparently everyone thought he was. But women were complicated, and above all he enjoyed the simplicity of his life; when he wasn't freezing his ass off at Armour, he was free to come and go, to see who he wished, and nobody much cared. Not so different from when he was a kid in Zagreb, before the Great War fucked everything up.

A light glowed behind the front window shade, where Sophie would be enjoying her afternoon tea, and he hesitated, thinking he'd get a sharp look, because if Martina knew, then who didn't? Well, *he* didn't, for one. He thought back and tried to piece it together, but each day rolled into the next. How many times with Stefani? Not that many, and he'd been careful. Except the one night when he might have screwed up. Actually did screw up. And when was that, exactly? She probably had it in her diary, had done the math. And then there was Lydia somewhere in the middle of all this. Which won't matter anymore, he thought sadly. Lydia, with her mysterious ways, just beyond his reach. Except the one time. But why obsess on all this? Life was about moving forward, regardless. Otherwise, he'd still be in Zagreb, or worse, buried in some trench in Serbia with a mouth full of dirt and a bullet in his forehead. Onward, he said to himself, dragging his thoughts past the house and away from any prying eyes peering out of the curtained living rooms along Barnett.

At the top of the hill, St. John's pointed a cross-tipped finger toward heaven where a moody cloud was spitting out some drizzle. Forget Morty's—enough about the goddam radio—and he didn't feel like being the token Croat at McGowan's. St. John's seemed safe enough, everybody having done their holy business for the day, so he slipped into the darkened church and sat in a back pew to think things over.

Vlado had never been much for prayer. His every personal message to God had always been some version of *Now what?*—exactly what he was wondering now. Light from the rack of red votives flickered beneath the statue of the Blessed Virgin, all beatific, hands folded, gazing into the merciful distance. But meanwhile her right foot was crushing the head of a snake! *She knows too.* He could just make out the Stations of the Cross hanging on the stone pillars and thought about Jesus taking that long walk up the hill. Now there was a guy who just kept moving forward, hoisting the cross and not worrying if he fell or not. A man with a purpose. A mission, so to speak. Of course, look what it got him.

A door squeaked open in the front of the church and Dorothy Penny floated out of the confessional. She was an angelic vision in a red polka-dot dress and tilted beret, auburn waves spilling over her lashy eyes, along with other assets Vlado could only guess at. He'd gone out with her for a while, but after a few fruitless evenings fumbling with her endless buttons, she made certain things clear, and that was that. Now what possible sin would she need to confess to a priest? Had he missed something? She walked straight and prim up the aisle and he slouched down, but too late—she pointed a finger and flicked it upward. *Holy crap, this town,* he thought, then realized he was still wearing his cap. He took it off, and she glided by without speaking.

Vlado eyed the confessional, thinking that if you confessed the sin and were forgiven for the sin, the sin would in fact be erased, which meant it never happened in the first place, right? Emboldened by this thought, he shuffled toward the open door and into the tiny house where he knew Father Kovac was sitting in darkness, just dying for some guilty soul to wander into his lair. Vlado worried that by entering the confessional he might have given up his "presumption of innocence," a phrase he'd read in the *Star* regarding the trial of some mob flunky who'd been caught standing over a body holding a gun and wiping blood splatters off his white shirt. But there'd been another thing about "plausible deniability," which apparently meant the legal right to say you didn't do it. Concluding that the law was probably on his side, Vlado closed the door and hunched in the darkness.

The panel slid open and there was Fr. Kovac's dim profile, like a face on a coin, his judicial nose hooked downward. Vlado was thankful that the screen between them guaranteed his own invisibility.

"I haven't seen you around much, Vladimir," said Fr. Kovac, before Vlado could even croak out a "Bless me, Father."

"Well, I guess I've been busy."

"So it seems."

Vlado wanted to kick himself. *Of course Kovac knew.* That's what he did all day, listen to everybody's secrets. Stefani had likely beaten him to the punch.

"So even if you know what's going on, you can't tell anybody, right?" No answer, so Vlado went on, "I mean, it's like attorney-client privilege, isn't it?"

"Vlado, if you yourself tell me something, I am forbidden by Church law to divulge it to any living soul."

"But if somebody else told you . . ."

"I do have other clients, as you might say."

"So, you know about Stefani."

It was so quiet Vlado could hear the whistling of Kovac's nose hairs.

"Is there something you want to tell me about Miss Lovick?" the priest finally asked.

"Well, apparently she's in the way."

"Of what, exactly?"

"No, I mean *the way*. Like the way a family is, if you get my meaning."

"She comes from a nice family."

"That's my problem right there." Vlado wondered if Kovac was just messing with him.

"Just say it, Vladimir. If you don't say it, I'm not obliged to keep it a secret."

So that's how it works, he thought. He could cop a plea, turn state's evidence against himself, and they couldn't use it in court. Maybe he could bargain Kovac down to some Hail Marys, then go and sin no more.

"All right. I did a thing with Stefani. And then another thing happened, apparently, as a result, even though I'd committed a second sin of trying to not make it happen, if you know what I mean."

"You used a rubber to have sex with Stefanija."

It was a relief to hear Fr. Kovac lay it out like that, although he wasn't sure whether the sinfulness of the second thing mitigated against the first. The fact that his protection had slipped off at a crucial moment perhaps weighed against the second sin while making the third more likely. He supposed it didn't matter, because you can only go to hell once.

"I guess it's the third thing I'm worried about now."

"You think she's having your baby?"

"If you're going to make me say it, okay, I'll say it. She's got my little baby in there."

Vlado waited for Kovac to yell at him or tell him it'd be okay. Or maybe the whole booth was going to burst into flames.

"So . . ." Kovac drew out the word. "You think it's yours."

"Is there reason to think otherwise?" Vlado didn't like what Kovac's doubtful tone implied.

Kovac coughed. "A word to the wise," he said, and while Vlado waited to hear what that word might be, Kovac muttered a Glory Be and waved his hand in the air. "Go now, and sin no more," he said, and the panel snapped shut.

Vlado sat still in the dark, trying to piece together what had just happened, when the panel opened again. "Ten Hail Marys," Kovac said, and Vlado got out of there.

3

Vlado was grateful that the Hail Marys miraculously acquitted him in the hereafter, but the problem was the here-and-now. On Monday, he spent the morning slicing T-bones, telling himself with each stroke that Stefani had probably done it a bunch of times after him. Tuesday night, at Morty's after work, he stared at every single guy along the bar for some sign he was being played as a chump. Wednesday at Armour, he ground up scraps that had been swept off the floor and stuffed them into pig entrails while telling himself that, except for some non-Catholic events only he knew about, Stefani was in fact a good girl. The following three days he repeated the same round of ruminations, which only confused him more, so Sunday afternoon, once he figured Stefani's family had finished their dinner and Ivan the Terrible was napping, he found himself climbing the worn concrete steps to their tiny bungalow.

The last of the fallen maple leaves skittered across the porch, pushed by a damp breeze. Lace curtains hung crooked behind the windows on either side of a rusted screen door. Vlado pulled on the latch, and a loud squeak announced his presence to the entire neighborhood. He paused for a moment, working up the nerve to knock, when the door swung open, and Stefani squinted at him out of the darkness. She muttered something that might have been a curse, then hurried out, steered him over to the porch swing, and sat down heavily next to him. Vlado hadn't decided what he would say to her, thinking he'd know at the time. But here was the time. His pulse throbbed in his forehead, and he could hear the nagging of Dorothy Penny's chickens over on the next block. A rooster crowed, and Stefani seemed to take that as her cue.

"I have nothing to say to you," she said. *Thank God.* But she went on. "I've thought about it, and the thing I'm *not* going to say to you is that you should feel sorry for me, or responsible for anything, or that, worst of all, you should think about marrying me, so if that's what you're here for you can just take off now."

"I thought you said you had nothing to say."

"I did. And I mean it."

"Well, I'm not thinking about marrying you, so you can stop worrying." He felt a flush of anger.

"Then why are you here?"

"Well, it's not so I can listen to some crap about you not marrying me."

He pushed up from the swing, turned from Stefani, and headed down the steps, leaving her to carry on with her wonderful life of not being married to him, because why would either of them want that?

Vlado tromped up the sidewalk, his thoughts misfiring. Instead of heading home, he cut down a path to the Kaw River where he kept a small rowboat stashed in the willows, just upstream from where the Kaw got sucked into the swift-flowing Missouri. On warm evenings he liked to sit in the boat with his cane pole, hook on some chicken liver or suet and toss the line into the eddying current, barely paying attention to the red and white bobber for a sign that a catfish had latched on. He never paddled out into the river itself, because why go to all the trouble?

But summer had fled, and Vlado sat shivering in the boat while the October sun dipped, the breeze sharpened, and the birds changed their song. Upstream a lone duck was paddling towards wherever ducks go at night. He tossed and retrieved his line, trying to let his mind drift like the bobber, but it kept snagging on one thought. *Why wouldn't she want to marry him?* Shouldn't it be up to him? Like everyone else, he had a decent job that he hated. Right? He was healthy, and women found him handsome, didn't they? He was clean, Croatian, and as Catholic as he needed to be, subject to shifting circumstances.

He'd been seeing Stefani off and on for several months, which mostly meant sneaking into her Aunt Josie's garage, knowing that dear old Auntie was deaf enough so they could do their business in peace. Otherwise, he was still free to man his seat at Morty's until last call, to go where he wanted and see who he wished. Of course, the only other woman he'd actually "seen" was Lydia, but just that once. He'd obsessed about Lydia for a long time—her flyaway black hair, her slim figure always draped in the latest fashion, her dark Myrna Loy eyes filled with the promise of things he had no inkling of. She lived on the other side of Quindaro but was regularly spotted here and there on the Hill, the subject of many Sunday morning discussions at Morty's. He never really believed such a woman would give him the time of day, so the night she appeared on a barstool next to him and ordered two rakijas . . . what else could he do? It was a mistake that anyone could make. Wasn't it? And who could blame him? Except for maybe Stefani. *Jebote.*

Incredible, he thought, how people got married all the time. Look at his cousin Joe, whose wife, Martina, was certainly no beauty queen. He recalled the day, already ten years ago, when he and Joe had been showing off on the high dive at the Strawberry Hill Swim Club. The four Vukovic sisters were lounging poolside beneath a large umbrella, and Vlado jokingly pointed out Martina, the youngest, shortest, and roundest of the bunch, who was waving around a cigarette and drowning out the other three with her cackling voice.

"There you go, Joey, the little one. But be careful, she might bite it right off."

Back then Joe was already balding and hadn't grown into his ears, still looking like the skinny seventeen-year-old who'd smuggled all his earthly possessions onto that boat in Rijeka.

Vlado steered him by the arm toward the battalion of Vukovic women.

"We could treat you ladies to an iced tea?" Vlado asked. *Was the English correct?* The sisters shaded their eyes.

"They don't drink iced tea," Martina replied.

"That's right, diving boy. We only like the hard stuff." Her sister Anna shot Vlado a demure look that the other two mimicked.

Martina scanned Joe up and down. "So, do you have the tea in your pocket?"

Vlado still had a copy of Joe's wedding picture. Martina's droopy eyes were framed by ringlets of black hair and a halo of white blooms, her pear-like figure wrapped in her mother's ample wedding dress. Next to her, in his vested suit and sporting a new mustache, Joe's expression was dark with resolve. Or maybe it was worry. And now, incredibly, after eight years and two kids, they still hadn't killed each other.

So it was possible. Stefani was a sweet girl. Wasn't she? She was several years younger, so she'd certainly defer to him in the ways of the world. After all, she'd just been learning her letters at St. John's when Vlado might well have been escaping the Austro-Hungarian Empire under fire, which would have been true if he and Joe had stuck around any longer. Stefani was going to have that little baby, and Vlado thought, what if it's a girl, and who would be responsible for insisting she be respected? Protecting her from people like, well, like himself he thought, then decided to stop thinking about it altogether.

But it was too late, and when Vlado tried to sleep that night, he kept seeing Stefani's sweet, plump face and honestly beautiful blue eyes.

4

Monday morning at nine sharp, Vlado waited on the sidewalk for Drago Grgch to draw back the retractable bars of the Jewelry Emporium.

"You look like a young man with a mission," Drago said. "Finally going to part with a buck and buy some earrings for that sweetie of yours? Cynthia?"

"Stefani. And no." Vlado had assembled a new trinity in his mind—priest, lawyer, and jeweler—three people a man could trust. He said, "This all falls under the protection of jeweler-client privilege, right?" Drago just stared at him. "Never mind, whatever. I need a ring. And don't tell anybody."

Thirty minutes later Vlado left, minus his watch and half of his roll of bills, fingering the tiny box in his pocket and already sick with what may or may not have been regret. He was late getting to the plant, where the Italian gave him the stink eye. The Italian was the floor manager who had the power to say if you'd be cutting pigs, cows, or heaven forbid, chickens. Or worse. He was always looking for a Croat to screw up, so it was best to stay invisible. But if you were late . . .

"Squeegee," the Italian said and smiled, displaying metal-capped teeth and too much happiness. He handed Vlado the pole with the rubber strip designed to sweep the pigs' blood into the grates after their necks had been sliced. The stink watered Vlado's eyes and the pointless drudgery of it made him wish he was in a trench somewhere fending off the Huns —well not really, but still, if nothing else, what a waste of perfectly wonderful blood, which, mixed with some rice and cooked just so . . . The worst was the smirky looks he was getting from all the neck slicers, who well knew that he was the best pig dissembler, could do the whole hog himself while they sat on the line and slit a thousand necks a day like a bunch of trained monkeys.

Three days later—after some badgering, which didn't work, and some begging, which did—Vlado convinced Stefani to meet him for dinner. When he got to Gino's, Stefani was already seated in a booth in the back. She had on the same baggy housedress she'd worn on Sunday, and her waist-length hair was tied up in some inscrutable knot. She held a crust of bread in one hand, while the other fiddled with a little vase holding a single yellow rose. Vlado sensed his own empty hands and slipped a rose from another table and presented it to Stefani with a look of feigned surprise.

"Looks like someone beat me to the punch."

"Good evening, Vladimir." Gino was there. He laid down two tomato-stained menus and plucked the flower from Vlado's hand.

"You're looking well, Stef," Vlado said. He busied himself with his napkin.

"Jesus, Vlado, if I looked any more 'well' there'd be two of me." She seemed about to cry, and Vlado felt a whiff of panic.

"It's okay, some nice spaghetti will make you feel better. It's Thursday, they got meatballs."

"Vlado, I don't know what you think—"

"First things first," he said and waved to Gino.

Vlado worked through a tangle of pasta and kept his mouth full to ward off any unnecessary chit-chat. He cleaned his plate with the last piece of the bread and washed it down with a glass of Gino's cloudy house wine. He eased back in his chair and watched Stefani poke at the rest of her spaghetti. How could someone who ate like a bird gain so much weight?

"You're not hungry?"

She hugged her belly and made a sour face.

Gino brought over a plate of yellow roll cake and two brandies.

"Here." Vlado nudged her glass. "Give the baby strong bones," he said and tossed back his. He wiped his face and folded his napkin in front of him and felt his trousers pocket for the outline of the little box. *Jebote*, what was he doing? Maybe Joe was right. It wasn't too late, was it? He could ease away from the table, back out the door, and hightail it off to the bus station to head off as far away as his remaining roll of bills would take him. Omaha needed butchers, right? But the hell with it, he wasn't going anywhere, and furthermore, there was no getting his money back for the ring. He opened his arms wide, like Jesus in a holy card.

"So, we have before us this blessed event. About which there's been some confusion."

"Oh, I can speak now?"

"It seems you've spoken to everyone else on the Hill about this, so why not me? I mean if you really think I'm the father then—"

"Vlado, just stop." Stefani bit her lip and looked down at the remnants of her spaghetti. "I saw Dr. Lesac yesterday. And I thought you'd be happy to know, the dates don't line up."

"Meaning?" But he knew what she meant.

"Meaning you're off the hook, so there's no reason for all this."

"You don't have to look so happy about it."

"Are you ever not sarcastic?" she said, and Vlado wondered if she wasn't being a little sarcastic herself.

"You're telling me it's not mine? That somebody else . . . while we were . . . ? Okay, then, who's the lucky guy?"

"I guess you are."

"Very funny."

"Well, *I'm* not laughing."

"You're not going to tell me, are you?"

"What does it matter, anyway?" She had the look of someone who may or may not be holding pocket aces. "Ovaltine."

"Come on, you just made that name up."

"No, you remember that guy, John Obersteen?"

Vlado had known Obersteen, an oafish, fast-talking salesman he'd run into at Morty's on occasion. "They call him Ovaltine? That's actually pretty funny. I haven't seen him around in a while."

"He got transferred to Topeka."

"That's convenient. You're telling me you did it with Johnny Ovaltine?"

She curled her lower lip down and sniffed back a possible tear.

"And that's his little package in there?"

She gave him an unconvincing nod.

"You don't seem too sure about it," he said.

"I know what I know," she said and placed her napkin on the table, indicating that the discussion was over.

Vlado folded his arms and leaned back in his chair and thought what a terrible poker player Stefani would be. If she was going to bluff, why would she pick some pathetic clown like Obersteen? He remembered him as a coarse loudmouth, with thick fingers that were always greasy from whatever he might have just shoved into his pie hole. Did she think he was an idiot? Jesus, just the thought . . .

"It doesn't matter whose it is," he said, *because why even argue the point?* He pulled the box out and slid it toward Stefani. She looked more angry than surprised.

"You just don't get it, do you?" Her frown softened, and she placed a warm hand on Vlado's cheek. "You know I've always been crazy about you, Vlado—" she said, "but no, just no."

"I'll give you a couple days to think about it." He slipped the box back into his pocket. "Don't worry, the offer will probably still be good."

Vlado resolved to ignore her for exactly two days, if she could even hold out that long. Women wanted something all the more if they were worried they couldn't have it. He imagined her at home, crying even, missing him, and wondering if she hadn't made some huge mistake.

Forty-eight hours to the minute later, he pulled off his work apron, stopped by his flat, rummaged through his dresser drawer for the box, hiked over to Stefani's house, and knocked decisively on the front door. It opened and Ivan the Terrible filled the space, unshaven, in a bathrobe, with an unlit cigar stub poking out beneath his handlebar mustache.

"I don't think you're here to see me, are you?" he grumbled in his rough, up-country Croatian.

"Ivo, who's there?" Mrs. Lovick, a tiny thing, edged around her husband. "Oh, hello, Vlado. Have you eaten?" Vlado caught a whiff of cinnamon and yeasty bread, but she made no move to invite him in.

"I'm fine, Mrs. Lovick, thanks. I was hoping I could see Stefani."

"She's not here. She's gone to visit her aunt."

"I see."

"Her aunt is very ill."

"I'm so sorry."

"Next time she calls, I'll say that you were asking about her."

Vlado was pretty sure that wouldn't happen, that in several months Stefani would return, refreshed from her trip, looking well as usual, and normal life would resume.

"Thank you, anyway," he said. Mrs. Lovick slipped back into the house and Ivan stood there looking down his considerable nose from his considerable height. He leaned down to Vlado.

"Paola," he grumbled.

"Paola?" Vlado asked.

"And Vlado, no offense, but I think Ivan is a better name than Vladimir." Ivan followed this with what was either a laugh or a belch.

Vlado wasn't halfway to the curb before he figured it out. He'd once been to Paola, a tiny town an hour south, with his softball team, where they played on the diamond at the Sisters of Ursula convent. He recalled the adjoining orphanage.

First thing the next morning, Vlado made the short walk to the Trailways on Minnesota Ave., drawing slowly on a cigar like a condemned man postponing the inevitable. Thirty minutes later, he was on a bus heading south.

5

The sign read "Welcome to Paola, Kansas, pop. 2006 and growing!!" Right away the flat fields gave way to elm-lined streets fronting white farm-style houses, here a church, there a grocery store. Vlado liked rural Kansas and its tiny towns where everything was so organized —purposeful, he thought—and told himself that he, too, could be part of this tidier world. Married to Stefani. A baby girl. He could see him and Joe opening their own butcher shop, then another, maybe one across the river. They'd steal some guys off the Armour floor, show them the ropes and pay them a good wage, and all he'd have to do was count the money every week—half for him, half for Joe, and half of his half for Stefani, plus a third half of the whole deal set aside for his baby, who he'd name Janet or some other American name. Plus, maybe a son (Ivan, to keep the peace), and then another girl, to round it out. They'd all move off the Hill, maybe even to Paola, where nobody spoke Croatian, to a house with a wide, flat yard, a swing set, and a weeping willow tree for climbing (and falling out of, he already worried). He'd smoke a long cigar on Sunday afternoons, watching his kids play, Stefani fat and happy in the kitchen . . .

Vlado got off the bus and squinted into the late morning sun. Across the street a neon sign above a blacked-out window said "Eat." It might as well say "Speakeasy." He figured Paola was like the Hill, where everyone made their own hooch and didn't give a fig about where or when they drank it. As long as you went through the motions, the cops were off chasing real criminals: kids with overdue library books, dogs off their leashes, the occasional mob murder across the river.

Tempted as he was, Vlado was on a mission, so he passed up "Eat," and after a short walk and more than a few sips from his flask, he was gazing through the arched iron gates and up the long driveway of the

Ursuline convent. A trim lawn and a parade of rusty pin-oaks led to the two-story brick-and-steepled home of the Sisters of Ursula of the Appearance of the Blessed Virgin at Lourdes, as the brass plaque advertised. He examined the Latin, a crest of some sort: "bring us your something, something, little lambs, something." He imagined what his own family crest might be. Maybe a crossed knife and fork over an American flag? He fingered the box in his pocket again—*why did it feel so heavy?*

Vlado felt the call of nature and slipped behind a cypress to pee. He was still zipping up when he came back around and saw a saintly black-and-white creature walking his way—or sliding, maybe, because he couldn't see her feet beneath her black robe. She was tiny enough that he could picture a breeze catching that white sail-like contraption on her head—a whippet? a whimpey?—and carrying her off into the grey autumn sky. Her head was down, and her hands were hidden in her robe—one hand no doubt clutching a rosary, the other probably a ruler. He could imagine, or remember actually, the sound of that ruler slapping against skin, his own skin if he had to be honest, and took a few instinctive steps backwards. She wheeled silently past him and pivoted toward the gate, where one hand emerged with a huge key.

"Let me help you, Sister." He leaned into the heavy gate, and she frowned and drew one finger over her tight lips. Vlado made the same sign over his own lips. He took stock of his dusty dungarees and sweat-stained shirt and whispered, "I'm to report to the groundskeeper." She gave him a familiar look, one that Vlado associated with distrust, and pointed to a shack in the far corner of the campus. The gate clanged shut behind them. Vlado thanked her and took note of her young, pretty face. He wondered about other things, so special they had to be hidden under layers of cloth and cardboard. Then he thought about having to confess to Fr. Kovac again and decided to wonder about different things instead.

The nun glided off down the promenade, and Vlado strode across the lawn toward the shack like he had real business. He imagined countless pairs of eyes watching from the windows, curious about this handsome man. *Ladies, please, one at a time.* He grabbed a rake that leaned against the shack and stabbed at the leaves strewn around the side of the convent, working his way toward the back.

He heard a cracking sound, like a bat hitting a baseball. He peered around a bush and saw a nun running hell-bent, her veil trailing out like a witch's cape, while several other black-and-whites chased after what in fact was a baseball bouncing into the outfield of a ball diamond. A row of hefty young women, dressed like real people, sat in lawn chairs along the first base line. Vlado thought how much better they might look in their nun-suits, until it dawned on him who they were. One chair was empty.

There was a tap on his shoulder and Vlado must have made a surprised sound when he turned to see Stefani standing there.

"Be quiet, you dummy."

"Stef, you're looking—"

"Don't say it, Vlado I swear—"

"This is the last place you want to swear," he said. Stefani's hair was shorter, and she wore no makeup and had tired circles around her eyes.

"Have you been crying?" he asked.

"Of course I've been crying, what else is there to do around this dreadful place? What's that smell? You been drinking?"

Vlado pulled the flask from his pocket and held it out with an apologetic shrug. Stefani took it from him, sniffed, and tipped it back for longer than Vlado thought might be wise. She flushed and choked a little.

"Our latest batch," he said.

"You and Joe, between the two of you—"

"Admit it, you missed me."

"It's been two whole days."

"Don't I know it. And frankly, Stef, I'm not happy about it. I'm not happy seeing you here, obviously unhappy. And little Janet—"

"Who is Janet?"

". . . or whatever I decide to name her, or we decide to name her, because after all, she's yours too."

"You're out of your mind."

There was another crack of the bat, and a ball crashed through the bushes and dribbled down next to their feet like a live hand grenade.

"Come on, they'll kill me." Stefani tugged at Vlado.

"Marry me."

"What?"

"I said, marry me."

"You're always telling me what to do. Now I'm telling you, we have to get out of here."

Vlado didn't budge. "I'm not *telling* you, I'm *asking* you." He fiddled in his pocket for the box, which felt larger than he remembered. "Okay, I can see you want the whole deal."

He dropped to one knee, held out the box to her and opened it. Inside were the silver cufflinks he wore to funerals and weddings. Stefani cocked her head and squinted at him, the way he'd seen dogs do. *Jesus.* He stuffed the box back in his pocket and picked up the baseball. "With this ring I do thee wed," he said, and folded her hands around the ball and pressed them into her bosom, then wrapped his arms around her and went in for the kiss. She dropped the ball and kissed him back. He felt the heat of her cheeks, the soft press of her chest, the promising bump of her belly, the strength of her arms squeezing him like a vise. He smelled her hair and skin, salty from the sun, smelled the grass and blooming flowers, heard more birds singing, music somewhere; he felt every hair on his arms standing straight up, his insides spinning like a merry-go-round.

"Okay. Now let's go," Stefani whispered.

"Okay what?" Vlado's pulse pounded in his temples.

"Vlado, come *on*." She tugged at him.

"Okay *what*?" Everything around him was humming and swaying.

Stefani held her arms out in an expression of disbelief. "Okay *okay.* I'm saying it."

"*Jebote.* Saying *what?*" He couldn't get any air.

She tipped her head back, closed her eyes. "I'll marry you, Vlado."

Vlado turned toward the shrub and puked out a half flask of homemade rakija. When he opened his eyes, he and his brand-new fiancée were surrounded by a herd of black and white creatures staring as if he might have just gotten off the boat from Mars. One held a baseball bat and didn't look too happy. Vlado picked up the ball he'd dropped and flung it as hard as he could into the air.

"It's a high, fly ball to centerfield . . ." he shouted in his best radio voice. Stefani giggled, he took her arm, and the two of them hightailed it toward the driveway. If there was any justice at all in God's green earth, the front gate would be unlocked.

6

Fr. Kovac was the last person Vlado had to see or wanted to see. He'd cleared the air with Mrs. Lovick, who had resigned herself to the inevitable; he'd suffered a round of shots with Ivan, who seemed a little less Terrible thanks to his approaching grandfatherhood. Vlado would take Stefani to city hall on Monday to do the paperwork, and hopefully the church was available the following Saturday.

"I'm sorry, Vladimir, it just doesn't happen that way." Kovac sat behind his desk and spoke as if he were explaining something to a child.

"Father, we have a legitimate reason for wanting to speed things along, and I'm pretty sure you know what that is."

"In truth, Vlado, the church frowns on marrying just because you got a girl pregnant."

"There's a better reason?"

"Marriage is a sacred commitment and mustn't be entered into for reasons other than the love between a man and a woman. The baby has to come, then you wait a year. That's church law."

"But that's only if I'm the father, right? Who says I'm the one who got Stefani pregnant?"

"I'm pretty sure you said it. In the holy confines of the confessional."

"If you're wrong about something it doesn't mean you're lying, right?" Vlado knew that lying in the confessional was probably a mortal sin but hoped that fibbing to a priest in his office at least wouldn't send him to hell. "What I'm saying is, what if it's not mine? I mean, here's this young lady who happens to be pregnant, and I want to marry her. The sooner the better, as I'm saying, for the sake of all concerned." Why was this simple solution to everyone's problems so hard to understand?

Fr. Kovac folded his hands prayer-like and rested his chin on his thumbs and stared into Vlado. "So, is it yours or not?"

Vlado returned his stare. "You tell me."

Kovac leaned back and exhaled loudly. "You know I'm not at liberty—"

"Right, but I'm just guessing you might have had one of your private conversations with Stefani about Johnny Ovaltine."

"Ovaltine?"

"Obersteen."

"Oh, John Obersteen, yes. They call him Ovaltine?" Kovac's eyes brightened, but only briefly, and Vlado knew he had him.

"So, if it's not mine, then it's just like a regular marriage, right?" He'd play poker with Kovac any day.

"Fine," Kovac said, then opened is hands in a gesture of helplessness. "But it's still six months, minimum. There's the classes, we need to publish the bans, and so forth."

Vlado tugged thoughtfully on his lower lip. "Okay, six months it is." He stood and turned toward the door. "And who knows, in the meantime, maybe Stefani will turn out not to be pregnant after all."

He had one foot in the hall when he heard, "Vladimir, wait."

Vlado turned back toward Kovac, who wore a pinched expression like he'd just eaten a bad oyster.

Kovac pulled a book and pencil out of a drawer. "We'll publish the third bans in Sunday's bulletin, and I'll see the two of you in church a week from Saturday, eleven o'clock."

"And the parish hall—"

"Is not available."

Vlado had squeegeed his way back into the good graces of the Italian, which meant he could rejoin Joe and go back to whittling carcasses down to the familiar chops and roasts and ribs he would later have the privilege of purchasing at the A&P. Today they were trimming spareribs, squaring them up to be wrapped and weighed. They worked quickly in the cold, littering the floor with globs of fat and gristle that the Chinaman would later sweep up for the sausage hopper. Vlado told Joe the whole business with Stefani.

"Unbelievable. You're marrying your girlfriend?" Joe said.

"Hey, don't have a heart attack," Vlado said. "And she's not my girlfriend."

Joe laughed. "I never thought I'd see it. I'm proud of you, little cousin. And Martina will be thrilled."

"Right, and you know how Martina likes to show off her back yard." He told Joe his idea about the party.

"It's November."

"So, we get a few more trash barrels and light them up. Plus, there's your front porch and the living room. If she balks, tell her Dorothy Penny offered her house."

"She'll never believe that."

"But it's true. She buttonholed me at the bus stop. She knew all about it. It makes me a little sad to say that I think she approves."

They paused for a moment out of respect for Dorothy Penny.

"Okay, I'll talk to Martina, but be prepared for the litany."

Vlado had heard the litany before, Martina's particular list of pains she was forced to suffer for the sins of others.

"No, that's just it, Joey. After this, I'm gonna be off the list for good. You'll see."

"And I suppose you think Martina will cook for everybody?"

"I've already thought about that, and no offense, but I figured we can do better than pigs' feet and bone soup."

Vlado sliced at a shoulder, cutting a little deeper than he should, and showed Joe the bit of meat stuck to the fat. "Whoops," he said and dropped it into the pocket of his apron. He repeated the move and Joe looked around and followed suit. By the time the whistle blew, both their pockets were stuffed with fat trimmings and meaty scraps. Vlado sliced two ribs off his last rack, stuck them down the front of his pants, and walked stiffly out of the plant.

That night they emptied their loot onto the worktable in Joe's garage. They sliced away any bones and hand-cranked the scraps through a grinder which spit out clumps of ground meat and fat. By then Martina and the boys were asleep, so they crept into the kitchen and sniffed around for additives—salt, black pepper, white pepper, sugar, other things they couldn't identify. Vlado grabbed a few heads of garlic.

"This'll take care of any undesirable smell."

Daily they repeated the process at the plant, filling their pockets, and duffel bags as well, and by the end of the week a row of wrinkly sausages hung from a line strung up in the tool shed behind Joe's garage. Underneath they positioned a barrel of glowing embers, and they fed in trimmings from Joe's cherry tree to keep up a cool haze of smoke.

The next day, they chose one of the reddened sausages and boiled it until it plumped out and perfumed Martina's kitchen with a stale-socks smell. Joe forked it out of the pan and sliced a couple of disks from the center. The sausage spit and steamed, squirting grease across the cutting board. Vlado poked at the inside garble of fat and pork like it might explode, sniffed at it, and tried to reimagine the stench as some exotic aroma. They each picked up one of the greasy pieces.

"On three?" Joe said. "One, two—"

"Hold on." Vlado reached above the sink for Joe's poorly hidden bottle of slivovitz and poured a splash into two growler glasses.

They solemnly drained their glasses. Then on Joe's "three," they each bit into their sample. Vlado was first overwhelmed by the taste of garlic and salt, followed by the firm resistance of the pork and the melted fat dribbling around inside his mouth. The meat rolled across his tongue and down the back of his throat until it changed from a mixture of spice and scraps and smoke into something profoundly pig-like. He swallowed, and only then did the pepper explode in his mouth like a time bomb. He took a deep breath and felt a heady vapor fill his lungs and leach into his bloodstream, finding its way to his heart where for a moment it was touch-and-go. He wondered if his own face looked as astonished as

Joe's, who grabbed the knife and furiously sliced at the rest of the link while Vlado reached for the slivovitz.

7

An organ was playing off somewhere, the sun was streaming bright through tall windows, and Vlado stood, with rakija-fortified resolve, as close to the altar as he'd ever been, listing as if he were still on the ship from Croatia, happy that his dear cousin had a firm grip on his arm. A parade of beautiful women moved up the aisle, somebody was throwing flower petals around; then the music swelled, and there was Stefani, all dressed up, looking small and round, hanging off the arm of Ivan, less terrible than ever in his stiff black suit, white shirt, and tie. Moreover, he appeared to be crying. They loomed closer, then Ivan kissed his daughter on top of the head and steered her toward Vlado, whose arm Joe pushed forward so Stefani could take it, and they both turned toward Fr. Kovac and his bad-oyster grimace. Vlado wondered if he was still annoyed but knew not to say anything. Joey had told him to keep quiet and repeat what Father says when it's his turn.

Two hours later, Vlado sat at a table in Joe and Martina's back yard, across from his beaming bride and scrunched between his new best pal Ivan and Stefani's mom. The afternoon was turning chilly, but no one seemed to mind. The slivovitz from breakfast lingered as a dull headache, partly relieved by the buckets of beer from Morty's that Joe was pouring for everyone. Morty himself had trucked his patched-up Majestic over to the patio, where it blasted out tamburitza music mixed with the occasional farm report and commercials for Ovaltine and First Wave Hair Oil. Martina and Dorothy Penny hefted bowls of slaw and boiled potatoes onto a long table where pans of steamed sausages sweated out a garlicky funk. Dinko Babic, Boxie Zellers, and a few of Vlado's other buddies from Armour drifted by to pay their respects, handshaking him a few bills and smooching Stefani on both cheeks, Inky lingering a little longer than Vlado might have preferred. Stritchie appeared at the table, all business in a vested suit and fat tie. He'd given the boys their first jobs back when, and now he handed Vlado a twenty-dollar bill and the keys to his roadster for the night. He wagged a single finger in front of Vlado, no doubt as a warning against any number of ways Vlado might screw all this up. Fr. Kovac, in his Count Dracula cassock and black biretta, commanded a card table in the back, flanked by Lubi Divac and Mae Jankovic, the three of them whispering and pointing in a technically non-confidential way.

"So, Vlado, you'll be moving in on Monday?" asked Stefani's mom.

"Actually, Mrs. Lovick—"

"Mom. Please call me Mom."

Vlado had never known his mother, who died two minutes after he was born. He barely remembered his dad—a bulldog of a guy with a huge handlebar mustache—who had been a firefighter, until a blaze at the Hotel Zagreb turned him into a hero and Vlado's ten-year-old self into an orphan. His Aunt Vera had taken him on and kept his belly full and the rain off his head. But she was a tall and opinionated woman, a good cook, and in every way unlike Stefani's mom.

"Actually, Mom," he said, *or should it be "fake-Aunt-Vera"?* "I was thinking of taking a few days, maybe borrow Stritchie's car for longer and go down to that new lake in the Ozarks."

Mrs. Lovick leaned in close to Vlado. "Do you think Stefani's up for a trip like that? In her condition?" she whispered, *like it was still a secret*. Across the table Vlado's new bride was a ruddy picture of well-fed health, glowing a little in her lacy dress, chewing a mouthful of sausage. She reached over and squeezed Vlado's hand.

"Mother knows best," she said and mimed a kiss.

"Maybe I should go without you?" Vlado joked, but nobody laughed.

"You really think you can take off work at this time," Stefani continued, serious now, "when you'll be having two mouths to feed?"

Vlado looked around the table and counted more than two mouths.

Loud static crackled from the driveway, then the smooth sounds of an orchestra filled the back yard, the mellow woodwinds of Guy Lombardo replacing the ratchety tamburitzans that had been croaking out of Morty's radio. Vlado squeezed out from between his newly minted set of parents and reached for Stefani.

"Time to dance with my bride," he said and led her into the driveway. People stepped back, he pulled her close and she lay her head on his chest, and they began to sway. His steps felt heavy, and Stefani's extra gravity was no help. Soon they were just rocking back and forth, not dancing at all, and Vlado wished someone else would join them, divert the attention. But everyone just watched, and Vlado sensed a general contentment in his surroundings, everybody happy, as if they were all part of it. *All in on it.* There were Ivan and fake-Aunt-Vera whispering together conspiratorially, the Armour guys nudging each other, Martina and Dorothy Penny giggling. Fr. Kovac sat back in his chair, with his bad-oyster face, arms folded, nested amidst his informants. Joe was moving around handing out shots of hooch. The music faded and Joe walked into the circle with a glass raised.

"On this solemn occasion . . ." he said, and everyone laughed, "a day we thought we'd never see . . ."

Vlado saw the laughter but couldn't hear it over the ringing in his ears. He stumbled toward Joe, snatched the glass out of his hand, and shot back the rakija. He grabbed Stefani's arm. "We gotta go," he whispered. Vlado steered his new bride out of the circle and down toward Stritchie's borrowed Speedster parked at the end of the drive, while the collective agents of his demise followed along, hooting and still laughing—with him or at him, it didn't matter. He herded Stefani in and squeezed next to her, then gassed it out of the drive and bounced along the potholes of Twenty-First Street as fast as six cylinders could take him. He swung onto Quindaro, heading toward the viaduct, and only then chanced a look at Stefani. She was crying and she pounded his arm hard enough to leave a bruise.

"I'm sorry, Stef, I couldn't do it," he said. "Too much excitement. Think of the baby. Besides, I could see Sinovic reaching for his accordion." She sniffed and hanked out a few more sobs, and Vlado draped an arm around her. "Come on, sweet potato, this is our night. Just you and me. Honestly, I'm sorry."

She pulled away and gave him a strange look. "What's the matter with you? You've never said you were sorry about anything."

"I guess there hasn't been a reason." In fact, he did feel sorry. It was a new feeling, and he wasn't too happy about it. But it was better than the immensely worse feeling he had when Stefani cried. *Jesus.*

His landlady (or, alas, former landlady) had popped for a room at the swanky Hotel Muehlebach, downtown on the Missouri side. The road ramped onto the bridge, and he hugged Stefani tighter, like she would fly out of the car if not for him. They bounced across the Kaw, leaping over the stockyards and packing plants. Vlado tried to think only of the moment—the brisk air whistling over the windshield, the looming Kansas City skyline, the warmth of Stefani next to him—but with each bump his stomach lurched, overstuffed with sausage and a feeling of what-the-hell-just-happened?

A short time later, Vlado was staring at the high, corniced ceiling, the Oriental rugs, and peach-hued wallpaper of their room at the Muehlebach. He ran his fingers along the finely tooled mahogany writing desk and polished chest-of-drawers. He pulled back the flowered drapes and gazed north toward the confluence of the Kaw and Missouri Rivers, at what looked like toy airplanes buzzing around the new Municipal Airport. The last of the day reflected pink off the downtown high-rises while lights twinkled on all over the city. Back across the river, Strawberry Hill was no more than a dark bump on the horizon. He sat on the high four-poster and bounced a bit.

"Quite a difference from your Aunt Josie's garage, I'd say."

Stefani ignored him and went into the bathroom and shut the door. *Of course, a girl needs her privacy.* There was an iced bottle of champagne and a cart with tiny edibles. He tasted one, a bland pastry, thinking how much better it would be with a slice of pork belly. He popped the champagne and poured two glasses, but ten minutes later when Stefani was still doing her business, he drained his, and hers as well. He didn't really care for it but liked following the bubbles to the top of the glass. Like happy little balloons, going up and up. Until they popped.

Stefani emerged from the bathroom, tucked into a tight negligee and smelling like a rose garden. They finished the champagne and ordered a second bottle, and after a room service dinner of poached lobster that neither of them ate, the two of them were sunken into the feathered mattress, tucked between silken sheets.

"It's been a long day, after all," Vlado said. "And the champagne, you know you can't mix."

"You go to all this trouble to seduce a girl, and now . . .?" Stefani threw the covers off the top half of her body and spilled herself toward Vlado.

"Maybe I'm just intimidated."

"You and your big words. You've never been intimidated by anybody."

"Till now. See? What have you done, Stef? Look at you. All of you. And this." Vlado leaned down and kissed her bulbous middle section. "Little Janet."

"Vlado—"

"I can't go poking my thing in there. That's our kid." He arranged the covers neatly over her bump and gave it a reassuring pat.

"Jesus, you're a mess, you know that?" she said, and turned away from him.

I'm your mess now, he was smart enough not to say. He draped an arm over her soft shoulders and pulled up behind her, kissed her fraternally on the cheek. She drew his hand tightly into her chest, but soon her grip relaxed, and her breathing slowed, and she began to snore softly. Vlado rolled onto his back, wide awake. He extended one arm and stretched his fingers toward the ceiling, but it was miles beyond his reach.

8

Monday morning Vlado stood next to Joe on the plant floor, carving away globs of fat from chicken carcasses as if the weekend had never happened.

"I'm telling you, Joe, it was this big." Vlado held out his thumb and forefinger two inches apart. Joe snickered, and Vlado said, "Breakfast, I'm talking about breakfast. Try to pay attention."

"Hey, a guy can get confused." Joe didn't dare look up from the cleaver he was using to chop the legs off chickens.

"Listen. Not *my* sausage. *Their* sausage, and not even theirs as you'll see. So, we come down for breakfast—"

"You and the missus?"

"Yes, thank you very much, Mrs. Novosel and myself, waltzing down the grand staircase into this fancy-schmancy room with about a zillion tables, nobody there, and they seat us at a tiny two-top by the kitchen door. The love of my life orders some complicated omelet and I go for over-easy with the works. So here comes some huge plate with little blue windmills on it and a couple of undercooked eggs in the middle, a single wedge of fried potato, and two sausages; like I'm saying, about the size of my pinky." Vlado put down his boning knife and held up his digit. "Meaning this."

"Was there toast?"

"Forget the damn toast, Joey. I'm looking at these shrively little things and thinking, 'Hey, I know that pig.' The menu said these were custom made on Old MacDonald's farm or some shit, but I could see they were the same little wieners full of floor scrapings that you and I stuff ten to a pack every Wednesday. Buy a ten-pack for a buck, wheel them through the Muehlebach kitchen, say some magic words, and look, now it's homemade sausage for ten cents a bite. Extra fresh because we're sitting close to the kitchen."

"Funny you should mention all this," Joe said. "Yesterday I was at Morty's, when after church Mae stops in and asks if there was any of that stuff left from the wedding."

"The sausage? Is there?"

"I think I remember Martina wrapping some up and putting it in the fridge. I'm not saying she took the leftovers off people's plates, but God knows she hates to waste."

"Wait. Mae liked it?" Mae Jankovic never had a nice word for anyone's cooking.

"Seems so." Joe whacked off another leg.

Vlado held up a handful of yellow, greasy chicken trimmings and let them slip down between his fingers. "That does it. We gotta get off this crap and back to the pigs. I mean, who's ever heard of chicken sausage?"

The weekly party was Vlado's idea. He and Joe got Inky and Bootnose on board, and by the end of the week they'd filled Joe's fridge with pilfered pig scraps and yards of intestines. Every Thursday night anybody who wanted a free shot of rakija and a way out of the house would meet at Joe's garage to grind and stuff sausages, which Joe then hung in his smoke-filled shed. Saturday afternoons they'd set up card tables and folding chairs on the sidewalk in front of Morty's if it was nice out, or inside if it was chilly, and then they'd boil up the garlicky links and serve them with whatever anyone brought along—a bowl of steamed potatoes or sauerkraut, maybe a nutbread or two from Martina. Fr. Kovac would always show up for the free feed, mutter some blessing about loaves and fishes, then disappear before the tamburas and slivovitz took over.

As one such afternoon lurched into evening, Vlado found himself dancing with Stefani, spinning her like a giant top down the sidewalk while Matt Sinovic went nuts on the accordion. Stefani had dispensed with the shrouded overcoats and today swung around her proud belly and its equally impressive counterbalance with abandon. Morty brought out his bass and Don Lesac unpacked a shiny golden saxophone, too new to have seen much use, and the two joined in to broadcast a klezmer-like cacophony. A few tamburitzas added themselves to the mess, and soon people were either up and moving or clapping along and singing, *Za vsaki smeh tvoj, fala,* everyone shouting the last word, *fala,* thanking the girl, the world, life itself, for its every smile.

Vlado slipped off Stefani's arm and into a seat next to Joe.

"Look at this, Joey. What do you see?"

"Happy, drunk Croatians?"

"Why are they happy?"

"Because they're drunk?"

"And why are they drinking?"

"They're always drinking."

"I mean today. Here. Now. Come on Joe, why are people even here at all?" Vlado speared a bite of sausage off Joe's plate and chewed it slowly, staring at Joe, chewing, staring. He swallowed and let out a small belch.

"I think we should have a talk with Stritchie."

Fifteen years prior, when Vlado and Joe arrived in Kansas City as teenagers, Ritchie Petrovic had been their first benefactor. He was a tall and solemn man twenty years their senior, with a hangdog face and a rumbling baritone that gave each of the few words he spoke the weight they deserved. He'd been born on the Hill and spoke English as well as Croatian. It was rumored he'd once been married, but his young bride had died from the flu, leaving him childless. At the time, he owned a boarding house near the trolley that led to the Bottoms and the packing plants. Vlado and Joe and most of the Croatians on the kill floors owed their jobs to Ritchie, who had become known as St. Ritchie, or Stritchie. Vlado knew that if you wanted something done and could get Stritchie on board, it would likely happen.

Stritchie preferred his cabbage wrapped around corned beef, so Joe and Vlado invited him to lunch at McGowan's, where they set up in a back booth with a bucket of "that Irish piss-water," as Vlado called it, and plates of pink, boiled brisket, soggy cabbage, and mushy potatoes.

"You put enough mustard on anything . . ." Vlado stared at the greasy thing on his fork. "Hey, I remember this guy. He was a fine lad who came to an unfortunate end."

Nobody ever remembered seeing Stritchie smile, and now was no exception.

"Look at them all." Vlado waved his still-full fork toward the window where they could see across the river to the Bottoms, the Armour sheds, and the hundreds of wooden pens where future briskets, ribeyes, and chuck roasts rustled around without a clue. "You gotta buy train tickets for these guys, put them up in the Armour hotel, then hire a guy to kill them, another guy to gut them, somebody to hack the whole deal in half, somebody to scrape off the hide—"

Stritchie stopped Vlado with a raised hand while he finished chewing a bite of potato. He swallowed, lowered his hand, and peered darkly at Vlado. "What are you trying to say, Vlado? You don't like your job? I can't get you anything more than your butcher status."

"For which he's grateful," said Joe, "and me as well. We have skills now, thanks to you. More skills than upstairs is willing to pay for, if you ask me."

"We're not here for a handout or a favor," said Vlado. "In fact, we're here to do you one. You get a third, no question."

He pulled out a pencil and scribbled lines across his napkin, a tangle of squares, diagonals, and cylinders, then pushed it across the table.

"These days you could hang junk like that in a museum," said Stritchie. Vlado knew his sister, Mijana, was an artist, who liked to paint scenes from the Hill—kids sledding, Christmas at St. John's, old ladies gossiping on their front porches, and so forth—but nobody in the neighborhood had any money to buy them. Vlado had once gone to the big art museum across the river, but nothing there looked like anything he recognized.

"Well, you're right about one thing," said Vlado, "it will be a work of art. Here's the front of the building, where we put the awning. Then inside, that's the meat case, shelves over here for canned goods." Vlado continued to point at various lines that in his mind created a clear picture of a small, brick market, with a gleaming glass meat display filled with smoked sausage, blood sausage, pigs' feet, shanks, ribs, oxtails; next to that, bins of fresh vegetables, shelves stacked with sundries, household items, a basket of hard candy for the kids. And beyond, the refrigerated carvery and the grinding table, where the magic would happen, everything stuffed and then hung in the proper smokehouse Joe would build out back.

Vlado drew a stick figure with a smiling face in front of the building. "See? It's Mrs. Divac, already here for some weenies." Then he took another napkin and set it off on the far corner of the table without explanation.

"Okay, I'll bite," Stritchie said. He looked tired.

"Maurice Starr's farm. In Bonner Springs. We were playing pinochle and he was complaining how little he was getting for his steers and hogs, what after paying transport and inspection fees, and all kinds of shit that Armour is making him do. He tried going with Swift instead, but the fix is in. I tell him, how hard could it be to get your chuck roasts the twenty miles to . . ." Vlado slid the napkin across the table to the architectural blueprint in front of Stritchie. "Point being, we know as much about what to do with a cow or a hog as those carve-monkeys and bean-counters across the river do."

"And we can do it quicker and cheaper," Joe added, "and without all that crap they sweep up off the Armour floor."

"Good, I'll be your first customer." Stritchie dug back into his corned beef as if the conversation was over.

"Just a kind word at the bank," Vlado said. "Tell Poochie I've changed. And that there was never anything to that business about his daughter."

Vlado was happy to be able to do Stritchie a favor for once, leasing out his little storefront on Sixth in exchange for Stritchie smoothing things over with First Federal. Stritchie hadn't even wanted a share, was happy to do it, and good luck to them. And don't be late with the rent. Well, that was Joey's department.

At the bank, Joe did the talking while Vlado sat uncomfortably, trying to avoid Poochie's gaze and smiling when he thought he was supposed to.

"And how can you guarantee payback?" Poochie, sounding all professional, if not a bit threatening.

Joe unfolded a document on the table. "This is my house on Twenty-First Street."

Joe. He'd learned well from Vlado. Always keep things moving forward.

9

VLADO had never been on a farm, and it wasn't what he'd expected. Before, he'd only driven past the golden expanse of wheat fields and acres of broad-leafed cornstalks that surrounded white houses and red barns, lovely little worlds all their own. He and Joe stood with Maurice in the damp weeds next to a barbed wire fence. On the other side, several horned steers loitered around the pasture gazing off in different directions, like they were pondering the universe's deepest secrets. It was a dull, grey afternoon with a bite in the breeze, and Vlado was cold and annoyed. One of the shaggy red beasts sauntered over to the fence and regarded him with affectionate brown eyes.

"I thought it would already be dead," Vlado said.

"Don't worry, he won't bite you," Maurice said.

"What are we supposed to do, anyway, ride them to the Hill?" asked Vlado. "And what is that terrible smell?"

Maurice shrugged. "You said you wanted fresh."

"Thing is, we gotta do the thing here. The deed. You know . . ." He pointed a thumb-and-finger gun to his own forehead and pulled the trigger.

"I don't have any kind of slaughterhouse here, Vlado."

"You're telling me when you kill a hog for your own table you first send it on the train to the Bottoms?"

"I got a spot over near the river, but it's small, and even if I did have enough space, how're you going to chill the carcass?"

"Let's have a look," Joe said.

They walked along the fenced pasture and past the pigsty, where the grunting beasts staggered around on tiny legs, chomping on hunks of field corn. Vlado wondered how living animals could reek so badly in their natural state. He was relieved when the stench of sweat and cowshit and mud and rotting silage was replaced by the more familiar stink of dried blood and offal that indicated many a hog had lived its last moment here.

Joe said, "We could put in some hooks, a winch. Like dressing a deer, right? Maybe bigger?"

"Inky knows," Vlado said. "He does this every day. We'll get Inky out here. And don't worry, we'll figure out how to keep it cold and get it to the Hill." He had no idea how they might do that, but one thing at a time.

"This can work for all of us," Joe said.

Maurice said he'd think on it.

10

Vlado had been living with the Lovicks for over a month, squeezed with Stefani into her tiny room in the back that shared a wall with Ivan and fake-Aunt-Vera. He'd gotten over his squeamishness about little Janet, and on the rare occasion that Ivan would be down at Morty's while Mrs. Lovick was out shopping, if Vlado himself wasn't at Morty's, or carving up animals, or plotting in Joe's backyard, he might enjoy a climb over Stef's mountains of love, wondering what he'd ever seen in those skinny women like Lydia.

Stefani was mostly cheerful and chatty. *We'll take the baby here and there. Dress her like so. Send her to school at St. John's.* It was a blur to Vlado, who liked to simply focus on the fact that she was happy, without needing all the reasons.

"Sometimes I think you're not listening," she said one Saturday night. His faux parents were out bowling, and he and Stefani were crammed together in her twin bed.

"How can I not be listening when your nose is in my ear? I'm thinking about other stuff is all. Like, how are we going to get out of here?"

"You don't like it here?" she said, and reached down for him, which only made the space tighter, but not in an unpleasant way.

"Not *here* here. But you know. Here." He waved his one free hand around in the air. "Every time, sneaking around like teenagers, like we're not even married. Before you know it, the baby comes, then you'll be all skinny again." He laughed, and she did too.

"Not only that, but if I have to keep eating your mom's cooking, or not eating it to be honest, I'm going to shrivel down to half my size." He didn't know why he was telling this to Stefani, who ate every piece of overcooked lamb or greasy fish her mom laid on the table. She was no cook herself, either.

"Well, as long as this doesn't shrink," said Stefani, giving him a significant squeeze.

When Vlado was a kid in Zagreb, he liked to hang around in his Aunt Vera's kitchen, where the smell of browned meat and fried onions kept him yearning for a taste of whatever might be simmering in the iron pot. At Christmastime he'd help her mix up rice and ground beef for *sarma*. She would toss in pepper and salt and chopped garlic, stir in a raw egg—*that's what you must never tell anybody*—and then they'd squish their hands into the greasy mixture and roll bite-sized balls that they wrapped in pickled cabbage leaves. These days, when he trimmed pork butts at Armour, wiping his hands to keep the knife from slipping, he often recalled the feeling of the slick fat on his fingers, and later, the taste of it that spurted into his mouth with the first bite. Sundays at Aunt Vera's were family dinner days; there would be his cousin Joey, his Uncle Goran and Aunt Lubi, other relatives, sometimes even Father Verbanic from the church of Kristova, elbowing around the oak table in the kitchen. The air was dense with cigar smoke and gamey, vinegary smells, and throughout the afternoon voices got louder as more wine was drawn from the barrel in the corner, mixed with water and poured generously, even to the kids.

Whether out of nostalgia or habit, the following Sunday after Morty's, Vlado drifted into the kitchen to watch his new mom liberate a lamb shank from its white butcher paper. She dropped it into a roasting pan, lit the oven, then pulled a beer from the ice box for Ivan, who was in the little back yard trimming the fig trees, probably cursing at the squirrels that often beat him to the ripening fruit. When she stepped out, Vlado hurried to the pan and removed the meat to a cutting board where he sliced off the better part of a layer of fat, then re-cradled the shank just before fake-Aunt-Vera returned. She frowned at the pan as if something wasn't quite right, then went on to toss in an unpeeled onion, a couple of carrots, and a few measly potatoes. To commence the cremation process, she put on the lid and shoved it into the too-hot oven, then removed her apron, poured herself a fresh coffee, and sat at the Formica table with Vlado.

"You look thin, lovey," she said. "Are you not feeling well?"

Vlado had gotten used to carrying around a slight feeling of nausea most of the time, now made worse by the threat of having to choke down a plate full of scorched animal and rock-hard vegetables.

"I'm fine," he said. "Smells good."

"Oh, you can't smell a thing yet, I just put it in."

That's the problem, he wanted to say. "So how long?"

"Three hours until it's done."

Vlado estimated the heat from the oven and multiplied it by three times sixty minutes. The resulting number explained everything.

"Well then, no point in waiting around here. Why don't we go turn on the radio?" He took Mrs. Lovick by the arm and urged her into the living room where she settled into her easy chair. Vlado lifted her feet onto the ottoman.

"You work too hard in that kitchen, and nobody appreciates it." He turned on the Motorola, twisting the dial through the static until they heard a tinny piano accompanying a birdlike voice that was singing something about birds singing.

They listened quietly for a bit, then she leaned back and closed her eyes. "Vlado, I know you're a better man than everybody says." He waited to hear more, but her head was drooping. "And for whatever reason," she murmured, "my beautiful girl loves you so." She exhaled greatly and let it all go, and Vlado tucked an afghan around her.

He took her eventual snoring as permission to return to the kitchen, where first thing he turned the oven way down and pulled out the roasting pan. He forked the shank onto a cutting board and made slits all around with a paring knife. He peeled some garlic cloves, sliced them thin and tucked them into the slits, just like he remembered Aunt Vera doing, and liberally doused the whole thing with salt and pepper. He took out the onion and peeled and quartered it; peeled and quartered the potatoes; peeled the carrots and chopped them into short lengths; then returned the whole shebang to the pan. He purloined some celery and a turnip from the fridge and an apple from the windowsill and sliced them all into the pan, added a bit of water and another shake of the salt, a sprinkle of paprika, and a bay leaf. Two bay leaves. He poured in half a beer, drank the other half, then made sure the lid fit tight and slid the pan back into the now-less-frightening oven and quietly toweled up his mess.

Two and a half hours later, when Vlado came back from a return visit to Morty's, he could smell the roast all the way out to the sidewalk. He found Mrs. Lovick at the kitchen counter, staring into the open pan with a puzzled look.

"Let a professional do that for you," he said, and lifted the roast out of its pan onto a cutting board. "I need a large platter. And a small bowl." She produced these and Vlado whittled juicy slices of meat off the bone and arranged them just so in the center of the plate. He spooned out the vegetables and placed them around the meat, then returned the pan to the top of the stove. He sprinkled in some flour and lit the burner and showed Mrs. Lovick how to stir the pan juices until they thickened and browned. He ladled some of the rich liquid over the lamb and poured the rest into a gravy bowl.

He gestured to their finished masterpiece. "It's all yours," he said. "I'll ring the bell."

Moments later Mrs. Lovick laid the platter on the table before her assembled family; ten minutes after that, half the roast had disappeared. Stefani was chewing away on her third slice while Ivan stared into his plate with a puzzled expression. He looked up at his wife and seemed about to speak, but Vlado beat him to it.

"Mom, you'll have to tell me your secret." He wiped his lips with his linen napkin and gave her a telling look that hopefully Ivan couldn't see. She pretended to frown at him.

"Then it wouldn't be a secret anymore," she said.

"Certainly not in this family," Ivan grumbled.

"Are there more carrots?" Stefani looked hopefully at the kitchen door.

11

Two nervous weeks passed before Poochie finally signed off on the loan and Stritchie gave Vlado and Joe the keys to the little storefront on Sixth. It had originally belonged to a cobbler named Stein. He'd gone bust during the Crash when his thrifty customers discovered that a layer of newspaper or cardboard in their shoes could block the holes long enough to get themselves from place to place. Vlado had always splurged to have his favorite boots resoled, but Joe swore that butcher paper could do just as well. (Maybe for him and the kids, but Vlado couldn't imagine Martina inconveniencing so much as a pinky toe.) In any case—cowhide, butcher paper; there was some sort of legacy at work in this place that seemed like a good omen.

Vlado could smell the familiar mixture of feet, leather, and shoe polish when they opened the door for the first time, and he half expected to see Stein sitting next to a junk pile of shoes, biting his lip and poking at something with his awl. But the cobwebs and dust indicated otherwise. Light through the soiled windows gave the room a rusty tinge, unappetizing, Vlado thought, and he imagined where they'd put the bright fluorescents and glass meat displays. And maybe some Christmas lights, come the season. For now, a dingy counter with a walk-through gate divided the room. With his finger, Vlado traced a stick figure in the dust, gave it a smiling face, and drew a knife in its hand.

"Look Joey, open for business."

Vlado and Joe moved through the space, mentally spending Poochie's money on new linoleum, paint, refrigeration, knives, band saw, grinder. Beyond the counter was what had been Stein's office and a storage closet, which Joe said they could combine into a walk-in refrigerator, with enough room on the side for a couple of worktables. The back door opened into a dirt parking space where Joe could build his brick smoker, with the alley beyond.

Afterwards Vlado and Joe adjourned to Morty's for an executive board meeting. They sat off at the end of the bar in front of a bottle of slivovitz, two glasses, and a notepad. Joe started scribbling across the page.

"So we have the loan payment, the rent to Stritchie, the wholesale cost of canned goods, the livestock slaughter guys, a counter boy, cleaners . . ." Joe went on writing numbers in columns, which was making Vlado nervous.

"Joey, you're making it all too hard."

"It has to add up or forget it. You know we can't do this and still work at the plant."

"Don't worry, if worse comes to worst, Martina can always get a job."

"Yeah, she'd love that. She and Stefani could open a bakery together."

"Martina does make a nice povitica." They laughed and Vlado poured two shots.

"To the muffin ladies and our early retirement." They drank and Vlado refilled their glasses. He took the pencil from Joe and a fresh sheet of paper, and in large letters wrote "X minus Y equals Z."

"'X.' That's the money people give us for our stuff. 'Y' is what we have to spend to make it all happen. Then, most importantly, there's 'Z,' which stands for money in our pocket. Actually, it's pretty basic arithmetic."

"Fine, Vlado, but what if this number—"

"What if? What if we'd never left Zagreb? Never came to KC and worked at that godforsaken plant? Never married our little muffins? Well, okay, who knows about that. But still, has it been so bad? Someday we'll laugh and say what if we'd never opened that butcher shop."

Vlado called to Morty. "Enough of this sissy crap. Bring us some of your nastiest homemade." Morty produced a dangerous looking bottle of off-color something and poured two shots. "And one for you," Vlado added. He raised his glass to Joe. "It's always been you and me, cousin. Thick and thin. Blood and liquor. As Morty is our witness, we're going to do this." Their three glasses met, and Vlado looked Joe in the eye, knew in that moment that he couldn't have done anything without Joe's steady hand. It was Joe who got them on the boat, who knew a guy who knew Stritchie, who was always the one quietly moving things forward. If Joe said no, it would be no.

"X minus Y, Joey. In the pocket."

Joe's worried look softened. He exhaled and spoke in a quiet voice. "As Morty is our witness." They all drank.

12

Vlado and Joe and most of the other packers avoided church. Vlado had long ago decided it was all too grim. He was still haunted by the Saints' book from his childhood with its image of St. John the Baptist's head on a platter, and the way his Aunt Vera used to finger the crucifix around her neck, with its little statue of the sagging, bleeding body, as if she too would be hanging on a cross if Vlado didn't straighten up.

If he and Joe didn't go to Mass on Sunday, at least there was the morning service at Morty's, complete with bread, wine, confession, and communion with their fellow carvers, who weren't going to waste their single day off listening to Fr. Kovac lecturing down his nose about how miserable they already knew they were. As long as the wives went to Mass, they could sit at the bar and drink and gossip, confident that their own paths to heaven were being skillfully negotiated.

Only twenty-four hours after Vlado and Joe had sealed their pact, they were again at Morty's. Joe was complaining, which wasn't like him.

"If I thought it would do any good, I'd buy flowers and swear off drink. Hell, I'd even go to Mass."

"Martina?"

"Is not on board." He went on to relate the substance of her argument, the detail and elaboration of which went on to great specificity, with a fair stream of expletives, and which ended with a night on the couch. For him.

"Cockamamie scheme?" Vlado repeated.

"Right, and swore on her father's grave—"

"Her father's still alive," Vlado said. Technically that was true, but a stroke had left the sixty-year-old Vukovich patriarch's body confined to a wheelchair and his mind consigned to a world of silence.

"Well, he might as well be dead. And her too, to hear her talk. 'Just put me in my dress' she says, 'and lay me out on a slab so my friends can come by for a beer and say how great I look.'"

"There's no arguing with that kind of logic, Joey."

"Then she wants to know, who will be left to take care of Tommy and little Donald?"

"Well, there's always Mae Jankovic," Vlado attempted to joke. Mae was an odd duck, six feet tall and thin as spaghetti, with a hunched posture. But she had large eyes that knew how to latch on and long, stringy hair that often veiled half her face in a way that made you wonder what she might be thinking, and if it could have anything to do with you. Early on Joe'd had a little thing with Mae, and Vlado thought they'd never quite got over it. Martina always suspected Mae was flirting with Joe, the way she'd brush a little dandruff off his shoulder or find a way to sit next to him at a party.

"You want me out on the street?" Joe laughed, but only a little. "Really, she's just afraid. I mean there's the mortgage on the house, which we wouldn't even have if not for the two thousand dollars her dad fronted us."

"Where did he get that?"

"Stashed it away before the depression hit. But there's no more where that came from."

"Okay, so she's afraid. We are too, right? But that's a good thing. It means we're onto something."

"Your lips to Martina's ears," Joe said. "And by the way, you're back on the list."

Just then Inky sank onto the stool next to them, which meant Mass was over and they were moving into the guilt-free part of the day, which called for another round.

"I hear there's going to be two job openings at Armour," he said.

"Why, are you and Bootnose finally going off to join the circus?" Vlado asked.

"Nice try. I heard all about it." He looked at Joe. "And about somebody who's not happy."

The word was out. That would be Martina, Vlado thought. It was just like her to first pitch a huge fit and then sign off on the plan by telling everybody about it.

"Fine, just between you and me and the Hill," Joe said.

"Cross my heart," said Inky.

"And what if I were to say I could offer you a job? Working in the great outdoors. Be your own boss, mostly."

Inky absently traced a finger across his wine-stain birthmark and leaned his beanpole figure down toward Joe, who explained the deal they were making with Maurice Starr to slaughter the cattle and hogs there, if they could get them to the shop without spoiling.

"I know you're a problem solver," Vlado said, more hopeful than certain. In fact, Inky and his cousin Bootnose were infamous layabouts and self-anointed comedians. If you ever found a bloody cow head in your duffel at the end of a shift, or a chicken hanging by its neck coming down the line between sides of beef, you'd figure those two were somewhere laughing their asses off. But the fact is they had the skills, knew how to hang and strip the carcasses and transform them into something a butcher could deal with.

"You'd be independent contractors," Joe explained. "We'll pay you by the pound for goods delivered and won't be chintzy about tossing in the occasional steak or two as well. And all the hides and whatever else, you can keep. Make them into belts or cow-skin hats or something."

Inky was cleaning his nails with the end of a matchstick. He stopped and gave Joe a happy look, as if his offer was just another fun thing. "Sure thing, Joey. I know Starr. And I already have an idea."

"Fine, we'll write up a deal later. Meanwhile, you guys can go out to Maurice's and see what we can do about hanging up some beef yardarms. And Mirko," Joe used Inky's real name. "Just one thing. Don't screw this up."

"Believe me, Joe, I'm touched. We got this."

"Thank the Baby Jesus I don't have to go back to that goddam farm," said Vlado.

The next morning, Joe and Vlado met inside the empty storefront. Pine two-by-fours were stacked along one wall; another wall had been crowbarred open so the plumbers could get the pipes in for the cooler. Sawdust floated up wherever they stepped. Vlado liked the smell of it—fresh, like the bright future he wished to imagine.

"You're not worried about those two?" Joe asked Vlado.

"Hell, we're talking about killing a six-hundred-pound beast, hanging it up, ripping its skin off, and cutting it in half. I think those guys'd probably do it for free."

Vlado knew that Inky and Bootnose, whose real name was Zoran, were designed for this kind of work. They were both loud and tall like their uncle Matt, Bootnose big-boned and Inky skinny but wiry, and seemed to take pleasure in any kind of destructive activity. Bootnose had briefly pitched on Vlado's baseball team but was shit-canned after he kept throwing the balls straight at the batters. Everybody called him Bootnose to his face but would never dare mention the odd dip in his nose that may or may not have been the source of the nickname.

"What do you think?" Joe toed a line in dust. "Maybe by St. Lucy's Day? What about the guys at Kavanaugh?"

Vlado had hired a company called Kavanaugh Destruction, which had started as a business with three brothers and a wrecking ball. But it turned out they were equally skilled at constructing things as well, so that became their new business model, but they kept the old name for chuckles.

"A week from now and we'll have our meat case right here, all the shelving in. Following week, they line the walk-in and hook up the cooler. It takes about five minutes to stack up some bricks for a smoker, so then we're all set," Vlado said. "Time to alert Maurice."

13

Joe and Vlado showed up to check on the store after the crew had left. It was one week until St. Lucy's Feast, December 13, which this year occurred on a Sunday, ideal for what they had in mind. They'd allow for Mass, then give Morty his due until four o'clock, at which point they'd open the doors to the new *Marevic and Novosel Meat Market and Grocery*. They'd be grilling sausages out front and steaming them with sauerkraut inside. Matt Sinovic was bringing his accordion, over Vlado's objections, but Joe said this wasn't about what *they* liked, but how to make people happy.

"Happiness is overrated if you have to listen to that crap," Vlado said. "We should be modern, get somebody like Hot Lips Page." He and Joe both liked listening to Bennie Moten's orchestra and his hot-licks trumpet player on Martina's little Victrola.

"Sure, Vlado, I saw him standing on the highway with a sign, 'Will work for sausage.'"

"You never know."

"I'm more worried about Inky and getting the meat here on time. The sausage isn't going to stuff and smoke itself."

"Inky still says tomorrow night as planned. At last count, two sides of beef and enough pork for fifty rings. He's got it going with Maurice. They found a tree to hang a winch on and tomorrow should be a cold day. The latest word is they'll cut out of Armour early and get to us a few hours after dark."

Vlado knew Inky's truancy from the plant was about to get him canned, meaning he'd be depending on them for a paycheck. Vlado and Joe had given proper notice for themselves, which gave Stritchie a chance to promote a couple more butchers so he wouldn't lose face with Armour. As for Bootnose, he didn't have a family. *He's your family now*, Vlado thought, suddenly nervous, like when he'd married Stefani, or when he'd gotten on that ship with Joe in Rijeka. And Joe, who had Martina on him about every damn thing.

"You're not worried?" Joe asked.

"Sure, I'm worried," Vlado said. "There's probably an asteroid heading to earth right now that's going to kill all life as we know it. But meanwhile, you know what I think?"

"What?"

"Green."

"Green?"

"Green is a great color for these walls." The paint still hadn't quite dried, and the whole room smelled like turpentine. Vlado wasn't sure the green walls made up for the fact that yards of electric wire were still coiled about the floor, that there was still no running water, that the compressor he'd gotten a deal on didn't fit the aperture.

But in fact, the green walls did look pretty great.

Late Monday afternoon, Vlado labored to screw the feed pipe into the refrigeration compressor. He could carve up a steer with his eyes closed, his boning knife always finding the path of least resistance, as if the corpse was collaborating in its own demise. But machinery confused him. Hardware. Steel.

Stefani had come by with sandwiches and hot coffee. She was like a balloon about to pop, floating around the place, stacking scraps of lumber into neat piles, poking at the cash register keys until she found the *chinging* sound, and in general, irritating Vlado, who was trying to focus on his own worries about keeping the meat cold when it arrived. If it arrived.

Vlado was muttering in Croatian, some rude comments about the compressor's mother, when Stefani drifted by for a look.

"Maybe it turns the other way," she said.

"Righty-tighty," Vlado said, struggling to engage the threads.

"I know, but if you stand on the other side . . ."

Two minutes later, with the pipe properly tightened, Vlado connected the last wires. He reached for the power switch, but Joe's hand stopped him. His head indicated Stefani, who cheerfully pulled the lever down to restore power to the room. Fluorescent lights flickered on, and suddenly Bing Crosby was crooning about Christmas from the tabletop radio back in the carvery.

"Turn that crap off," Vlado said. Joe found the volume control, which he turned, first righty-tighty and then the other way, and the music disappeared. But instead of silence they heard a low humming, like a vacuum cleaner covered with pillows. They opened the heavy door into what used to be Stein's closet and office, now re-framed with layers of insulation and steel, and Joe held his hand up to the air vent. He smiled at Vlado.

By six o'clock Stefani had gone home, and the cooler's thermometer had inched downward to the requisite thirty-nine degrees. Joe set the thermostat accordingly, and Vlado watched him wipe the stainless carving table for the umpteenth time, wipe down their new glass and steel display case, wipe the keys on the cash register, the top of the scale. He turned toward the empty shelves and Vlado put a hand on his shoulder.

"It's all ready, Joey. We just have to wait for Inky."

"You know how scary that sounds?"

Vlado was dreaming about sausage. He and Stefani were in the kitchen where she was cutting the ends off the links and squeezing the ground mixture out like toothpaste. He reached a hand toward her, but she drifted back with a sad look. He bent to grab at the pork, but he slipped on the grease and fell headlong.

He came to sprawled on the floor next to the folding chair he'd apparently snoozed off in. A nearly empty bottle of slivovitz rested next to the other chair, where Joe was slumped back like a dead man. Vlado pulled out his watch, and in his dreamy haze he could see it was a little past one in the morning. He became aware of a sound he'd probably been hearing all along, a persistent banging on the back door. He nudged Joe, who groaned and muttered a curse. Vlado got up to investigate and found Inky bobbing up and down and blowing on his hands.

"Jesus, Vlado, I'm freezing my ass off."

Behind Inky a large, squared-off vehicle was backed into their lot. Vlado could just make out the golden embossed letters on the door: "Sandusky and Son Funeral Home."

Vlado rubbed his chin, wondering in his half-awake, semi-sober state if Inky had misunderstood what sort of meat they were expecting. Bootnose appeared from around the side of the hearse. He had on an army greatcoat and Russian Cossack hat with the earflaps down. Vlado thought he looked like a giant dog dressed as a person.

"Sorry we're so late," Bootnose boomed out, like he'd just arrived at a party already in full swing, "but the traffic was terrible." He laughed and pulled a flask out of his coat and offered it to Vlado, who refused; to Inky, who didn't; then helped himself to a long gulp.

"Christ, it's as cold as Dorothy Penny's—"

"Shut up," Inky said. "She can probably hear you all the way over on Eighth."

Joe appeared at the door next to Vlado. He squinted at the hearse. At Vlado. At Inky and Bootnose.

"Don't even tell me," he said to no one in particular. Inky twisted the handle on the tailgate and swung it open and there was a polished mahogany coffin. Lacy filigree was carved into the edges, and ornate brass handles on the side matched the brass crucifix mounted on the top. Bloody handprints were scattered across the lid, like clues to some horrible misdeed.

"What, no flowers?" Vlado said. He pulled on one handle and the coffin rolled easily out on its rack. Joe propped open the shop door, and the four of them lifted.

"How many bodies you got in there?" Joe groaned.

They staggered in and thunked it down onto the floor next to the cooler. Bootnose picked up a crowbar, but Inky waved him off and reached to unclasp the lid. He splayed his arms out like he was Jesus. "A sacred moment, gentlemen."

Vlado and Joe raised the lid and a cloud of icy humidity rose up to expose the awful remains. Vlado gazed with both horror and admiration at the curving spine, the exposed ribs, the pink flesh of the skinned torso that narrowed to the white, fat-covered neck. Chunks of ice were stuffed into every space. There was no head.

"Where's the rest of it?" Joe asked.

"You said we could keep the head," said Inky.

"No, I mean the rest of the—"

"It's like that song," Bootnose said, "about the railroad guy who gets his head lopped off one night, then keeps coming back, swinging his lamp on moonless nights—"

"'Just a-lookin' for his head,'" Inky sang, and Bootnose joined in.

"No you idiot, Joe means what about the rest of the order," said Vlado. "And no, you can't keep the head."

"You said we could have the head."

"We'll talk about it later," Joe said.

"Are we going to say a rosary, or what?" Vlado asked, and with some effort they maneuvered the corpse out of the coffin to its final resting place, hanging by its neck from a hook in the ceiling, where at last, it looked more like a side of beef than a horrific act of mob retribution.

Outside the cooler, the empty coffin lay open. Its velvet lining was stained with blood and body fluids, with bits of fat floating in a pink, icy soup.

"How are you going to return this to Sandusky?" Joe asked Inky. "Does he even know?"

"Sure, he does. After he sold you the coffin, he didn't mind lending us the truck."

Vlado eyed their newest expense and wondered what column Joe would put it in.

"Did I have to buy the fanciest one?" Joe said.

"You know, Joe," Inky said, "you start skimping on the little stuff and pretty soon it adds up and you're as bad as Armour." He and Bootnose lifted the mahogany box like it was nothing and slid it into the back of the hearse.

"Back to the scene of the crime," Inky said. "We'll see you in a bit." He and Bootnose slammed the tailgate, climbed into the front, and with an engine roar too loud for that time of night, they bounced down Sixth in the direction of Bonner Springs.

"Where do you think they got the ice?" Joe asked Vlado.

"Who knows, maybe you bought an ice company too."

"Why is it always 'me' and not 'us'?"

Vlado produced a full roll of bills from his pocket. "Obviously I haven't bought anything."

14

THE night before St. Lucy's Day, Vlado checked their inventory. The pork shoulders had been ground and stuffed into yards of entrails and tied off into sausages that now rested peacefully in the cooler. Newly carved sirloin steaks, T-bones, rib steaks, chuck and round roasts were chilling on the shelves, ready for the display, while racks of spareribs were slow-smoking out back. Stefani was home making nutbread, as certainly was Martina, and not to be outdone, probably Dorothy Penny as well. He figured if they sold the whole deal, they could pay Inky and Bootnose, make a dent on the rent, and set aside something for Poochie. It was after midnight, and Joe had left to have a drink with the meat morticians. Vlado took a last look, then turned off the lights and locked the door.

Back home, the house was dark but for a single light in the kitchen, where Vlado found Stefani absently stirring a cup of coffee and staring off as if he wasn't there. The air smelled sweet and bread-like, and he saw four sadly misshapen poviticas sitting on the counter. He poured himself a coffee, added a swirl of milk, then sat down next to his dear bride, who didn't move or acknowledge him. He placed a hand on her shoulder, and she stiffened and turned toward him. The circles under her eyes were darker than ever, and Vlado knew what she was thinking. If she said it out loud, would he be willing to cancel the whole deal, give everything to Joe, beg for his Armour job back? Who did he want all this for, anyway? For himself? For Stefani, who was frightened? For little Janet, and all the rest? *Jebote.*

He said the only thing he knew for sure.

"The nutbread smells good."

Stefani rested her crossed arms on her belly and gave him a long stare. A pipe creaked. A horn honked in the distance. Vlado's stomach rumbled. Finally, she blinked, and what might have been a smile tugged at the corner of her mouth.

"Go take a bath, Vlad." She kissed him on his cheek. "You smell even more like a pig than usual."

Twenty minutes later Vlado lay in the bathtub, drinking from a quart bottle of Schlitz, staring at the ceiling and wondering what the hell he had done.

If there was a beautiful sunrise the next morning, with pink reflections on the early cloud wisps; if there was a mockingbird improvising a daybreak aria; if golden leaves were falling and the morning star glowed over the eastern horizon, Vlado did not notice. He fidgeted for his keys, then opened the shop; listened for and heard the compressor motoring in the distance; smelled the drying paint and turpentine that was now overlaid with a smoky aroma, of grease and soot, and the metallic tang of dried blood. He turned on the lights.

Unfortunately, no magical *vilas* had appeared during the night to straighten out the mess. Canned goods were disarrayed on the shelves while their boxes littered the floor. Construction dust had shaken itself out of the walls during the night. He grabbed a mop and some rags, and by the time Joe rolled in a half hour later, he'd wiped the whole place down, stacked the boxes in the alley, and checked the temperature of the cooler a dozen times. Joe produced a pair of cinnamon rolls from a bag and the bottle of slivovitz from behind the counter, then pulled out his notebook with the final to-do list. Vlado took it from him and scanned it.

"The boys will be here at noon. Not to worry."

Joe snatched back the list and jabbed his finger at the items.

"Really, is Inky going to set up the grill and do the sausages? Wash the windows? Put up the sign? Is Bootnose going to slice the nutbread? Pick up the vegetables from Maurice?" He continued down the list with mounting agitation until Vlado covered it with his hand.

"Yes, Joey. That's exactly what's going to happen."

As it was, the boys were an hour and a half late, but toward four o'clock most everything had been punched out and they thought they were ready to go. Stefani arrived with a little jingle-bell for the door, and Vlado steadied her on a step stool while she nailed it in above the jamb. Moments later the bell rang, and Martina appeared in the doorway with two paper-wrapped bundles.

"Go away, we're closed," Vlado shouted.

"You, in particular, look like hell." Martina thrust a package into Vlado's hands. Inside was a stack of starched white shirts and four bow ties. "Go on. You two as well," she said to Inky and Bootnose.

All four stripped down to their sleeveless underwear and struggled into the shirts, and then Stefani helped them clip on their ties. Martina opened the other package in which there were four new, black aprons, with a name stitched on each: *Josip. Vladimir. Mirko. Zoran.* Beneath each name larger letters spelled out *Big Sausage*.

"At least you'll look like you know what you're doing," she said. Then she sighed dramatically, as if to wash her hands of the whole affair.

Vlado stared at the apron. "Whatever happened to *Marevic and Novosel Butcher Shop and—*"

"Do you think I have all goddam day to spend with a needle and thread?"

"But *Big Sausage?*"

"You're the one who's always talking about the size of your goddam sausage," she said. The room went dead quiet, and Vlado knew better than to make eye contact with Joe.

"What?" asked Martina.

Inky had on his *Mirko* apron and was holding a chef's knife up as if it were a new, bright idea. "How do I look?" Joe carefully removed the knife from his fingers and handed him a mop.

"Better now, I think."

Just then Stefani's mom and Ivan jingled in. Ivan brought a box camera and herded everybody out front where they posed beneath the new awning—Vlado and Stefani at one end, Joe and Martina at the other, with Bootnose and Inky (who was somehow brandishing another knife) in the middle. But the picture that would end up in the *Kansas City Times*, heralding the grand opening of Strawberry Hill's own *Big Sausage*, was the photo of the four new brothers-in-arms, neat in their shirts, ties, and aprons, with their right hands stacked together on the end of a baseball bat and looking like they meant business.

Out front, Bootnose began forking rings of sausage onto the grate over the gray coals. Vlado handed him some tongs—*don't waste the juice*—and then he and Joe brought trays of cut meat from the cooler to the display. Joe called out the prices, which Vlado scribbled on squares of cardboard that he tooth-picked into the leading cut in each row. They each pulled an armful of smoke-reddened sausage rings out of the coffin and spooned them together up one slope of the polished glass case. A strong scent of pepper and garlic wafted through the store, and the front door jingled.

It was Mrs. Divac. She stepped hesitantly through the doorway. Bootnose stood on one side of her, Inky on the other, to escort her to the counter where Joe and Vlado stood, ready to serve. The door rang again and in came Stritchie, dressed in a black topcoat and fedora. He strode right past Mrs. Divac and up to Joe.

"I said I'd be your first customer." He looked Joe up and down, scanned the room, and ran one finger along the chrome trim of the display. He took a piece of the nutbread Joe had sliced onto a plate and bit in. "Nice," he said, then pointed to the sausage. "I'll take three of those."

"Who says you get to be first?" Mrs. Divac said to Stritchie, who ignored her efforts to edge between him and the counter.

Joe set the rings on the scale, then started to scratch out the math on his pad.

"Never mind that," said Stritchie. "Just wrap them up. It's on the house." When Joe looked surprised, Stritchie said, "What? You don't expect me to be paying my own rent, do you? Don't worry, you boys will do a good job. We'll all be happy."

Vlado wrapped the sausage in white paper and handed it to Stritchie, who turned and bumped into Mrs. Divac.

"I apologize for the intrusion, young lady," he said, then handed her the package. "With my compliments."

"Christ," Vlado said to Joe after Stritchie walked out. "I hope he doesn't get to be a regular."

Dorothy Penny waltzed in next as if she were in a parade, decked out from Mass and glowing with the goodness of the Holy Spirit. She hefted a grocery bag onto the counter and unloaded tiny sacks about the size of a single sarma, tied at the top with curled green ribbons. Vlado opened one and saw the wheat seeds that the kids in the neighborhood collected all year down at the tracks, where the railroad cars filled with grain would spill a bit as they rounded the curve at Kaw Bottoms. On St. Lucy's Day families would plant the seeds in a pot, and if they sprouted by Christmas it meant prosperity in the coming year.

"For your customers," she said. "And don't forget to plant one here."

She looked at the sausages in the meat display and wrinkled her nose. "Is this the dreadful stuff they're cooking outside? I suppose I should buy one."

"Let me treat you," Joe offered. "With our thanks for your good wishes."

"In that case, I'll take two," she said, and Joe wrapped them up. He and Vlado reverentially watched Dorothy Penny sashay toward the door.

"We're not really very good at this, are we?" Vlado said.

There was a commotion outside—no doubt the gang from Morty's —and Bootnose stuck his head in the doorway. "More samples, Joey. Vlado, you've outdone yourself."

Joe frowned. "They're not samples."

"Too late now," said Bootnose. "The Armour guys are going nuts. Come on out and have a beer."

Joe propped the door open and followed Bootnose outside with more rings, leaving Vlado alone behind the counter. A charred, smoky aroma filled the empty room. Vlado inhaled deeply and closed his eyes. He listened to the first notes wheezing out of Sinovic's accordion, the lively jabber of Croatian, and the honking laughter that meant the same thing in any language. He pulled a couple of plump sirloins from the case and headed out to the grill, hungrier than he could ever remember.

A little after midnight, Vlado and Joe finally closed the door and dimmed the lights. They pulled stools up to the counter and sat down with the last of the links that by then had browned and shriveled on Inky's grill.

"You know what would go great with this?" Vlado said. He sawed through a burnt end that felt more like jerky than kobasa.

"I don't know, homemade sausage?" Joe said.

"Very funny. I wonder why we don't have any?"

Joe gave him a dim look. "Because you gave it all away?"

"Exactly! That's the way it works now, Jozo. It's modern times. Just think, right now Marijana Divac is snugged up tight in bed with her loving hubby, thinking, 'You know what I want, more than anything else in the world?'"

Vlado knew they were both picturing old man Divac, with his withered face, withered attitude, and probably withered everything else.

Vlado stuck a fork into the wrinkly remains of his dinner. "Not this, that's for sure." Vlado held the fork up and moved it toward Joe's mouth. "Go on, eat it. Come on Joey, bite it."

Joe pushed his hand away and started to laugh, as did Vlado, and in an instant the two of them were convulsing. Vlado wondered if this might be the finest moment in his life. He reached for the slivovitz bottle, but it was empty. Probably for the better. He looked at the empty room, the empty meat case, and felt the fullness inside himself. That's the way it works, he thought, some mysterious deal that balanced it all. Like Stefani, who needed everything, and here he was to provide it.

"Who'd-a thought, Joe, when I convinced you to leave Zagreb—"

"Wait, you convinced me? What about that guy—"

"Okay, let's just agree it was complicated. Point is, here we are, and there's no going back to that bullshit."

They'd stopped laughing and had cleaned their plates. In the space Vlado suddenly felt an overwhelming affection for his cousin.

"Joe . . ."

"I know." Joe stood and turned away so Vlado couldn't see his face. "Come on. It'll be morning before you know. We don't want to keep the Divac family waiting."

15

THE next morning, Vlado woke at six, freezing, curled up against Stefani, who necessarily had claimed the lion's share of the covers. He heard a ghostly moaning sound, was relieved when he realized it was only the wind, then distressed when he shivered across the cold floor to the window and saw a horizontal blast of snow pelting the already whitened sidewalks and streets.

Twenty minutes later, the same wind urged him down the icy sidewalk to Big Sausage, where he had to fiddle a bit with the frozen lock. He turned on the light, wondering in his not-exactly-hungover-but-mostly-exhausted state if it might have all been a dream. But there it was: the compressor humming, the gas heater pumping the room up to a toasty sixty-five degrees, everything gleaming under the fluorescents. He checked the temperature in the cooler and put on a pot of coffee, shrugged out of his herringbone overcoat and reached for his apron.

The front door jingled, and a colorful figure lumbered in, brushed snow off his shoulders, and stamped his galoshes. Vlado had to admire Martina's handiwork: the crocheted green and red tasseled cap tied tightly under Joe's chin, the blue mittens with the lace filigree, and once he took off his coat, the red-and-white knit cardigan with a crucifix over one breast and a lamb over the other.

"You look like a Zagreb housewife," Vlado said.

Joe ignored him and pulled two strudels out of a paper bag.

"You're welcome," he said.

"So, Martina didn't get up and fix you a big breakfast, give it a little squeeze, and say 'Have a nice day, dearie'?"

"No squeeze, little or otherwise. And you?"

"No squeeze."

They silently chewed their sweet rolls until Joe pulled out his pocket watch.

"Seven o'clock."

They straightened their aprons, Vlado licked back a sprig of hair, and Joe flipped the window sign to "Open." Vlado cracked the door and looked out onto the empty, snow-streaked street. The snow had stopped but the wind rattled in the bare trees. If the sun had crested the river there was no way of telling, with everything so gray and gloomy. No lights glimmered through windows; no smoke fingered out of chimneys. It was like someone needed to flip a switch and get everything going. Vlado reached up and jingled the bell above the door, but all he heard in response was the distant clank of the trolley delivering his former compatriots to their carving stations across the river.

"You're letting the air out," Joe said.

Vlado closed the door, and the bell jingled again.

"That goddam bell is going to drive me crazy," he said.

"You mean the one that's not ringing now?"

"Yeah, that's the one."

"Everyone's just going to be a little bit late today. We'll be fine."

As if to underline his point the bell rang again, but it was just Inky.

"Sorry I'm late, gentlemen, but you know, the weather." Beneath his pea coat he already had on his "Mirko" apron and bowtie.

"Hang on. What are you doing?" Vlado said.

"I said I'm sorry. Anyhow, you guys look like you've been fine without me so far, so no problem, right?"

"So far?" Joe said, and gave a concerned look to Vlado, who had in fact seen this coming and handed Inky a broom.

"Fine. But put your coat back on." He opened the door and indicated the snow-covered stoop and sidewalk. "And by the way, where's your partner in crime?"

From the alley behind the store they heard the clanking of a vehicle bottoming out. A crunching sound, then silence. Out the back door they found the Sandusky and Son's tailgate lodged against the corner of

Joe's brick smoker. The engine revved and the tires spun without purchase, so they shouldered into it until it cleared the bricks far enough to open the back. Bootnose hopped out of the driver's side wearing a monogrammed "S & S" chauffeur's cap and a smile way too big for the time and circumstances.

"Good news, we didn't even need ice."

Sure enough, the coffin this time was lighter, and they easily managed it into the shop, where Vlado reached for the lid. He opened it and recoiled from the sight of a gruesome corpse, some terrible mistake, with a mangled face and flayed limbs that jutted out from beneath a black shroud. It took a long, horrifying few seconds for Vlado to recognize the shroud as an apron that said "Zoran," the face as a pig's head, and the body beneath the apron as a careful arrangement of butts, shanks, trotters, and ribs, at which point Inky was laughing like a hyena, Joe was smirking, and Bootnose was frowning with pretend puzzlement.

"I must have got my orders crossed," Bootnose said, shrugged, removed his hat and positioned it on the pig's head. "Hey, it's our new night watchman."

This, of course, called for a round of shots, only after which did Vlado think he ought to soundly kick Bootnose's ass, but when he looked at their newest uniformed employee dismembered in its silk-shrouded mahogany bed and considered what it had been just a few short hours ago, he decided to think again.

Just then the bell jingled and the four of them looked at each other like guilty schoolboys.

They hustled the coffin into the cooler, then Joe went up front to investigate. Vlado retied his apron and hurried after him, ready to do business, to carve steaks, to weigh sausage, to grind beef, but his partner was standing in an empty room staring at the open door.

"The wind," Joe said, and closed it quietly. But it was too late, and a chill entered Vlado's bones.

"Nobody's coming, are they, Joey?"

Joe didn't say anything, but Vlado recognized the uncertain look on his face as the same one he had the night they'd realized they had to flee Zagreb, which seemed like a lifetime ago. But that had worked out, right? At least they weren't dead in some goddam Serbian trench. He knew one thing. He'd never go back to that goddam plant, where—he could see now—the beast he'd been carving up was himself.

He stared back at Joe, waiting for a word. A joke? An A-okay? Absolution?

Joe shrugged. "Let's get to work."

They unloaded Bootnose's pig parts onto the carving table and began slicing and piling up the fat from the shoulders and shanks. They skimmed the hair off the trotters and set them aside for pickling, then got into a familiar rhythm with their knives, carving the loin away from the ribs, squaring out the belly and salting it for the smoker.

Meanwhile the head sat morosely on the counter giving Vlado a perplexed look.

16

On Tuesday, the weather broke, the wind died down, the sun came out, and the birds were all over the place. At ten thirty-two a.m. Dorothy Penny bought a can of green beans and a half pound of ground beef. That afternoon, Joe and Vlado played forty-three hands of pinochle.

On Wednesday, it was lucky that Vlado got there to open promptly because Mrs. Divac jingled in at seven sharp, looking for fresh tomatoes, which they didn't have, and settled for a can of Heinz tomato paste, which they did have, along with a half-pound of ground beef and a box of spaghetti. She'd forgotten her wallet, so Joe obligingly wrote down the amount in his ledger. A few hours later, a stranger wandered in to ask for directions to Morty's. By the end of the day, the chrome-trimmed meat display was polished to a mirror finish, the knives were sharpened to a paper-thin edge, and the cuts of meat had been alphabetized on the shelves of Stein's Office.

Thursday was quiet well into the afternoon, until at three-thirty the bell rang sharply and four young girls in St. John's plaid skirts and white blouses tumbled in, jabbering like a nest of baby sparrows. They helped themselves to the wrapped candies in the jar and counted out enough pennies between them to buy a bottle of Coca-Cola with four straws. The coins rang hollow in the cavernous cash register and the unfamiliar sound of the *cha-ching* seemed to startle everybody.

On Friday, Mae Jankovic came in looking for fish. They had no fish.

Saturday was nice enough that they could leave the front door open, which made it easy for passersby to wave or shout a hello without having to even enter the store. Vlado had boiled up some of the garlicky sausage for his and Joe's and Inky's lunch, which caught Lubo Grisnik's attention as he lumbered past the open door.

"Smells good," he shouted in to them, flashed a thumbs-up from his three-fingered left hand, and continued on.

"People are so friendly," Inky said with his mouth full.

Every night that week, Vlado returned home exhausted from having done nothing all day.

The next day was the last Sunday before Christmas, and like a Christmas miracle, it seemed as if half the Hill magically reappeared around Inky's grill at the stroke of four o'clock. The weather had brightened, and it was unfortunately warm enough for Matt Sinovic to be pumping his accordion, cranking out Christmas favorites such as "Roll Out the Barrel" and "The Croatian Sword Dance." Vlado wondered why the instrument needed all those buttons and keys to play the same five notes over and over. He poked at the sausages, which were already beginning to split and sizzle.

"That's funny," he said to Inky, but louder than he needed to, "I could have sworn everyone had moved across the river."

"Why would you think that?" Inky said. "Obviously everybody's still here."

"Obviously," said Vlado, and headed into Stein's Office for more rings of everyone's favorite free sausage.

Inside, Joe was perched on a stool behind the counter. He wasn't smiling. Vlado reached past him to pull a ring of sausage out of the case and Joe hit the *ching* on the cash register. Another ring, another *ching*. And again. Then one more time, at which point Vlado said,

"Okay, I get it, cousin. But people are eating, and that's always a good thing."

Joe clearly worried too much, which was his business, of course—his actual business, Vlado thought—except that it was rubbing off on Vlado. He decided Joe could sit there like a pouting baby while he, Vlado, would return to the grill and turn his sorrows over to the warm embrace of the neighborhood. He walked away with his plate of links, heard one more *ching* behind him and answered by swatting the bell above the door, which flew off and landed on a shelf next to the canned corn.

Outside he scanned around his crowd of happy customers—well, not customers, exactly, but people eating and laughing and trash-talking, apparently enjoying the sausage, and the day in general, despite the accordion. But the stone in his gut did not shrink, and in fact started to swing back and forth, because there on the far side of the grill was Lydia—his Lydia, or his former Lydia—nibbling on an end-piece and talking to fake-Aunt-Vera like they were new best friends. She looked like the devil herself. Way overdressed for a Sunday afternoon poaching sausage on Sixth Street, but without a doubt, she looked fantastic in a low-cut whatever, her skirt glued to her hips, and heels that she didn't need in order to be taller than Vlado.

Vlado had tried to put Lydia out of his mind. He hadn't seen her at the wedding, no surprise, nor had she been to any of the sausage events. She hadn't dropped by Morty's, and if she'd been at church, Martina would have made some smart remark. It had ended abruptly, not badly . . . well, badly, too, but was it his job to make everybody happy all the time?

She didn't look up until he was almost upon her.

"I had to see it to believe it," she said.

"It's pretty nice, right?" He looked at the new brick storefront, the plate glass window, his hungry neighbors. Maybe too hungry.

"That's not what I meant," she said, and tipped her head toward where Stefani was spread out on a folding chair, drinking beer with Inky (who needed to get back to work this very second).

"Excuse us, Mom," he said to Mrs. Lovick and steered Lydia away from the crowd and down the sidewalk. "What are you even doing here?"

"You married her?"

"I'm going to be a father."

"Oh really." She gave him the same skeptical look he'd been getting his whole life. Thinking about Stefani and Ivan and Mrs. Lovick and little Janet on the way and his deal with Joe and quitting the plant, and

75

the whole conspiracy that meant he was no longer free to roam the streets at will, he realized that, no, he shouldn't even be talking to Lydia.

"What if I told you I was pregnant?" she said.

"What if you did?" Vlado said. Then. "Are you?"

Lydia looked off in the far distance and rubbed her belly. Vlado started to get a sick feeling.

"No," she said.

"You look a little—"

"I'm bloated today." She definitely looked a little heftier. "Your damn sausage."

"I didn't know you knew Stefani."

"We went to St. John's together. And not that long ago." She flipped her hair like a schoolgirl. "How is it you're too dumb to know what an idiot you are? I'd try to explain it, but I don't think I have a prayer."

Vlado had foreseen this turn of the conversation and had the good sense not to say anything stupid, like, *You wanted it*, or, *We didn't make any promises*. Or even, *How's your sister?* Christ.

"So, where've you been, anyway?" he asked.

"In my bedroom sobbing, what do you think?"

"Seriously."

"I didn't tell you I was moving across the river because I knew you'd come chasing after me."

"And if I did, where would I find you?"

"You wouldn't."

She smelled terrific, something way better than smoke or sausage. He'd gotten used to Stefani's bread-and-perfume aroma, but now Lydia's woodsy, clove-like scent triggered a sense memory in Vlado so deep that he wanted to get on his knees and beg her to take him away to her Missouri hidey-hole.

She flipped her hair once more, then turned from him and walked deliberately down the sidewalk, a statuesque silhouette in the twilight. He didn't go after her, though he wondered if she would turn around, and if so, what he would do. But she didn't, so he stood there watching and reassuring himself that he was glad he'd ended it. After all, a guy needed his freedom.

With Lydia gone he was free to see if his sweet petunia needed anything, even just a glass of water, because *why get up when I'm right here?*

By eight o'clock, Inky had extinguished his grill and gone home to his suffering wife. Joe and Vlado were wiping down the counters to the refrain of some song that Bootnose was outside singing to himself.

"We've done it again," Vlado said to Joe.

"Exactly. We didn't sell a damn thing."

"Right, but nobody went home hungry. And you know what, Sinovic really isn't so bad on that squeezebox of his once you get used to it. Like our sausage, you know?"

"Did I see Lydia out there?"

"Who didn't see Lydia out there? Doesn't she ever get cold?"

"You know," Joe said, "there's Dorothy Penny . . . and then, there's Lydia."

"Lydia," was all Vlado could say, which sounded enough like a toast that they drained a couple shots. "Well, she's gone, Joey, I swear. I only want what you have." He wasn't totally sure he wanted what Joe had, or what it was exactly, but he knew he had to lay out his sentiments in front of a witness, otherwise . . . well, there would be no otherwise, that's what he was saying.

Bootnose had apparently finished his aria, and the only sound Vlado heard was the hum of the compressor, then the slam of the front door—unannounced, as the jingle bell was still loitering in the vegetable aisle.

"What did Inky forget?" he said to Joe, who was tinkering with the thermostat. He went out front where a shadowy form stood inside the doorway. He stepped forward and Vlado saw that it was Stritchie, hands in the pockets of his trench coat, fedora centered, face frozen.

"Hey, it's our first customer," Vlado said, but Stritchie didn't respond, just set his hat on the counter and moved his fingers to his head to check on his perfectly parted hair. He looked around the store and seemed to be thinking. Stritchie always seemed to be thinking, which unnerved Vlado, who was more comfortable once he knew what people were thinking about. This time, Vlado didn't need to ask.

"The rent was due yesterday," Stritchie said, then cocked his head like a curious dog.

"Has it been a month already? Joe, has it been a month?" The look on Joe's face told Vlado that yes, it had been a month, and no, the rent hadn't been paid.

"What, no grace period?"

"You get your grace in church. I get my rent on time."

Joe *chinged* open the cash register and fished for the few bills and coins they'd stocked it with to make change.

"Forget that," Stritchie said. "This way." He gestured toward the heavy metal door of Stein's Office, which Vlado unlatched and tugged open. Vlado followed Joe into the chilly room, with its thick, no doubt soundproof, walls, and he wondered—irrationally, he hoped—whether he would freeze to death before he ran out of air. Already he couldn't get a deep breath.

It was a good sign when Stritchie came in as well and took a close look at the shelves that held the steaks and roasts and pig parts that had been neglected by the good people on Strawberry Hill, who apparently were only hungry on Sundays. Stritchie patted a few rump roasts like he was some food inspector; he picked up a ribeye and sniffed it; he ran one finger along the metal shelf, then rubbed the finger against his thumb as if he was feeling the quality of everything. Stritchie knew his shit, whatever that was.

"Wrap it up," he said.

"Which one?" Vlado asked.

"All of it."

"What do you mean?"

Stritchie peered down at Vlado as if to say *how do I explain this to a small child*. He dangled the ribeye in front of the cousins.

"You think this will last forever?"

They got to work loading the meat onto the steel table and Joe broke out a fresh roll of butcher's paper. Vlado was imagining how they could reassemble the entire cow, then noticed the missing ribs—Inky and Bootnose, no doubt—so, no infrastructure, and he stacked his wrappings next to Joe's. With that finished, Vlado went for the remaining smoked sausage.

"Not that crap," Stritchie said. "Let's load it up." Apparently "let's" meant Vlado and Joe, who stacked the packages into the trunk of Stritchie's roadster.

"We're going for a short ride," Stritchie said. They squeezed in and he drove up the hill past St. John's and parked at the foot of the stairs leading to the old Scroggs house next door, a stone and brick mansion built in the last century by a prominent attorney. Upon his death, the house was converted to an orphanage, but you'd never know it from the wide porch and elegant leaded glass windows that peered out over the confluence of the rivers, over the stockyards and carving plants, over the Hill in all directions.

It wasn't until they pried themselves out of the car that Vlado noticed Father Oyster-Face standing in a pool of streetlight at the foot of the stairs, in his black robe, like some prince of darkness. Nothing about seeing Vlado and Joe improved his miserable expression, but he did his best to give Stritchie a smile, more of a grimace really, and suddenly Vlado was thinking about Lydia, wondering if his possibly errant thoughts about her, his actual encounter with her, his awakened desire that he was determined to ignore was something Kovac could sense, sniff out, and hold Vlado accountable for. He shivered and took a step backwards.

"You know my friends Vladimir and Josip, right?" Stritchie said. Of course, they all knew each other, Vlado thought, what the hell? "Well, they have something for you," he continued, and beckoned toward the trunk, which he unlatched and opened with something like a flourish. The stack of glossy packages glowed snow-white beneath the streetlight.

Then Stritchie actually did smile, not a big, toothy grin, but his lips tightened and curved upwards in an unnatural, but not completely unwelcoming, way.

"Merry Christmas," he said. "From Big Sausage."

A half hour later, Stritchie dropped them back at the store. He produced a money clip and gave Vlado and Joe each a five-dollar bill.

"Get your wives something nice. God knows they deserve it."

Vlado felt the crisp bill, new enough to give you a paper cut.

"Do you by any chance have ones?" He liked his roll of bills to have some bulk.

Stritchie ignored him and held up a single finger. He slowly moved it back and forth, casting his Stritchie-spell.

"I know you boys can do better," he said. "I'll see you in a month." He pointed at Joe. At Vlado. And then he was gone.

17

VLADO and Joe opened dutifully at seven the next morning. They didn't bother with the bowties. All they had was sausage, which they didn't bother to load into the case. Vlado gave their five-dollar bills to Inky and Bootnose and dispatched them out to Starr's, hoping for another animal.

"No chickens," Vlado warned them. "Maybe some eggs, but nothing with any goddam feathers."

It felt like an intrusion when Vlado heard the jingle of the reinstalled doorbell that announced Mae Jankovic's arrival. She wandered down the vegetable aisle, toting a wicker bag and eyeing the cans of beans, tomatoes, corn, and whatnot with suspicion. She approached the counter, exasperated.

"Nothing fresh?"

"It's winter," Vlado said without enthusiasm. "We have cabbage, but it's pickled."

She bit her lip and hunched over her open purse, pushing the coins around with one finger. She looked at the list of prices posted on the counter and sighed as if she were the Kaiser surrendering.

"Okay, I'll take two."

"Cabbage?" Vlado said.

"No, that whatever-it-is sausage of yours."

"You want to buy some?" Joe was suddenly alert. "I'll go—"

Vlado stepped on Joe's toe. "I'm sorry, Mae." He gestured to the empty case. "We just sold out the last batch. Christmas, you know, everybody stocking up."

He enjoyed her visible disappointment for a moment. "But we've got another dozen or two in the smoker. Ready Thursday. I tell you what, we'll put you first in line." He tore a page from Joe's notepad, wrote her name on it and taped it to the white tile wall behind the counter. He held up his pencil.

"How many rings did you say?"

"You better make it three," she said, and Vlado wrote down the number. "Christmas Eve for sure?"

"I promise. We'll be opening at noon and closing early, so don't be too late," said Vlado. She fiddled again with her coins. "No need, pay us when you pick it up." She turned to go. "And Mae," he added, "Don't tell anybody we're running low. Makes us look bad."

She jingled out, and Joe looked at Vlado like he was a crazy man.

Vlado beamed back at him. "I give it about two hours." He tore off four more sheets, wrote a name in small and illegible script on each one, and beneath that a number between two and five. He lined these up on the wall to the right of Mae's order.

In fact, it was only forty minutes later when Dorothy Penny jingled in and marched straight up to the counter with a disturbed look.

"What a pleasant surprise," Vlado said, which he meant, despite the frown that was scrunching her fulsome eyebrows.

"You big dummies. You give all your sausage away and don't save any for your loyal customers?"

Vlado nudged Joe. *You take this one.*

"I'm sorry, Dorothy, we had no idea it would be so popular," Joe said. He took out paper and pen. "But we're taking advance orders."

She looked suspiciously at the five orders posted to the wall. "Are you sure there'll be enough?"

"I tell you what," Joe said, writing her name clearly on the paper. "I'll put you so you're next behind Mae." He moved the note after Mae's to the far right and taped Dorothy Penny's paper in its place. "How many rings?"

"One. No, two."

Joe wrote it down. "Done. We'll see you Thursday, noon sharp."

"Merry Christmas," Vlado called out after her.

They were closing up when Inky and Bootnose rolled in with another corpse—an enormous hog with a lot of jowly fat—along with a crate of eggs, mercifully minus the chickens that laid them. Vlado and Joe went to work, trimming off scraps for sausage, slicing the shoulder to be ground, separating the ribs and hanging them in the smoker.

They knocked off just before midnight and made it to Morty's for last call. There was a fair crowd for a Monday night. Vlado recognized a few guys from the plant sagging over the bar, but he was beat, so he and Joe sat at the other end, closer to the radio that was broadcasting Joe Nemitz's "Moody Kansas City" show. A mellow flugelhorn was noodling over a sparse piano accompaniment when Morty came over. He looked as weary as Vlado felt.

Vlado waved away the bottle Morty was setting down. "I'll just have a beer." Joe followed suit and Morty brought over two mugs.

"Where you guys been?"

"Busy," Vlado said.

"I hear it's been slow," he said.

"It's not like we've seen you over there."

Morty opened his arms to indicate the room. "And when would that happen?"

"Don't worry, it doesn't matter. First, we sell out all our beef, now the sausage is gone too. And Christmas is coming. Going to be a lot of disappointed *slavskis*."

"Maybe Sadie Goran can give you a deal on some chickens," Morty said. "I'd personally come in and buy a plucked version of that fucking rooster of hers. In fact, I'll go over and shoot him for you myself."

Vlado flinched at the very thought of touching a chicken and swigged deeply on his beer to erase the persistent memory of chicken fat, feet, feathers, and other parts better left nameless that all added up to create such an odious creature.

Morty topped up Vlado's glass. "You really out of sausage?"

"We'll have more by Thursday," Joe said, "but people are putting in orders like crazy. I don't know what we're going to do."

Vlado looked at his cousin with proud admiration. "That's right, but keep it under your hat. I hate to have to say no."

Morty shrugged. "Who would I tell?"

The next morning, Morty's wife Petra was their first customer. She reserved four rings and was followed later in the day by Maja Stipovich, Lucy Tomasic, and Lubo Grisnik, whose orders were duly taped onto the wall. The day before Christmas Eve, the preorders continued until a large swath of the tile wall was covered with paper. Vlado left Joe in the front to take care of business while he pulled a sour head out of the bin and peeled off the briny cabbage leaves. He scooped steamed rice into a bowl along with a fat-rich mixture of ground pork and a this-and-that selection of spices. He thought of his aunt Vera and remembered to crack two eggs over the mixture, then massaged the whole mess into a gooey consistency. He spooned a knob of stuffing onto each cabbage leaf and wrapped it into a tidy two-bite bundle, which he set onto a rimmed baking sheet. He continued until he had a nursery of tightly swaddled pigs-in-a-blanket—he preferred the more colorful American term—which he then covered with a can of chopped tomatoes, the juices of which turned the whole deal slightly pink. It looked and smelled right as far as he could remember, and he placed it in Stein's Office for later.

Vlado was finishing his third tray when Joe came back with his notebook to count the sausage rings.

"What'll we do with all that?"

"New Year's Day is coming. We need something new to run out of."

18

The morning of Christmas Eve brought snow, large flakes that clung to Vlado's eyelashes as he blinked his way to the store just before dawn. Today it would happen or not, and although he figured the weather would be one more check in the "not" column, at least the snow was gentle and not blowing around—calm and Christmas-like, wasn't it?—and he whistled the "Dancing Nutbread" song and tried to think happy thoughts.

He was glad to see the lights already on at the store and his cousin poised behind the counter, apron on, bowtie in place, ready to ring up a can of lima beans or tomato sauce or sardines should Mae or Mrs. Divac decide to brave the slippery sidewalks.

"I'm here for my sausage," Vlado announced, stamping his feet in the doorway.

"Go away, we're all out," Joe said, and reached for the slivovitz.

By ten o'clock the entire place had been scrubbed spotless. They had pulled the last batch of sausage out of the smoker and stacked all the rings together into the meat case. Vlado laid a bed of sauerkraut onto the bottom of a roasting pan and nested in his little piggies. He topped it all off with more sauerkraut and poured over another can of tomato juice for good measure. Joe opened the vents on the smoker to up the temperature and they slid the pan in.

Inky showed up, and Joe gave him a long shopping list.

"French bread? Potatoes?" Inky moved a finger down the list. "Butter? Milk? Where are we supposed to get all this?"

"If it were me, I'd go to a fucking grocery store," Vlado said. "Try the A&P on Minnesota and put it on Poochie's account. They'll know. And pick up some beer."

Forty-five minutes later, Inky and Bootnose unloaded boxes of tomatoes, head lettuce, radishes, turnips, red potatoes, cartons of milk and orange juice, and still-warm loaves of crusty bread that Vlado arranged along a sawhorse table, turning the boxes backwards to hide the A&P logo. He got the prices from Inky, subtracted a nickel from each one, and posted the new prices on the sides of the baskets. He put the beer in Stein's Office to chill and positioned a batch of sarmas on the counter next to a plate of sliced nutbread.

The bells of St. John's began to ring the noontime hour. The cousins stared at the front door, willing it to open, willing their own little jingle bell to ring. Vlado could hear the slight buzzing of the fluorescent lights. He could hear Joe scratching the side of his face with the back of a fingernail. He could sense the lettuce wilting and the sarma chilling into a pool of fat, and the nutbread drying out in the winter air. There was nothing else he could do.

Then he heard a light tapping at the front door. He looked at Joe, who shrugged.

"You unlocked it, didn't you?" he asked Joe, then realized that the "Open" sign should read "Closed" from where he stood.

"*Jebote*," Joe said, and went over to flip the sign and unlock the door and was almost knocked over by Stephani, pushing her way in hoisting a large bag, and Martina, who was dragging along little Donald, followed by nine-year-old Tom.

"Maybe you should be open for business and try to sell some goddam sausage for a change," Martina said, putting her hands over Donald's ears. "At least this way they get to see their father."

Behind Martina, a line of neighbors filed into the shop, stomping the snow off their feet and pulling their hands out of mittens and gloves, unwinding scarves, and pressing forward to the counter. The room filled with a loud mix of English and Croatian. Stefani unloaded four nutbreads from the bag. Joe pulled Tom behind the counter and showed him how to hit the "ching" key on the register while Vlado tried to herd everybody into a line, without much success, but so what, don't worry, everybody gets sausage. Bites of sarma disappeared, grocery sacks were filled with fresh produce and loaves of bread ("Cheaper than up the street," Mae said) while Joe and Tommy wrapped up the rings in butcher paper and rang the beautiful bell on the cash register.

Vlado looked at the little pot where Stefani had planted the seeds on St. Lucy Day. A tiny green leaf at the end of a pale stem was pushing its way up out of the soil.

19

Vlado never smoked cigarettes, had always thought it was stupid, and probably unhealthy, not that health was the decider, but still, why not stick around to enjoy the fun as long as possible. But he was smoking now, some godawful unfiltered thing, coughing and pacing the concrete-block hallway of St. Margaret's Hospital. Stefani had been in there almost an hour, *and why were the doctors so slow about the whole deal?*

"Vlado, it'll happen when it happens. Which, believe me, is never soon," Joe said.

Joe should know. He'd done this twice already, not him, actually, but Martina, as she was bound to point out. And now, Stefani. When he thought about what might be happening, he had to shut his eyes and shake away the image. A baby's going to come out of *there?* He sucked in another drag, and the room took a quick spin.

He was worried about Stefani. He was worried about the shop, where he could imagine Martina and Inky getting into it with sharp knives around. Stefani's parents were sitting on a bench in the hall, and the clicking of fake-Aunt-Vera's rosary beads was getting on one of the nerves that wound through his innards like a stretched spring.

"Maybe you should go back to the shop," he told Joe.

"Let's go for a walk," said Joe. "It might not even happen today."

Outside, the sun was low in the hazy February sky and the bleach-and-urine hospital smell was replaced by a damp whiff off the Kaw and the outgassing of wet soil and mulched leaves. Vlado shivered in his herringbone overcoat and walked a little faster.

Three blocks up Vermont, they reached Junior's Delicatessen, where Joe steered Vlado through the doors and into a too-bright room steamy with bodies and beer. Men in work shirts and caps just off their shift sat or stood two-deep at the long bar, so Joe and Vlado took a table in the corner. Joe held up two fingers and soon Junior's daughter Emily came over with a couple of pints. Vlado noticed the swollen bump under her apron. Jesus, was it contagious?

She set down the beers and Joe said, "You're looking well, Em." She rested one hand on her belly and gave them a tired smile.

"Haven't seen you guys in a while."

"We've been busy, especially this one," Joe nodded to Vlado, "who has his own blessed event taking place right now."

Vlado stared at Junior's daughter, who he'd always thought of as being a kid, and wondered when all this had happened. Here she was a grown young lady, about to do this thing, and suddenly he felt older than dirt.

"Yeah, we get a lot of that, being near the hospital. Congratulations, Mr. Novosel. This one's on me," she said and turned back toward the bar.

Joe laughed and clinked Vlado's glass. "Cheers, *Mister Novosel*, here's to the start of a great dynasty."

Vlado sat up a little straighter and tried on the name for size. "Mr. Novosel": responsible father and husband, patriarch and provider, a shining example for his little girl. He downed his beer and waved for two more.

"You don't think I can do this, do you, Joey?"

Three hours, four pints, and a pastrami sandwich later, Vlado suddenly remembered in a panic where he was and where he was supposed to be.

"Joe, we gotta get out of here," he said, taking a final swig. Joe pulled out his watch.

"Probably should while we still can."

Vlado stood and sagged against the table. His gaze traveled to the bar, where he didn't know anybody. It was mostly the Swift boys who went to Junior's. He thought he recognized a face at the far end, but it was hard to see past the corned beef sandwich, the entirety of which the guy was stuffing into his mouth. He was hefty, with mitt-like hands that clutched his Junior's triple-decker like it was the last life buoy on the Titanic. What was his name? It fizzed around in his brain but didn't rise to the surface.

Vlado was quiet on the way back to the hospital, mostly just trying to stay on the sidewalk. He knew he had something important ahead of him. *Don't worry everybody, Mr. Novosel is here, and everything is under control.* Joe was opening the glass door of the hospital when the image of the guy in the bar floated unannounced into Vlado's brain. The broad, humpty-dumpty silhouette. The fat, grabby fingers gripping the sandwich.

"Ovaltine." He whispered the three syllables like an unholy incantation.

"What?" Joe said.

"Ovaltine. Obersteen. I think that might have been Johnny Obersteen back at the bar." He turned back and tugged Joe's sleeve. "Come on, we've got to—"

Just then both doors flew open and there was Mrs. Lovick.

"Vlado, come quick. It's the baby."

"The baby." He followed her in. "The baby, is it okay? Is Stefani—?"

"Just hurry." She took off down the hall and Vlado staggered after her.

"Wait, what's wrong," he yelled after her, and she stopped and turned.

"Nothing's *wrong*, Vlado. You have a beautiful baby girl. You're a daddy." She took his hand and pulled him through some swinging doors and down to a large glass window that looked in on a room full of tiny beds with plastic shells.

"That one," she said, and pointed to number four in the first row, where an impossibly small human-looking thing with purple skin and wet, black hair wiggled its arms and kissed at the air.

Vlado stared and the thing stared back, and suddenly it wasn't just a thing. *I know you*, he thought, with no idea how he knew, but that was unmistakably his little girl. He might have been staring for seconds or hours when little Janet's new grandma tugged at him.

"Come on, Stefani wants to see you."

20

Vlado stood with Stefani next to the white marble baptismal font at St. John's in front of Father Oyster-Face. Godfather Joe held little Janet, whose mercifully less purple face poked out of a vast swath of white satin, the same dress Stefani and her mother before her had worn on their own blessed days. Godmother Martina was worrying her beads. Vlado felt itchy in his starched white shirt and necktie, sweating heavily into the one dark, wool jacket he wore to weddings and funerals, and now baptisms, apparently. Half the congregation had stayed after Mass and moved into the front seats to witness the blessed event. Father cleared his throat and waited for the rustling and coughing to stop; he made a showy sign of the cross and looked at Vlado.

"And what name have you given this child?" he asked.

Surely, he knows the baby's name, Vlado thought, and gave Joe a concerned look. Joe gestured with the baby toward the priest and shrugged. *Okay, so this was part of the whole thing.* Vlado stood up straight and looked Father in the eye.

"Janet," he said.

"Janet?"

"Janet."

Father blinked slowly and suddenly looked very tired. "Is there more?"

"Oh, right," said Vlado. "Janet Ivan Novosel." He loved how that sounded. Like a poem. He heard a sniffing behind him and turned to see new-grandpa Ivan finger a tear out of the corner of his eye.

Upon hearing herself summoned to the stage, Janet Ivan Novosel began a long, moaning cry that amped up like a fire siren to a shrill peak, followed by choking sobs until she caught her breath and began again.

Joe handed the quivering bundle to Martina, who held it away from herself and gave it a few quick shakes, to no avail, and passed it over to Stefani, who pressed it tight to her chest and swayed back and forth, but the screaming only took on a more ambulance-like quality.

"Here," said Vlado, and reached for the baby, which he nestled into the crook of his arm like a football, rocking her back and forth until the crying ramped down to tiny gasps. He held her out toward Father.

"Janet Ivan Novosel," he repeated, as if to start it all again.

Vlado tried not to fidget while Father went through the ritual and prayers and gave a little speech about water and the Spirit, dropped a few names like Matthew and St. John the Baptist, and tried to explain the ridiculous idea that baby Janet was born in a state of sin and that everything would be set right now. At the mention of sin, Vlado smelled something that, if sin had a smell, would smell like that. He'd seen the worst parts of chickens, but nothing had prepared him for the sight and stench of this tiny human that seemed to poop about every five minutes.

"Sorry," he said to Father, who took a small step backwards and rubbed his nose with the back of his hand.

This sped up the proceedings, and soon the Holy Oyster was going to work on Janet Ivan's tiny forehead, pouring water and rubbing on oil and muttering some Latin; a final prayer was said, everyone stood and clapped, then hurried toward the door.

When Vlado and Stefani and their little bundle of joy arrived at Big Sausage, their neighbors were already malingering around Inky's grill. Vlado held the baby high above him and pushed into the store where Joe was collecting quarters in exchange for index cards on which people were writing their guesses about the baby's weight. Stefani had cleaned her up and wrapped her into a blanket like a giant sarma. Vlado stood behind the meat counter with her, swaying back and forth and bending to sniff the top of her head before it would be overshadowed by more unspeakable scents.

Martina banged at the bell over the door with a broom handle and everybody quieted down. On the counter was a scale with a scooped top. Vlado cradled little Janet Ivan into it and bounced her up and down so the scale dial shot back and forth

"If she spits up, that changes everything," Mae Jankovic yelled from behind a box of cabbages, and Vlado stopped and let the needle settle. Joe peered at it.

"Eight pounds . . . one ounce."

"Bingo!" It was Dorothy Penny. She strode through the crowd, which parted like the Red Sea, to receive the promised three rings of sausage, one povitica, two sour cabbage heads, and a five dollar "gift certificate." ("It's like making your own kind of money," Joe had told Vlado. "They think they've won something, but we're going to get it back.")

Joe verified her number. "Anybody else?" he called out, and suddenly Bootnose was in front of him.

"Bootnose, you can't—"

"Right here, boss," he said, presenting his card.

Vlado saw a faint, erased vertical line in front of the eight. "Really, you thought it was eighteen—"

"Eight. It says eight."

"And that crooked one looks like it was once a seven."

"Besides," Joe said, "You work here."

"Well, I'm not working today."

Vlado handed him a broom.

By the end of the day, they'd sold out of sausage and nutbread and made a good dent in the ribs and chops. Since Christmas, Vlado's strategy of never making quite enough sausage had paid off, to the point where Joe had to find a couple more hog farmers, because Maurice only had so many pigs, or so he said, maybe running a little fake-shortage game of his own. Inky had somehow made a deal with the A&P produce manager to siphon a bit off the daily delivery, paying a wholesale price instead of having to buy it at the A&P for more and then mark it down. Most mornings during the week, Mrs. Divac was first in, sniffing the tomatoes and squeezing the melons, usually followed by Lubo Grisnik in his meat-cutter overalls, picking up one of the liver or smoked beef sandwiches Joe prepared for the increasing number of carvers who stopped in on their way to the Bottoms. Later in the day, it was not unusual to see Dorothy Penny and Mae Jankovic and their crocheting partners huddled up at the end of the meat counter helping themselves to the ever-present slices of nutbread and analyzing the sins of the less fortunate. The bell over the door jingled often enough to annoy Vlado, but this was finally mitigated by the corresponding ringing of the cash register, and over the two months since Christmas, they'd paid their back rent to Stritchie and even had to purchase a heavy safe for the leftover cash that Vlado wouldn't trust to a bank.

21

Despite—or because of—the success of Big Sausage, there was still the thing of having to work every day from six a.m. till God-knows-when, followed by a quick drink, and then home and the baby stuff, and all again. Vlado looked forward to the one time each week, Sunday morning, when he could collect his thoughts at Morty's and perhaps even share them with his close associates.

One morning, he was sampling Morty's finest with Joe and Bootnose —not Inky, whose wife had dragged him off to Mass—when Lubo Grisnik sat down with a pinochle deck, notepad, and a bottle of rakija. They all reached into their pocket for nickels while Joe took the ever-present pencil from behind his ear.

"Not much of a day off," he said, as it went without saying he'd be the scorekeeper.

"What can I say, Joey?" said Vlado. "Thank God you went to University so you can count to ten for the rest of us."

"You went to University?" said Lubo.

"When would I have gone to fucking University? I've been cutting meat since I was nine years old."

Bootnose dealt the cards then turned over the queen of spades in the middle. Vlado tossed down a ten of spades and took the first trick.

Bootnose and Lubo had both been born and raised on the Hill, and Vlado knew they held him and Joe in a sort of strange regard, these two cousins who could rattle off Croatian faster than anybody could understand and who seemed to be able to absorb inhuman amounts of plum brandy as if it were part of their very bloodstream. He poured a round of shots, looking to press any advantage against his tragically less skilled opponents.

They played quietly for a while and the coins piled up in front of Joe and Vlado, until Vlado had to pee. He pointed to his money, "Joe, take inventory," then listed a bit on his way back to the toilet. He stood at the urinal and took in the so-called "phone book." Some names had up to five stars next to them. *Pretty fucking childish*, he thought, then recognized his own handwriting on a few entries. And there was Lydia, with her phone number crossed out. Good to know someone was updating the roster. He knew Stefani was there somewhere but didn't want to see it. He also knew without looking that he wouldn't find Dorothy Penny, because what pencil wouldn't explode into flames from the pure sacrilege.

When he returned, Morty had joined the table. Inky had arrived from church, and everybody was sitting back in their chairs; Joe and Lubo had lit cigars, and Joe was talking:

"So Vlado and I are at the Green Man Bar," he was saying, meaning the divey place in downtown Zagreb they used to sneak into when they were sixteen. "Vlado's going on about our little cousin Lubi, who was just fourteen at the time, and like hell would he ever let her date a Serb —"

"Last time, Vlado said it was the Kokoruda Café," said Inky.

"You know this story?" Joe said.

"The entire congregation of St. John's knows this story."

"That's another story."

"No, it's the Serbian guy and Vlado's big mouth—"

"Well, I haven't heard the story," said Morty. Inky sighed.

Joe went back to it: "So Vlado and I are at . . . let's just say it's the Green Man Bar. We're about sixteen, and we'd had a few shots—"

"See, it wasn't a café," Vlado said to Inky.

"Anyhow, Vlado and I are talking about our little cousin Lubi, who was only then fourteen, but you knew she was going to be a beauty, and Vlado's saying how he'd never let her go out with a Serb, and he's getting louder—"

"Odd how I can picture this," said Morty.

"Yeah," Vlado said, "well you guys weren't there. Suddenly the place smelled like a pigsty, and I was only saying—"

"Only saying to the whole bar that you were ready to fight anybody whose nose had a little more hook than your own," Joe said. "So, this young guy a few seats down—who's actually really fucking big, probably a Serb but who can tell—comes over to where we're sitting, walks up to Vlado, gets right in his face and tells him, 'I think I might want to go out with your cousin. You got a problem?' So Vlado just says that if you're going out with my cousin, at least let me buy you a drink, we can get to know each other and whatnot, and the guy gives me a nasty look and elbows in next to Vlado. They clink and then drain their shots, and Vlado asks the guy if everything's okay, and the guy says sure, so then Vlado says, 'Good, now go back to the shithole country you came from.' Holy Mother, I think, but the Serb—he had to be a Serb—just looks at Vlado, points a single finger, then turns back into the crowd. Vlado shuts up for a while, but of course they were waiting outside. Three of them. One sucker-punches me then pins my arms while the other two go to work on Vlado. They have him down and are kicking him right there on the side of the road, until a streetcar comes by, and they take off, but Vlado looks like hell. I get him home, and you can't even imagine our Aunt Vera, hysterical and yelling about blood everywhere and who did this to her baby boy, but we get him cleaned up and it's not too bad. Some nasty bruises, but anyway, it wasn't the first time his nose had been broken. My cousin may be a short loudmouth, but he's built like a tank."

Bootnose had a serious look on his face and spoke through a mouthful of boiled egg:

"Don't worry, if those guys want any more trouble . . ." he clapped Inky on the back, almost knocking him out of his chair, "this guy'll take care of it." He laughed and a bit of egg shot out of his mouth and landed next to Vlado's pile of nickels.

"You dummy," said Inky, "that was fifteen years ago. How many times you have to hear this story?"

"Actually, I think I have heard it before," said Morty, "But this was good. I could really picture the streetcar and all that." There was silence and everyone took a swig of whatever they were drinking. Lubo gathered up the cards and began to shuffle.

"None of you have heard the whole story," Vlado said then. He didn't like to think about it. But suddenly he felt the same need people probably felt when they went to talk to Father Oyster in the dark, private box, that somehow by talking about it you could get some kind of a do-over. He looked around the table, at his cousin Joe, as close to a brother as anyone could have; at Inky and Bootnose—his new partners, he had to admit it; at Lubo, one of the most enthusiastic Big Sausage converts. And Morty, who had his own priest-like way of presiding over this congregation. Vlado folded his hands prayer-like and rested his chin on his thumbs.

"I just have to say up front that I was only trying to scare them," he said. Joe shot him a look.

"It's okay, Joey, what happened, happened."

"Scare who?" said Morty.

"Those same stinking guys. I saw them in the billiards hall a couple weeks later. I just wanted to tell them don't fuck with me, or my cousin Jozo. Don't fuck with us, because we'll fuck you up. Then one grabbed for me, but I had the pool cue and took a couple of hard swings, then got the hell out of there." He swigged his beer and looked at Joe.

The laughter went out of the room and the smoky air compressed itself around the table, until Joe finally spoke. "Yeah, I'm pretty sure you haven't heard this part. It was a bad deal. That night Vlado shows up really late, maybe two, three in the morning. He's drunk and he's crying, and he's got this stick of wood with blood on it."

"I just wanted to scare him," Vlado said again, which was the truth, right?

"I know, Vlado," Joe said.

Joe went on: "You gotta understand what a crazy time it was. I mean, you look back on the Great War and think it worked out okay and we won, right? But it's different if you were there when it was all starting to fall apart. It didn't make any sense. Everybody had their thing—Serbs, Jews, Turks, Russians, everybody ready to throw a punch, or worse. People had guns. Secret meetings. It was stupid to mouth off in a bar like that, but it was happening everywhere.

"We later found out Vlado'd shattered the guy's knee; in fact, he was a year younger than us, some big football star at his high school, and who knows if the leg would ever heal. Vlado took off on my bicycle and hid out at his girlfriend's, Radic, what's her name?"

"Dijana Radic," Vlado said. Spooky Dijana, with the dark rings around her eyes and her cold, skinny fingers. "She kept saying over and over how they're going to kill us all. Whoever 'they' are. And I knew she was right; that shithead Emperor was going to take us and make us fight for some goddam thing he was pissed about. We'd be up to our assholes in mud just shooting at each other for God knows what reason."

"I wasn't so sure," said Joe. "Maybe it would blow over, the kid's leg would heal, and we'd go back to minding our own business."

"Like we ever minded our own business," Vlado said.

"But when that Gavrilo guy, who unfortunately turned out to be a Serb, shot the Archduke—"

"You mean the Archbishop?" Inky said.

"No," said Joe, "The guy who was going to be the next Emperor. Our guy, right? I know, it's confusing, I still don't get it all, but they went nuts in Zagreb, pulling down flags and burning stuff. Everything was crazy, you didn't know who to trust. Vlado was still hiding out, but he'd bike over at off hours, when he'd go on and on about boat tickets and New York." He smiled at Vlado. "And bright-lipped American girls."

"Bright-lipped American girls?" said Inky, and Bootnose snorted out a laugh. There was a moment of silence when Vlado figured everyone was reckoning with their own American-girl fate.

"Anyhow," Joe continued, "The more he talked, the more it all seemed possible, and we started to count our *kuna*."

"Admit it, Joey, the whole deal was my idea," said Vlado.

"I know, I was nervous about it, but you'd won me over." Joe turned back to the room. "Finally I told Vlado, 'If you go, I go.' Then one night the two of us are having a drink in the kitchen when my dad comes in late from work. He doesn't look happy. He tosses an official-looking envelope onto the table addressed to me. I open it and when I see the emperor's seal at the top and the typed words below, I know right away what it is. I had one week to get my affairs together and report to the army. What could I do? I remember looking at Vlado and feeling sick, thinking how can I tell him I can't go now.

"Then my dad picks up the letter and curses, which was not like him. 'Why did we even fight?' he says and rips it in half, then in half again, and stacks the squares on the table. 'This is not for you, Jozo,' he says and sweeps the paper away. Then he gives me a large envelope. I open it and first see the hundred-*kruna* notes and behind that the two certificates with the Cunard Line heading; "Josip Marevic" typed on one, "Vladimir Novosel" on the other."

"Train tickets?" asked Lubo.

"Boat tickets," said Vlado.

"Well, we did take a train early the next morning to Rijeka," Joe said, "where we had to wait for the boat."

"We didn't know if somebody was after us, or what," said Vlado. When he thought back on those three nervous days hiding out in their cousin's apartment, fearing every passing footstep and knock on the door, it seemed like a made-up story. Was that really him and Joe then, pulling their caps low, climbing the gangplank, finding their hammocks in the lowest reaches of the boat? He remembered shivering in steerage, thinking the ship would never leave, and only when a horn bellowed and he felt a swaying movement did he chance a climb to the aft deck. He would never forget that moment, squinting through the sunlight that bounced off the Adriatic and danced on the receding cliffs, like a semaphore message from the beyond. *Goodbye to everything you know and love. Forward, always forward. You fucked it all up.*

Vlado remembered the endless, sickening trip across the Atlantic, the first look at the giant statue of the lady, the crowd and confusion of voices spilling off the gangplank until somehow somebody had stamped some papers and they were in New York, looking for the bus station.

Bootnose leaned forward. "So how did it all end?"

Vlado shrugged. "We're here, aren't we?"

"What about the kid?" said Lubo.

"The kid?"

"You know, whose knee you broke."

All Vlado knew was from a letter from Aunt Vera who told him the kid's entire family moved south when it was no longer safe to be a Serb in Zagreb. He hadn't thought about him since then.

"Who knows, maybe it kept him out of the war."

22

It was inevitable that they would cross the river. Joe was hesitant, but Vlado kept at him. That's where the money was, not here with their tightwad neighbors, *God love 'em, but God forbid we should bump the price a nickel.*

"Do you even remember your kids' names?" he asked Joe one exhausted evening, while they were closing up. Vlado thought about Janet Ivan, not so little anymore; at six months, she was a chubby eating machine. She'd wiggle her fat fingers and giggle when Vlado would pretend to give her a spoonful of whatever that green mush was and pull it away at the last minute. Her eyes had grown to huge dark orbs with awning-like lashes, and big black pupils that would follow Vlado around the room— he could feel them on his back like an accusing stare when he headed out the door early every morning. At night, when he came to gaze at her in her crib, wondering about this tiny creature, she'd open them again and before she could cry, he'd scoop her up and wrap her in an afghan and sit with her in Ivan's big chair in the living room. Many nights, he'd wake around two or three o'clock to Stefani picking up little Janet and shooing him off to bed, where his thoughts swirled for a while before he'd drift into a half sleep, and then what seemed like moments later, he'd drag himself out of bed and start it all again.

Vlado hadn't forgotten that breakfast at the Muehlbach Hotel. Now he asked Joe for the umpteenth time, "Why are they so special that they can charge five times as much for those little wieners?"

"Nobody wants a big sausage for breakfast," said Joe.

"There's a joke in there but for once I'm not going to make it, but truth is, we're the ones getting dicked around," Vlado said.

"The problem is," Joe said, "it's the same amount of time and effort to do little sausages as big ones. All those tiny sheep casings."

"Or don't go to so much trouble, curing and smoking." Vlado looked at the clock above the countertop, which read ten-fifteen. "Wait here," he said and went into Stein's Office for a chunk of pork shoulder, which he sliced into pieces that would fit into the grinder. He set the plate for a quarter inch and cranked it through once, then again. He added the usual amount of salt and black and white pepper. A little garlic. Some nutmeg. Inky hadn't finished stocking the shelves last night so Vlado had to reach around stacks of boxes for the sage leaves that were hanging up to dry. He ripped off a few bunches and crumbled them over the pork and massaged the whole deal. It smelled great with the fragrant sage, but maybe too much. Unwilling to start again, he looked around for something to counter the herb's oily bitterness and saw an opened box of Log Cabin syrup. Thinking sausage always goes great with pancakes, he cracked out a bottle and drizzled it over the mixture. He massaged it until the pork was sticking to itself—let Armour mess with the sheep intestines—and hand-rolled it all into cigarillo-sized lengths which he lined up on a cookie sheet. He carried it out to the counter and looked at the clock.

"Twelve minutes," he said to Joe.

"Now we smoke it?" asked Joe.

"No. Now we cook it." They went to the back and heated an iron skillet and tossed in a handful. Soon they were sizzling in their own melted grease and in ten minutes they were golden brown and filling the room with a thick, porky aroma. Vlado forked them out of the skillet, singing "This little piggy went to market," like he would sing to Janet Ivan while trying not to think what it was really about.

Joe looked skeptical. "No cure, no smoke . . ."

Vlado ignored him and took a bite, which crumbled nicely in his mouth, and when his tongue searched for the flavor, he found that he tasted neither syrup nor sage, that somehow, they'd combined with each other and the pork to create a flavor he had no word for. Mostly it tasted like pig. Like really good pig. And if money had a flavor, he thought, it tasted like that too.

Joe was chewing his, and his eyes lit up. "What's in this, anyway?"

"The point is what's not in it. All that cure and salt, and sheep guts even, they get in the way of what you really want to taste. Let me ask you this. What does Mrs. Divac want almost every time she comes in?"

"Fresh tomatoes," said Joe.

"Why doesn't she just buy canned?" Silence. "Exactly."

Vlado stood in front of the full-length mirror in their bedroom and buttoned the starched cuffs of his white shirt. Monday was the slowest day at the store, so he felt only slightly worried about handing the keys over to Inky, knowing Martina would check in later. Stefani wrapped around him from behind to adjust his bowtie, pressing into his back a little tighter than necessary, which was not unpleasant, but he needed to focus. She moved her hands down to smooth his shirt, then past that to a more suggestive area and kissed him on the back of the neck.

"My handsome boy. I don't get enough of you." Janet Ivan let out a wail from the laundry basket where Stefani had left her in the kitchen.

"How does she always know?" Vlado said.

"Kids just know. She doesn't want a little brother. She wants you all to herself. Just like I do." She faked a pout into the mirror, her hands drifted away, and Janet Ivan immediately went quiet.

"Maybe I'll be home early," Vlado said, raising one eyebrow to Stefani in the mirror.

"Why, is Morty's closed tonight?"

"No," he said, wondering why she would think that, then the light came on. "Oh, right. Okay, you've got a point. But maybe if your mother —"

"You know the baby makes her nervous."

The whole deal makes me nervous, he wanted to say. "Well, there's always the orphanage," he said, and Stefani gave him one of her hard punches. "Hey, at least they eat well." Stritchie's miraculous Christmas delivery had continued as a monthly tithe, part of Vlado's genius business plan of always giving stuff away.

Stefani sighed dramatically. "I suppose they do have visiting hours."

"And we could probably take her out on Sundays."

A siren cranked up from the kitchen.

Vlado slipped on a gray satin vest and Stefani handed him his straw boater, which he installed at a provocative angle, until she straightened it and gave him a light slap on the cheek.

"You be a good boy over there," she said.

Joe was waiting outside in the hearse. *Their* hearse now. Sandusky had given them a good deal, maybe thinking it was unseemly for a single vehicle to be performing that sort of double duty.

Vlado climbed in the front, and Joe looked him up and down. "You look like you work in a carnival."

Vlado took in Joe's dark suit, necktie, stiff grey fedora. "Yeah, well, who died?"

Vlado felt queasy as they bounced across the viaduct toward the looming skyline. They exited onto Broadway and cruised through the shadows of the downtown buildings, which seemed to be leaning over too far, like they could collapse at any moment. He scanned the women strolling the sidewalks in their pillbox hats and tight skirts, suddenly terrified by the thought that any one of them could be Lydia. He felt short of breath, not wanting to fully inhale, afraid he might accidentally rebreathe some of the air that she'd breathed, and there they'd be, sharing air and God knows what else.

"What's the matter with you?" Joe asked. "Don't puke in the car."

Joe turned onto Ninth St. and soon pulled up in front of their first stop at the Wolferman Grocers building. He went around back to retrieve the samples while Vlado stepped out onto the sidewalk and tugged at his tightly buttoned collar.

"Hey, Joey, do you smell perfume?"

23

The day had turned into an afternoon scorcher by the time they headed toward their fifth and final appointment. Joe had slipped out of his suit jacket, and Vlado's boater had left a sweat ring around his head that dribbled into his eyes. So far, nobody had shown the least interest in distributing any Big Sausage product to restaurants or grocery stores on the Missouri side of the river, thank you very much. Nor did they want to see any of the samples, which were not improving in the melting ice chest in the back of the hearse.

Joe pulled into a loading zone in front of the imposing Power and Light building, where Morton's Food and Beverage Company claimed the entire twenty-first floor. It was the tallest tower west of the Mississippi, featuring an arched façade adorned with concrete lightning bolts that seemed to be blasting the whole thing skyward. At its pinnacle, a glassed-in bell tower cast out a nightly illumination, a testament to a new era of "power and light," which, from across the river, had always looked to Vlado more like the glowing tip of a cigar. The cousins lifted their ice-packed chest of samples into a little red wagon Vlado'd borrowed from Janet Ivan and towed it through the cavernous lobby and into a bronzed elevator. A thin man in a double-breasted jacket, epaulets, and service-station hat yanked on a lever and they groaned skyward, like three birds in a cage, shooting up the center of the great building.

After what felt like a journey to the moon, Vlado stepped unsteadily into an ornate hallway, wondering if there might be less air or less gravity to account for a new sense that none of this was entirely real. His boots looked scuffed and dirty against the shiny, pink marble floor that stretched beneath pendulous Tiffany lamps and led past important-looking mahogany doorways. He was conscious of his and Joe's heels echoing off the stone as they approached a large door that looked more like the entrance to a church than an office. The name Frederic Morton was carved right into the wood.

"Do we knock?" Vlado asked. Joe shrugged and tapped a single knuckle lightly on the door. They heard a muffled high-pitched voice and hurried footsteps until the door was opened by a gray-haired woman. She peered at them over the top of her half-moons with a distrustful look that would have done Martina proud, then bustled back toward a desk where a telephone was clanging.

"For heaven's sakes, come in," she said, waving them toward an overstuffed divan.

An hour later, Vlado and Joe were still sitting quietly on the sofa, their wagon at their feet, wondering how to get the attention of the woman who had been talking nonstop on the phone, when she finally hung up and glared at the two of them. She jiggled a finger at Vlado, and he realized he was still wearing his boater.

"Mr. Marevic and Mr. Novosel," she read from a notepad, and fortunately that's who they were because it wasn't a question. "Big Sausage," she added, which made Vlado smile while her own lips pursed downward. "Go," she said, and they followed her gesture down a hallway to another oversized, carved door.

"How big is this guy, anyway?" Vlado said.

Joe nudged the door open, and they entered a dim, hushed room, lined with floor-to-ceiling bookshelves and dominated by a broad mahogany desk with a globe and a model of a TWA airplane poised on a stand. They pulled their wares across the plush red carpet toward the desk and the man behind it, who stood with his back to them, a tall silhouette against a large window. Vlado could see past him to the quilted prairie, the wide twists of the Missouri River, and the clouds that drifted like unmoored boats about to collide.

Fred Morton turned from the window and squinted at them. His height was accentuated by his thin frame and the vertical blue and white pinstripes on his burgundy-vested suit. His dark hair was oiled and parted in the middle and a half-smoked cigar jutted out from beneath a thin mustache.

"Gentlemen." He removed the cigar with one hand and extended the other to Joe, then Vlado, who winced at his bony grip. "Brothers in sausage. *Mes frères des saucisses.* The French, they know. The tarragon. The dill"—he wrote the words in the air with his cigar—"*Les espices du poignante. Alors. Bienvenue. Aloha.* Velkum, no?"

"No?" said Vlado.

"Yes," said Joe, "and thank you for your time."

Fred Morton gestured to the two leather lounge chairs in front of his desk, and they all sat. He pulled out a pocket watch, frowned at it, and set it on the desk.

It occurred to Vlado that maybe they should have given more thought to this moment and what they might say. Suddenly he heard himself saying,

"Do you like eggs?"

"Do I like eggs? I eat two eggs every morning."

"So, these eggs. Do they come in a can?"

Fred Morton twisted the tip of his 'stache and seemed to consider. "Eggs from a can? From a can? No, *certainmente.*"

"That's what we're saying. Fresh. We all want fresh. Like the eggs."

"Why are we talking about eggs?"

"We're not exactly talking about eggs."

"You keep saying eggs."

"Not eggs. This," Vlado said, "this is what we're talking about."

He leaned down and unlatched their makeshift cooler. The lid wasn't halfway open when Joe's eyes met his with a horrified look, but it was too late to get the pig back into the barn.

"Oh my fucking God," said Morton, standing from his chair and backing away, holding a handkerchief over his nose and waving his cigar like he was banishing vampires with a crucifix.

Two minutes later, *les frères des saucisses* and their little red wagon were back on the street. Staring at an empty space in the loading zone.

"Probably towed," said Joe. "I'll talk to the door-man."

"It's a hearse, Joey. What if there was a body in there?"

They dragged themselves over to the river side of downtown and a fenced-in parking lot where they shoved some bills through a window slot to a surly looking kid who slid them their keys. Vlado pushed a couple dollar bills back at him, and they headed for the car.

"Did you actually tip the guy?" Joe asked.

"Here's the thing, Joey, it's circumstances like these where you need to show some class. The guy who pays for lunch is the boss. You can give me your half later."

For a late lunch they opted for Katz Drugstore, a gaudy emporium famous for its ornate soda fountain and swirly marble lunch counter. They settled in, and Vlado eyed the long, laminated menu.

"Amazing, you can get breakfast any time of day. Who'd-a thought of that?"

He ordered eggs and sausage, and Joe got a pastrami sandwich. Vlado's eggs were perfectly sunny, but he poked at the pathetic sausages. "I swear, you need a steak knife to cut this thing."

They ate in silence, until Joe said,

"I guess there wasn't enough ice."

"Who knew we'd have to sit there forever?"

"We'll get it next time."

24

Vlado didn't tell Joe about his idea, or about the "Help Wanted" sign he'd seen on the way out of Katz. They were closing the store a couple nights later when Vlado put on a sad face and puffed out a tired sigh.

"You know, Joey, I can't keep going on like this. I swear, it's coming at me from all sides. This thing," he pointed to the bulge of bills in his pocket, "is just not big enough for all concerned. I mean, that kid . . . not just feeding her, but other stuff. These little dresses she grows out of in five minutes. And you ever hear of a pre-ambulator? I don't know, I gotta fatten the kitty. Maybe we could ask Inky to put in some extra hours in the mornings and I could get another job."

"What else do you know how to do?"

"You know, that really hurts. Don't worry. Like always, I'll think of something."

And so it was that four days a week Vlado rose at 4:30, and after kissing Janet Ivan and tucking the covers around the snoring Stefani, he ruminated over a cigar on his way to Minnesota Avenue, where he caught the bus downtown. Thirty minutes later, he was behind the counter at Katz Drugstore, donning his butcher's whites and a mushrooming toque, which seemed more fitting to his position than the white paper hats worn by the second shift. To a boning-knife acrobat such as himself, a spatula was child's play and he had no trouble dispatching eggs—over easy, sunny, scrambled—to the suited businessmen with their noses in their newspapers, who only half filled the counter on a good day. If the order called for sausage, he cooked the Swift prefabs to a cinder and served them hard and shriveled in a pool of their own grease. If anyone complained he'd tell them, *what can I do, this is what they give me? Times are tough.*

Vlado kept his mouth shut and did his job so that after a week his boss, Regina, stopped looking over his shoulder and stuck to her stool behind the cash register, fiddling with her nails, reading beauty magazines, and ringing up the checks. At this point, Vlado brought in a cooler—well-iced—with a few "freshies" and tucked them into the fridge. He waited until he found the perfect victim, a well-fed guy who daily ordered the "Three-times-three." Vlado fried up three of his own sausages into a fresh golden brown and positioned them next to the three smiling eggs and a stack of pancakes. The guy slid one of the sausages between his fat lips and gazed off at nothing in particular. He picked up the second one and popped it whole into his mouth. Then he took the third and stared deeply into it, as if it might predict the winner of the fifth race at Shawnee. He wiggled it at the waitress.

"Clarisse, can I get another order of these?"

The next day, Vlado snuck in three-dozen more, and at the bottom of the chalkboard that advertised the day's specials he wrote, "Side of fresh sausage, 50 cents." By late morning he was sold out.

"You're doing what?" Joe was not amused when Vlado told him the deal. Joe was closing up the store while Vlado rolled freshies for the next day. "You can't steal from Katz like that."

"I'm not stealing, they're getting all the money."

"Then how do we make anything?"

"Don't worry, we'll jump off that bridge when we come to it. Now give me a hand with these, I have an early day tomorrow."

After two weeks of successfully selling out his freshies every morning, Vlado decided it was time to inform the Katz brothers of their future careers as sausage impresarios. He interrupted a pinochle game in the cramped storeroom that served as the office for Isaac and Michael Katz —"Mike and Ike, the kings of cut-rate," like their ads said. These two Ukrainian immigrants had created a small empire smack in the middle of the Great Depression by taking the idea of a drugstore and expanding it into a sort of destination resort for all shoppers, selling not only pharmaceuticals but also cheap cigarettes and fishing tackle and magazines and hair coloring and secret ladies' items and one time even a monkey, purchased by a lonely widow from Raytown. A trip to Katz Drugstore was always an occasion, where on weekends, families would wait beneath the tall, hammered-tin ceilings to sit at the long counter for a hamburger or a shake . . ."

". . . or a full breakfast any time of day, now accompanied by Katz's own fresh breakfast sausages," Vlado said, completing his irrefutable pitch.

"You're doing what?" Isaac Katz, like Joe, was not amused. He spit out a Ukrainian-sounding word that had to be a curse and pointed his cane at Vlado with an unsteady hand. "You're fired."

"Okay, so I don't have to work here, but—"

"Get the fuck out."

Vlado flushed with humiliation, then anger, and yearned to take the cane out of the old man's hand and give him a good whack, but instead he reached past him for a notepad on the desk, wrote down a phone number, and tossed it to the possibly more civilized of the two brothers.

"Here, you'll be wanting to know who your sausage supplier is," he said and turned out the door.

A black Bakelite telephone perched on a stool next to Stein's Office, mute and judgmental, like a piece of religious statuary. Inky and Bootnose had strict instructions to never touch it. After a while they ignored it, except for Vlado, who would pick up the receiver and listen for a dial tone, annoyed by the irritating buzz that said it was indeed working.

Two weeks later on a muggy afternoon, they all sat around the table in the back for the monthly status meeting. Vlado toed open the cooler for a bit of chilled air. Bootnose was tipped back in his chair, newsboy cap pulled low, his legs stretched out to where his dirt-caked boots rested on the carving table, something Vlado always warned him about, but what could he do. Inky was busy rolling perfectly formed cigarettes from a bag of shag tobacco and stuffing them into an empty Chesterfield pack, while Joe mumbled numbers to himself and scanned his ledger. Vlado's eyes drifted shut in the sweaty heat and he fell into a half dream, where a phone was ringing somewhere but he couldn't move his arm to answer it. Then he realized a phone actually was ringing, and his eyes shot open just in time to see Inky thoughtlessly pick up the receiver next to him.

"Hello?" Inky said. Then his face blanched as he no doubt realized what he'd done. Vlado reached for the phone but Inky held out one hand, bobbing his head to an insistent voice that Vlado couldn't quite make out. "I guess you'll want to speak to our meat manager . . . um . . . *Boyko*." He handed the phone to Joe like it was a newborn baby.

Boyko? Joe whispered, with his hand over the mouthpiece.

My wife's sister married a Ukrainian. His name was Boyko.

Joe held the phone to his ear. "Boyko here . . . um hmm . . . no, English is fine . . . right . . . okay." He began scribbling on a sheet of butcher paper, nodding and writing, nodding and writing. "Tuesday and Friday? Let me check," he said and noisily crumpled some papers next to the receiver.

Count to ten, Vlado whispered, and Joe nodded and mouthed the numbers, then said,

"Okay, that should work. Cash on delivery and we'll see you then."

He hung up the phone and his eyes were glistening.

"They want sausage."

"How much?" Vlado asked.

Joe wrote a number on the butcher paper and showed it to Vlado, who thought there must be some mistake.

"That many freshies?"

"That many *dozen*. Twice a week, to both locations."

"Joey, do the numbers." His voice quavered.

"Well, you know these cut-rate guys aren't going to pay much, but maybe we can get a bulk price on the pork shoulders, if we can even get enough . . ." he scribbled, "times twelve divided by two . . . subtracting . . ." he muttered and scribbled some more then leaned up from the paper. "I'd say we're looking at about a nickel per."

"Per dozen?" Vlado asked.

"Per sausage."

"Fuck you."

"No, fuck *you*."

Vlado leapt out of his chair, grabbed Joe and danced him around the store, gave him a quick spin, then went over and gave Inky a big smooch on top of his head. He kicked Bootnose's feet off the carving table.

"Wake up, *Boyko*, you got a new job."

The following Monday night, they all had new jobs. The whole crew assembled at closing time to roll Vlado's freshies for their first delivery. Martina and Stefani came by to help, along with Janet Ivan, who was happy to sit in an empty potato crate and chew on a soup bone while following Vlado around with her big eyes. Joe's boys, Tom and Donald, were in the alley with Bootnose, who was screwing a new sign onto the side of the hearse that said "Boyko Meats." Inky was ringing up the day's final customers out front while Joe sliced cubes of fatty pork shoulder that Vlado fed into the grinder. He massaged in the spices and syrup and savored the heady aroma, wondering at how these simple flavors could combine into something so complex and wonderful, something greater than any single thing. He thought about the flavors of his own life, his sweet dumpling Stefani, the always salty Martina, and little Janet Ivan, forever the secret ingredient, and his thoughts extended to his new brothers, and to Ivan the Not-So-Terrible and fake-Aunt-Vera, the stunning Dorothy Penny, and Mae and Lubo and Morty, of course Morty with his own combination of spices, and then beyond that to St. Ritchie and St. John's, and the Holy Oyster, with his cohort of gossipy housewives who thought every detail of everyone's life was worth sharing—which meant at least it was worth something—and everybody he knew by name, and everybody who knew his name and to Strawberry Hill itself, all of it adding up to something he'd never known as an orphan in Zagreb, and it was with a sense of disbelief that he considered how he'd come to find himself in this place.

The room blurred—probably the onions—and he wiped his watery eyes with a sleeve and looked at his cousin.

"Come on Joey, hustle it up, we can't keep tomorrow waiting."

Part 2

25

In late February of 1932, Janet Ivan turned one year old, and the expected party occurred on a Saturday afternoon, at Vlado's new house. The venture with the Katz brothers had miraculously continued, and for months, the cousins raked in more money than they'd ever seen. Joe had finally convinced Vlado that all that Boyko Meat cash sitting in the safe was doing nobody any good, and when the house next door to Ivan and fake-Aunt-Vera's came up for sale, Joe brokered a deal on Vlado's behalf.

"If I own the house, why do I still pay rent?" he'd asked Joe.

"Think of it like paying rent to yourself."

Their new home was like all the others on Barnett: a narrow bungalow with two bedrooms, a small kitchen and living room, and a backyard with space for his little girl to toddle around. Stefani had festooned the generous front porch with potted geraniums. In the back, Vlado flipped sausages and pork steaks on a charcoal grill.

After the festivities, the newly walking-and-talking center of everyone's attention collapsed into the arms of Grandma Lovick, who looked around for whom she could pass Janet Ivan off to, but Joe and Martina and Vlado and the happily liberated Stefani were already making a break for Vlado's chromed-up new Studebaker. The car was a splurge, but worth it for the feeling he had when he would cruise slowly up Barnett or Eighth like he was the mayor. Or somebody. Somebody, as opposed to the nobody who'd been swept into this country like part of a horde of anonymous ants. He tapped the pedal, and the eight cylinders of Detroit iron answered with a commanding rumble.

They crossed the river to the Lo-Ball, a speakeasy on Twelfth Street that featured some of the most refined gin around and usually a small combo of Negro musicians messing with songs in the new jazz way. It had been a long day, and Vlado looked forward to the no-crying-babies quiet and the cool basement air. They slipped down the stairs and through the velvet curtain, but the room was loud and smokey and still simmering with the day's heat. The bartender indicated a table near a small stage where a piano trio was riffing out a drowsy blues. A mason jar filled with amber liquid and four small glasses appeared and Vlado did the honors.

"You can take that off now," he said to Stefani, who was fingering the beady-eyed dead fox draped around her neck. He couldn't think what she saw in the thing, but it had been part of the negotiation for the new car. She only clutched it tighter around herself, despite the heat, and mouthed him an air kiss.

"Maybe it'll crawl off by itself," Martina said, and turned to Vlado. "And why is that thing twice as big as your head?"

Vlado removed his new fedora and displayed it at arm's length.

"You know what they say, big hat—"

"Tiny sausage," Martina said, giving out a toothy laugh.

Vlado couldn't help laughing too. "*Jebote*, I need a witness." He draped an arm around a giggling Stefani and held his glass out to Joe.

"*Until the annihilation . . .*"

"*. . . yours or ours*," Joe answered, and they drank and slammed down their glasses.

It was an old toast they laughed about now, so different from their teen years in Zagreb, when those words were uttered in secret meetings and printed in the slough of political rags that foretold the coming chaos of war.

A couple at the next table gave the side-eye to Vlado, who realized he might be disrespecting the musicians. The pianist was playing alone now, flirting with a familiar melody— "Night and Day?" He turned to the small stage and was surprised to see the player was a young woman —a tiny figure, with honey-colored skin and black, lashy eyes too large for her thin face. She wore a drapey burgundy dress that followed her modest curves. Her long, skinny fingers roamed lightly across the keys, and her dark red lips were slightly parted as if she were about to speak. The piano notes twinkled like starlight, and in that moment Vlado was a kid gazing up into the speckled night sky, thinking that the gravity of the billions of stars could pull him straight into the heavens.

"Joey, look," he whispered.

Joe followed his gaze. "She's lovely," he said.

"No, I mean . . ." He wasn't sure what he meant. She was certainly beautiful, but not like Dorothy Penny was beautiful, or Lydia even, but something more, maybe not even beautiful, another thing altogether. He listened to the melody, rambling around the piano as if it couldn't find its way home. And the woman looked lost as well. He felt sad for her, for this person he'd never seen and had never imagined.

Vlado looked at his empty glass and thought how quickly the previous year had slipped from his grasp. How every five minutes it was another Monday, or a crying baby, or another drink at Morty's, moments that flipped through his mind like cards in a ruffled pinochle deck. It seemed like a century ago that he'd married Stefani, but now suddenly here he was, this spiffed up stranger; a good father, wasn't he? Devoted husband; business owner. With a fancy car, a house, and a bank account of all things.

He thought back to his life before all this and wondered, who was that guy, running around like one of Starr's roosters, crowing at all the ladies. He'd always thought of himself as a ladies' man, but truth was he hadn't been very good at it. Despite spreading his charms generously around the hill, other than Stefani, there'd only been Lydia. He couldn't remember why Stefani had been angry with him that night. Those days, it could have been most anything. But there he'd been, alone at Morty's on a cold and quiet night, and there was Lydia, leaning into him, matching him drink for drink until they both knew what would happen next. He remembered waking the following morning in her bed with a dreadful "what-have-I-done" feeling. It must have been plain on his face as he struggled into his pants.

"Don't worry about it, Vlado," Lydia had said, "in a hundred years, we'll all be dead."

He'd laughed, relieved to be let off the hook. But now he remembered that moment and the look in her dark eyes—not so different from the eyes of the small woman on the stage exploring the piano keys like she was all alone in the world—and realized Lydia hadn't meant to be funny.

Then it struck him. It wasn't that nothing mattered. It was that *everything* mattered. *Every fucking thing.* Every cry from Janet Ivan or complaint from Stefani or jab from Martina or shine-on from Inky or Bootnose, or Joe even; and every note this woman conjured from the piano was, for its tragically brief existence, the most important thing in the universe. He closed his eyes and willed with his entire being that she would never stop playing and that the bittersweet beauty of the song, of the world itself, would never end.

A ripple of applause brought Vlado back to the moment. The woman had vanished, and the musicians were packing up.

"Where did you just go?" Stefani looked at him strangely.

Vlado tried to answer but his thoughts wouldn't condense into words. Sweat streamed into his eyes, and the smoke-hazed room took on an unreal aspect, like it too could disappear at any moment. He grabbed onto Stefani's hand and held tight while his own began to shake. Joe leaned in with a worried look.

"Vlado—"

An invisible fist punched Vlado in the chest then reached into his breastbone and squeezed, hard, twisting *"righty-tighty"* he could only think, a pain greater than he'd believed possible. *Christ on the cross.* He opened his mouth and tried to suck in a breath but there was nowhere for the air to go. He struggled up out of his chair and pitched over to his left and felt his head bang against the floor.

Vlado was at Maurice Starr's farm, lying on his back in a pool of mud surrounded by chickens that were scolding him with their clattering voices. An elephant stood over him and had one foot pressing against his chest.

That's ridiculous, Starr doesn't have an elephant, he thought, and the foot turned into a boot, and he was staring up at Bootnose, who laughed and spit out a stream of indecipherable Ukrainian. *Boyko*. To his left, Morty fiddled with his cathedral radio. He heard an announcer's voice:

". . . made with fresh cold milk and sweet, chocolate-flavored Ovaltine. Mmm, what a treat on a warm summer day . . ."

The boot on his chest was now a knee and Vlado looked up into the chubby face of Johnny Obersteen, who licked his thick, greasy lips and wiggled his stubby fingers like he was playing an invisible piano. Ovaltine!

"So, how's my little girl," Ovaltine said, moving his squiggly sausage-fingers closer to Vlado's face.

"How's my little girl?" he kept saying again and again, each time with a harder thrust of his knee—

Vlado opened his eyes and recognized Stefani's concerned face hovering over him.

"Ssh, your little girl is fine," she said. "It's you we're worried about."

"Hey, who's awake?" It was Joe speaking. "Go tell the nurse." Vlado saw Martina hustle out of what he realized was a hospital room. He was lying on the most comfortable bed he'd ever felt and gazed with curiosity at the needle stuck into his arm which was connected to a tube that disappeared somewhere behind him. His chest throbbed with a dull ache, like he was bruised from a fight, but his pieces still seemed to be connected. And looking into Stefani's worried face he felt . . . happy. Overwhelmingly happy.

"It's you," he said to Stefani. "I feel so happy."

"Well, you shouldn't," she said, and he could see she'd been crying. "If you think you can just go off and die like that . . ."

"Nobody's dying," Vlado said. Why did everyone look worried?

Joe laughed. "It's the morphine. Don't worry, Vlado, soon you'll be as miserable as we are."

"They think you had a heart attack," said Stefani, with a what-do-you-think-about-that frown, and then Vlado remembered: the girl at the piano, the crushing pain, and his urgent need to . . . to what?

"Not a heart attack!" A voice rang in from the hallway and a balding, bespectacled man in a white coat came in waving a long sheet of yellow paper. "Nein," he said, "Your heart is strong like a bell."

"A bell?" Joe said.

"Ya, mit da horns?" He pointed index fingers out from his forehead.

Vlado knew three different recipes for braised beef heart.

"See?" He showed them all the paper with its cipher of zigzags. "Very good lines."

"Then what the hell?" Joe said.

"Allow me to declaren," said the doctor, whose name was Leichenberg, according to the stitching on his white coat, and he "declarened" in bright Anglo-German how many things can grip the heart that are not gripping the heart at all, how the chest is full of many cranky muscles, how noxious acid churns in the stomach, how things can go up instead of down, how every thought rings something in the body, and what a lovely day it is for a healthy young man to go out and enjoy his family and continue on with his promising life.

He listened to Vlado's chest through a stethoscope—"Beat, beat, beat, so boring"—and lightly touched Vlado's forehead, which apparently was wrapped in a bandage. "Strong head, strong heart," he said and gave Vlado a light slap on the cheek. He wrote on an invisible notepad with an imaginary pencil, then pretended to tear it off and hand it to Vlado—"My subscription for you"—then pulled it back. "Here, I read it. 'Don't vork so hard. Don't vorry so much.' Now go home, this is place for sick people."

He vanished, and a nurse came in and cheerfully yanked the needle out of Vlado's arm. Then somehow Joe and Martina were squeezing him into the back seat of the Studebaker next to Stefani. His soft, lovely Stefani. It was weirdly bright outside, like daylight, and in fact it was day, late morning from the looks of it. And a beautiful, blue-sky morning at that.

Vlado relished the damp river breeze whisking across his face and the soothing thrum of the tires as Joe steered them back across the viaduct, and he abandoned himself to the wonderfulness of it all.

Vlado moaned on the divan while Stefani applied a towel full of ice to a tender spot on his forehead. Everything was too bright, and the smells coming from the kitchen were making him sick. Janet Ivan was crying in the other room, and he had a bitter, acid taste in his mouth.

"So Obersteen is back, I saw him," Vlado said, wincing at the thought of that knee in his chest.

"What do you mean? Where did you see him?"

"He was asking about my little girl."

"Oh Vlado, that was a dream. There's no Obersteen. Where do you think this even happened?"

Vlado thought for a second, and of course it made no sense. A dream, definitely. But he'd been in the hospital, right? That much was true. "So, the funny doctor with the German accent. He was real, right?"

"German accent?" Stefani's brow narrowed. "No, he didn't have an accent."

Did he dream the whole goddam thing?

She laughed. "Who was that guy, anyway? You know, I hear all their smartest ones are coming over here, so he's probably some genius and is right about you."

"Right about what?"

"You need less work. And more of your *seksi djevojka*." Her fingers slid down the buttons of her blouse, liberating them one by one, and she lowered herself onto Vlado, who had the good sense not to complain about his pounding head or spinning stomach, or his inability to breathe for that matter, because if he had to die like this, then so be it.

26

The next morning, despite Stefani's protests and Janet Ivan's doleful gaze, Vlado wrapped himself in herringbone and fedora and set out for the store. Drizzle fogged the air around him, and the damp chill tightened his bones. His chest hurt, and by the time he jingled in the front door he was out of breath and sweating. Joe seemed surprised to see him.

"You look like hell."

"Yeah, well, I feel absolutely fantastic," Vlado said. He tied on his apron and grabbed his boning knife, which quivered in his hand as he shuffled toward Stein's Office. Joe caught up and relieved him of the knife.

"No hurry," Joe said. "Inky and Bootnose came in yesterday morning, and we're all set for Tuesday. Inky even convinced Tereza to let him skip Mass."

"Great, now I'm going to get it from Tereza. Like it isn't bad enough always being on Marti's list."

"Ha, when you were sacked out in that hospital bed, she probably said enough rosaries to where you can bypass purgatory and go straight to the front of the line at the pearly gates."

"But that's just the thing, Joey. I don't want to go anywhere."

Joe produced a bottle and poured two shots of Morty's finest, and they raised their glasses. "Okay, but none of this bullshit about the annihilation," said Vlado.

Joe shrugged. "*Zivjeli.*"

"*Zivjeli.*" They tossed it back and were both quiet for a long moment.

"I saw Obersteen," Vlado said. "Not actually, but in a dream, apparently. Like he'd come back for his little girl. And then she'd be gone. Like all those notes from the piano, just disappearing."

He didn't know how to explain it to Joe. He remembered the feeling just before he was struck in the chest—a panicky sense that everything could vanish in a blink. And then it did.

From the alley came a familiar squeal of brakes. Joe was out of his chair.

"Come on, mister sad man. Maybe the smell of a dead pig will cheer you up."

Vlado looked up from the carving table and saw from the clock that somehow eight hours had passed. He took off his apron and called to his cousin, who was whistling some too-happy tune and ringing up orders in the front.

"Joey, I'm out of here."

"Good. Go get some sleep."

He washed up, grabbed his coat, and headed into the damp twilight. The same drizzle was hanging around, refuting any idea that the world would ever again be green and warm. He considered Morty's but didn't want to have to answer a bunch of dumb questions that he didn't have the answers to. He tugged his lapels closer and headed downhill to Junior's Delicatessen, where he'd be just an anonymous face. And where he'd maybe seen Obersteen. A year ago already? It was early yet, most of the meat cutters still slaving on the line across the river, and he found a seat by himself at the far end of the bar. Junior's daughter Emily put down the glasses she was washing and came over to him. She had a sling around her neck that cradled a tiny human.

"Hi, Mr. Novosel," she said and pulled back the sling to reveal a pink, possum-like face. "Say hello to Junior Junior."

"Looks just like his grandpa," Vlado said.

Emily laughed. "Let's hope not." She drew Vlado a beer and slid over the jar of pickled eggs.

"Well in any case, good for you. Hey, I got a question. You know that guy, Obersteen?"

"Obersteen?"

"Yeah, John Obersteen. They call him Ovaltine."

"Ha, good one."

"So, you know him?"

"No, I don't think so. What's he look like?"

She's in on it too, he immediately thought, then thought again. "Stout guy. Pudgy fingers. With a big mouth that can eat one of your dad's double-stacks in about two bites."

"Well, that could be almost anybody."

It was true that Junior's clientele skewed towards the well-fed.

"Never mind, then."

"If I meet him, I'll tell him you were around."

"No, don't say I was here." He drained his beer and tossed down a bill. Then another. "Something for the college fund. Take good care of that little critter." He buttoned up and headed back out into the gloom.

Vlado took the long way up the river road towards Barnett. What had he expected, that Johnny would still be sitting there a year later? And if so, then what? *Jebote*. He gazed across the murky Kaw to the vast stretch of prison-like pens and factory sheds, ghostly in the fog-misted twilight. A train rattled along the river, piping out warning whistles, and as if in response, a long horn blew from the Armour plant, releasing its inmates, who would then be free to cozy up in the bars and continue on with whatever congenial bullshit they'd been slinging the whole day. He didn't miss the long shifts on the kill floor, but some things . . .

Past the Bottoms, he could see the glowing cigar tip of the Power and Light tower and the surrounding buildings where lights twinkled out of impossibly high windows. He imagined the cars cruising the streets with important purpose, the speakeasies and dance halls and high-toned restaurants and well-dressed women and free-flowing booze, all of it stitched together as a single, mysterious beast lurking over his little world of Strawberry Hill. He thought of the piano player, lost somewhere in all this.

Her image weighed on him as he climbed the steps to his little house. When he reached the door, he was clobbered by an unpleasant aroma, no doubt from the kitchen, and felt the bile rise in his throat. He thought about what lay on the other side—smelly diapers and an annoyed Stefani, shushing him so she could hear the sad story of Little Orphan Annie bleating out of their new Majestic. He already knew what it was like to be an orphan, one without a rich "Daddy."

He stood with one hand on the knob, past the point of exhaustion, aware only of his aching, shaky legs, the arthritic pain in his fingers, the molasses in his veins. He pushed open the door but the flood of light and heat was too much. He closed it quietly, turned from the porch, and descended the steps toward the Stude. He got in and checked himself in the rearview mirror, dragging a comb through his oily hair, then started the engine—too loud, a sure giveaway, but never mind—and soon he was bouncing along the viaduct toward the tall buildings.

27

The Lo-Ball was nearly empty when Vlado sat down at the bar. He looked for the musicians on stage, but no one was there.

"Give me a shot of whatever you got," he told the bored-looking bartender, "and a glass of milk."

The bartender returned, and Vlado slugged down half the milk and sniffed at the shot then set it back on the bar.

"No musicians tonight?"

"Just the one." He indicated a table in a corner of the room where a small figure blended into the darkness.

"The pianist?"

The bartender nodded. "Helene. We can't afford her guys during the week."

Vlado shot back his drink, picked up his milk and walked slowly toward the table, with no idea what he would do or say. He stood there and she looked up at him with a vacant gaze. Her bony cheeks and the squint around her eyes said she was older than he'd thought. She nudged a chair with one foot and Vlado sat.

"You got a cigarette?" she said. The candle from the table flickered too shiny in her eyes.

"I quit."

"So does that mean no?"

"I could buy you a drink."

"If I wanted a drink, anybody could buy me one. Pick a song and give me a dollar."

Vlado pulled out his roll of bills and peeled off a five. "Your choice."

Her unreadable gaze remained fixed on Vlado as she rolled up the bill and tucked it into her bodice. She stood and sashayed toward the stage and positioned herself at the baby grand. She closed her eyes and extended her thin fingers toward the keys, and tinkly bells fell from heaven.

Vlado sat on the edge of a bed in a ramshackle hotel room with a drink in one hand and a burning cigarette in the other, listening to a trumpet blowing a mournful ballad out of a small Victrola and watching the pianist hug herself as she slow-danced around the room. His eyes watered from the smoke and from the bright overhead lights that exposed the shabbiness of the place. An opened suitcase was the centerpiece of the room. Thin dresses were draped over chairs and crumpled on the floor.

Despite the alcohol, the fatigue of an impossibly long day was grounding him, and he dizzily tried to reassess his moves, unsure now whose idea it had been to visit her room for "just one drink." She'd walked the two blocks to the coloreds-only hotel while he drove around, parked in the rear, and found his way up a back staircase. He'd expected something, but somehow not this—had he thought there'd be a piano? An insane corner of his mind was considering how he'd explain this all to the Holy Oyster or tell Stefani about the nice piano player he'd met and had drinks with. He could see Joe's "you dummy" shake of the head and imagined Martina bursting into the room with a baseball bat.

The song scratched to a finish and Helene sat down on the bed next to him. She took the drink out of his hand, sipped it, and her other hand drifted to his knee. Vlado hadn't been this close to another woman since he'd married Stefani. He felt like he'd been holding his breath for an hour, and exhaled as silently as possible, to not disturb the wild beasts inside his chest that might awaken and devour everything. She used a long finger to turn his face toward hers.

"It's okay, cher. I won't bite you." She smiled slightly, but her eyes still drooped, and he wondered what she must be thinking or remembering. She touched his ring finger and gave the gold band a slight twist.

"You worried about this?"

I'm worried about everything, he wanted to say, *every little goddam thing,* but his tongue was peanut-buttered to the roof of his mouth.

She touched her fingertips to his cheek, then took his hands and raised him to his feet. She could have been twenty-five or forty-five; she seemed frail—as breakable as an old woman—but her lips were full and bright and here he was, here they were, nowhere, on their own planet, where the only rules were the ones they agreed to and everyone else be damned. She reached one arm behind her back, Vlado heard the zipper work its way down, and the satiny drapes of her dress dropped away from her thin body to reveal a lacy white bra and white panties.

She held one finger up to his lips. "Wait," she said, needlessly, as Vlado was terrified by the thought of moving at all. "Stay," she said, not a command, but a request, and he could tell she, too, was nervous. She turned off the overhead lights and picked up one of her discarded blue dresses and draped it over the table lamp, casting the room in a violet shroud that seemed to grant everything a fictional aspect, like something from a movie, and for a ridiculous moment Vlado thought this must be how it feels to be an actor in one of these scenes. "Stay," she whispered again. She reached for the bathroom door and disappeared inside. He heard water running and knew that when it stopped, that was his cue.

Vlado could never have been an actor; he was clueless how to follow a script, and tonight was no exception. When the woman left him alone in the bedroom, the spell paused and he felt the blood returning to his veins and locomotion to his legs, which propelled him out the door pronto and into the cold night. And then he was bouncing along the empty viaduct through the what-the-hell-time-was-it toward Strawberry Hill, whatever awaited him there, afraid to look back lest he turn into a pillar of salt. *Christ on the cross.* He'd left behind his herringbone topcoat and was freezing, but he sure as hell wasn't going back. He understood the look she'd given him and how the story was supposed to go. They'd do it, and he'd fall all the way into her oily-dark eyes and . . . what? He gassed the Studebaker, which skidded on the icy road and veered close to the railing that was the only thing between him and a fatal drop into the Kaw's bleak waters. But what did it matter? *In a hundred years we'll all be dead.* Fucking Lydia.

Stefani was asleep when he got home and barely stirred when he slid into bed. He lay there awake, worried that his heart was too loud. Why hadn't he gone through with it? Who would ever know? He imagined the guy in the movie who would have made love to the piano player, left ten dollars on the nightstand, and walked out feeling like he'd done the world a favor.

He heard some whimpering from Janet Ivan's room and got up and went to her, thinking he could head off whatever she might be worrying about in her tiny life. He scooped her up and took her to the living room, where he turned on the radio, down low, and settled into their easy chair. She quieted, he closed his eyes, and a moment later, it was morning.

28

Vlado sleeved the sweat from his forehead and stropped his boning knife for what seemed like the zillionth time. "Joe, I swear I don't even know what day this is."

"It's yesterday, and soon it's going to be last week if we can't find some more fat hogs. Those skinny things from Deke's are muscled up like they were bred for racing."

The door jingled, startling Vlado, who'd been twitchy since his delinquent night across the river, as if he had to worry about who might be coming through the door. Which was silly, because there was a whole river between him and whatever it was over there he had to worry about, which anyway would have to wait its turn behind all the other worries he had to face right here. Like, for instance, who just came through the door? *Jebote.*

Vlado hadn't told anyone about the dizzy moments that sometimes occurred if he moved too quickly, or that odd sense of "we've-been-here-before" that would have him wondering if he was awake or dreaming. So when he heard a familiar voice, he wondered if it was just a thought ringing in his head. *How's your little girl?* He peered around the corner at the counter and felt again the knee to the gut when he saw an exact double of Johnny Obersteen standing across from Joe. He couldn't make out what they were saying, but the whiny voice was unmistakable. Vlado turned off the grinder so he could hear.

"Okay, not to be presumptuous, but you fellas done good, and I just want you to know if you need somebody to push your product out there a little more, well, I'd do what I can, which sometimes has been a lot."

"It's Johnny, right?" Joe said. "I haven't seen you around."

Obersteen, stepping right out of the dream.

"Yeah, well, I been itinerant, if you know what that is, in and out. I have business in a lot of places, but I miss the Hill."

The Hill? Jebote. Vlado knew Obersteen was from the Argentine neighborhood and didn't know *halva* from *hvala*. He put down his knife and came out to stand next to Joe.

"Vlado," Obersteen said.

"Johnny, I didn't know you were still around."

"Well, I was just telling Joe—"

"I heard what you were telling him. I'm thinking maybe you need to go talk to the guys at Boyko Meat."

Obersteen stretched his thick lips into a pretend smile and pinched a piece of nutbread, which he popped into his mouth and chewed on thoughtfully—like one of those damn cows at Starr's. He and Vlado were the same height and Johnny looked him straight in the face.

"Everybody knows it's you guys, Vlado. And if you want to continue to go around pretending to sneak sausages here and there in a reconditioned hearse like a couple of small-timers, that's your business."

Vlado slid the plate of povitica out of Obersteen's reach. "Well, you're right, it is a business, our own business, and we're minding it, if you know what I'm saying." He recalled the feeling of Johnny's knee in his chest and could imagine putting a fist in his arrogant face, wondering if it would even connect with bone.

"Hey, no need to get hot about it, and no offense meant, but I'm just saying, when I eat over at Wolferman's, and I got a big plate of spaghetti with some kind of overpriced mystery meat, I look at the menu and wonder why something like this"—he pointed into the sausage case— "isn't on it." Vlado was going to speak, but Obersteen held up a finger. "It's because you gotta know a guy." He reached across Vlado and pinched another slice of nutbread. "And I'm the guy."

"You're the guy?"

"Yeah, I'm the guy. I mean, I'm the guy that knows the guy."

Vlado gave Joe an exasperated look.

"Look, Johnny," Joe said. "We're pretty busy now. Why don't we meet later on, when we're not up to our armpits in pig fat. Gino's does a nice lasagna if you don't mind going small-town."

"I'm all yours," said Obersteen.

He squeezed himself out the door and Vlado peered at Joe, wondering if his cousin had lost his mind.

"Joey, the dream. He's back, like I thought. And he knows." *About what? Their pretend Ukrainian business? Janet Ivan?*

Joe rubbed one hand along his receding hairline. "Who knows what he knows, but maybe we should find out. Besides, he's here, and there's nothing we can do about it."

"Joey, I swear, you're like some fucking prophet."

Ovaltine was already waiting for them at Gino's. They grunted out some small talk over clumps of pasta soaked in red sauce and a stack of lasagna, which Vlado thought could have used a spicier filling, but why make Gino feel bad. Then Obersteen got to the point. Big Sausage could penetrate the restaurant game, especially—he gestured with a foot-long dangle of spaghetti—if they could crack the market on the other side of the river, and why just settle for selling your tiny wieners to Katz? Despite Johnny's lame attempt at humor, Vlado started to relax a bit. He didn't like the guy, for a million reasons, but maybe there was no big conspiracy here. His dream was just some random thing. Vlado knew Stefani by now, was more certain than ever she'd never . . . well, he didn't even want to think about it anymore. He interrupted Johnny's monologue.

"If you're sure, Johnny, that you don't mind hanging out with a couple small-timers—"

"Honestly, I meant no offense, Vlado. Look, I've never been a creative guy. I can't even scramble eggs. All I know is how to talk to people, convince them of stuff."

Vlado looked at Joe and suspected they were both thinking back to their own—okay, admittedly small-time—effort when it seemed that the city itself had chewed them up and spit them back across the river. Fine, next time let it be Obersteen.

Coffee and gelato appeared. Obersteen lit a cigar, passed one each to Joe and Vlado, and soon they were talking business inside of their own smoke-hazed room.

"Bottom line, I can get you on their menus," he concluded.

"Out of the goodness of your heart, I suppose," Vlado said.

Obersteen picked up a paper napkin from the preemptive stack Gino had provided, wrote down a percentage and slid it across the table. Joe reached for the ever-present pencil behind his ear, but it was gone, and Johnny passed him his. Joe wrote down another number and slid it back. Vlado had a panicked sense that this would go on forever, had always been going on, and he grabbed the pencil in mid-pass to break the spell.

"What, are you guys playing tic-tac-toe? Here's your number, like it or not." He scrawled it down and showed everyone. "Take it or leave it."

"Done," said Obersteen, who seemed too happy, and Vlado again felt the knee and imagined with a shudder Ovaltine's greasy fingers reaching into Vlado's pocket for his roll of bills.

He shook away the image, and said, "Okay, then. Gino, bring us your best and strongest."

Gino shuffled over with a murky liquid and Vlado poured three rounds, with a little extra for Obersteen, and they raised their glasses.

"To Obersteen, Novosel, and Marevic," Johnny said.

"To Big Sausage," Joe said.

"To the annihilation," Vlado muttered, and they all drank, and he had the satisfaction of seeing Ovaltine's smile disappear, his eyes water, and his chest heave up in a desperate grasp for air. There followed a gas-warfare-sized belch, and Vlado covered his nose with a napkin and got up from the table, as did Joe.

"We'll be talking to you," Joe said. He and Vlado made for the door, passing Gino who had the check in his hand. Vlado's head indicated Ovaltine, who still hadn't extracted himself from his chair, and the two of them hightailed it out of there.

29

Vlado didn't know what he'd say to Stefani. Had Obersteen been around all this time? He hadn't mentioned her to Johnny, and she'd not spoken his name since that day in some previous life when she tried to claim he was Janet Ivan's father.

"So, guess who's back?" Vlado was helping Stefani with the dishes after their Sunday afternoon meal. Janet Ivan sat in her highchair, fiddling around with leftover pieces of boiled short ribs.

"What?" said Stefani.

"Not what. Who?"

"I mean, what did you say?"

"I said Ovaltine, or maybe I didn't, but in any case, he's back. Did you know?"

She scrubbed especially hard at a greasy plate then held it up to the light and inspected it like it was the Hope Diamond.

"He came by last week," she finally said.

"Johnny came by. Here?"

"Where else would I mean?"

"And what did he find?"

"He found me, obviously."

"And where was I?"

"Where are you ever?"

"And Janet Ivan?"

"Was here. She's always here, you know." She reached for the gravy bowl and gave it a soapy swipe.

"And?"

"And nothing."

"It's not nothing."

"Oh, Vlado, it's not anything. He knows now it's you and me."

Apparently, Stefani was determined not to elaborate, and Vlado didn't know what to say. *What did he know about what happened when he wasn't around?* Meanwhile, Janet Ivan was happily babbling to herself in what might as well have been Ukrainian, grasping shreds of meat with her chubby fingers and stuffing them into her chipmunk cheeks. *Her chubby fingers.* Vlado took a hard look at her, and she put down her meat and wiggled her fingers at him, giggling. He lifted her out of the chair and hugged her close, pushing his face into her neck and inhaling her bread-like aroma. Then he marched her into the bathroom and hoisted her face up next to his, and they both stared into the mirror. He ran his finger down the ridge of his own hawk-like proboscis, then wiggled Janet Ivan's little pug nose, pulling on it just a bit, but it snapped right back. *Oh, well, Stefani doesn't have much of a nose either, so there you go.* He felt his own angular cheekbones, then ran one finger across her inflated, peach-fuzzy cheeks and she puckered herself up into a kissy face, her fat lips blooming out so different from Vlado's thin smile. In the mirror she didn't look at herself, but at him, and he felt the tug of her gravity, something that was all her and came from nowhere else.

"If it were me, I'd kick his ass," Bootnose said.

"Something you know that I don't, Boyko?" said Vlado. The four of them were at Morty's and it was creeping toward midnight.

"I know there was talk once and I heard some things about him and Stefani, which I didn't like, and didn't believe even if it was true." He raised his chin toward Vlado. "And I don't like it when you call me Boyko."

"Forgive me, *Zoran*, the name will never again cross my lips," Vlado said. "And anyhow, he's been to see Stefani and she set him straight. What's past is past, and we'll never know anyway."

"And we can't kick his ass, he's our new business partner," Joe explained. "Or will be, if he can make a sale."

"What sale?" Inky, finally showing some interest.

"Any sale," said Joe. "We're loading him down with samples tomorrow and he's going to hit up Union Station, the Oyster House, Shakey's, and a few other places. What do we got to lose?"

"Why should anybody listen to him?" asked Inky.

"He's a salesman, that's why," said Vlado. "Besides, look at him."

"I can see how he might know all the restaurant guys," Inky said. He rubbed his neck thoughtfully. "But how does he know so much about us?"

The next morning, Obersteen showed up just after they opened. He was draped in a baggy glen-plaid suitcoat, with oversized shoulders, sagging pants, and a red bowtie and matching vest that weren't quite up to the task. His face was already sweaty on this cool morning, lips shining like he'd just tossed down a few dozen links.

"You look like you went shopping with Dorothy Penny," Vlado said.

"Who?" said Johnny.

"Never mind. Here's your stuff."

Joe brought a cooler out of Stein's Office with a well-iced selection of smoked kobasa and ten-packs of freshies, when they noticed Johnny had a cooler of his own. On the side was stenciled "Johnny's Smokehouse."

"What the hell," said Vlado.

"Hold on, I knew this would be a thing." Johnny must have had lifts in his polished two-tone brogues because he was just tall enough now to look down and around his bulbous nose at Vlado. "But I gotta say, these are classy joints, you know, and they can be fussy."

"We're counting on it," Vlado said.

"God knows I love you guys to death, and I don't know how to say this the right way, but nobody's gonna buy expensive meat from a bunch of Croatian *paisanos* from across the river. And hey, that's them talking, not me."

Vlado looked at Joe. "You knew about this?"

Joe's lips tightened. "Nothing's carved in stone."

Vlado tried to imagine his next line in this ridiculous script. But whatever it was, it would only make him as much of an ass as Johnny, so he turned from them and stalked back to the carving nook. He picked up his boning knife and went to work on a pork shoulder, neatly separating fat from meat. Then he grabbed a cleaver and attacked the pile like an ax-wielding maniac, metal biting into wood, sending shreds of gristle and muscle everywhere, until he'd bludgeoned it all into a greasy mishmash of mangled sinew and mush. He used the back of the cleaver to scrape the whole gooey mess into the trashcan.

30

With Obersteen gone on his mission, Vlado was left to meditate on what had just happened. Throughout the day he kept going back to what Inky had said. *How did Johnny know about their whole deal?* It wasn't until late afternoon that two thoughts came together as one, and without a word to Joe, Vlado took off his apron and headed for home.

He found Stefani in the kitchen making tea.

"What are you doing home?" she asked.

"I'm sorry, do you have company?" Vlado peeked past her into their tiny living room. He noticed happily there was only one teacup.

"The Pope dropped by earlier, but he couldn't stay," she said. He eased into a chair at the Formica table and Stefani reached for another cup. She poured the tea and sat down with him. Her hair was tied up into a tidy bun and she was wearing the pearls he'd given her for their anniversary. Was that perfume he smelled? Vlado sipped and looked at Stefani as if she were a stranger he was meeting for the first time.

"What?" she said.

"I don't know. You look nice today, that's all."

She gave him a skeptical look. "You came all the way home just to tell me that?"

Vlado would have preferred to not have to deal with any of this, to just enjoy a surprise afternoon off with this lovely creature. Just the two of them, Janet Ivan apparently asleep. But the image of Obersteen's grubby fingers appeared between them until he blinked it away and searched for some words.

"So, am I not providing for you?" *Here we go.*

"What do you mean?"

"I mean, have I ever denied you anything?"

"Of course not. You know I'm happy. Why would you have the idea —"

"Obersteen. You told him the whole deal."

"Johnny?"

"Johnny? Yes, *Johnny*, who's suddenly everybody's new best friend."

Stefani gave her tea a few thoughtful stirs, then tilted her head back with either a confident or stubborn look that said she was digging in and would quite happily drag Vlado into the hole after her. At least he was on familiar ground.

"We had a nice talk, like old friends do," she said. "And why shouldn't I brag on my talented husband?"

"You know business is business."

"And so it is. But why shouldn't you be famous across the river?" She leaned forward and enveloped him in her perfume. "Why can't you let somebody help you? I mean, Johnny knows what to do."

"Johnny's an idiot, Stef. I know what to do. I've always known what to do, even when I don't. Believe me, if you're not eating well, it's only because of your mom's cooking."

"I don't know, I guess I thought it would be nice to go to the Savoy and there you are on the menu."

"First of all, that's a seafood restaurant. And secondly, it won't be *us* on the menu, it'll be Smokehouse Johnny. Is that what you want?" In the next room a desperate howl pitched upward. "And Janet Ivan. Why is she always crying when I come home? What do you guys do all day?"

"I don't want to hear you asking about my day when yours is filled with all this stuff that has nothing to do with me. Or with Janet. And for that matter, where were you that night?"

"What night?"

"The night I didn't ask you about and that you're thinking of right now, wondering what sort of lame-ass explanation I'm going to fall for. It was Lydia, right?"

Vlado stiffened at the sound of her name.

"Lydia? Why would you say Lydia? Who says anything about Lydia?"

"So, it *was* Lydia."

"What do you mean *was* Lydia? There is no *was*. I mean, at one point certainly Lydia was . . . well, you know, so let's not even get into it. I mean, I went across the river, sure, but not to see her."

"Well, you'd been drinking."

"I was drinking, so what?"

"So, I've never seen you drink alone."

Obviously, because if you were there to see me then I wasn't alone. But he knew that wouldn't win the war.

"I see what's going on," she said, tears welling. "Ever since that night at the Lo-Ball. And the hospital. That damn doctor who told you to just go out and enjoy your life and to hell with everyone else."

"He didn't say—"

"I can see something has changed. Even when you're here, you're not really here. Well, if you're going to be catting around with your old girlfriend, don't get all huffy that Johnny came by in the middle of the afternoon, in front of God and everybody, to offer to make our lives a little better, not sneaking around at night."

Vlado knew how this worked, that the more he protested, the more guilty he'd look. He could swear on the head of John the Baptist, but Stefani would only reach for her rosary to do what she could to keep her lying husband out of the jaws of hell. Which proved that she cared, right? That she'd never leave him. That he could tell her about the night in the hotel room with the pianist—*See, like you and Johnny, nothing happened*—or the way everything in his life now seemed like it could disappear. He was afraid he could close his eyes and open them again and Stefani herself would be gone. He reached for her hand, but she slid it away.

By then, Janet Ivan was bawling so loud that any more talk would be useless, and besides, Vlado suddenly had important places to go. Things to do. And if he was going to do the time, he thought with soul-soothing anger, then maybe he should go ahead and do the crime.

31

Every morning, Obersteen showed up to fill his sample cooler while Vlado lurked outside by the smoker, like the bad kid expelled from class. At home, when he was home, he mostly avoided Stefani, insofar as that was possible in the tiny house. Often, he'd go next door and smoke a cigar or drink a beer with Ivan on the back stoop before calling it a night. If they were enjoying each other's company, neither one gave any indication.

After two weeks of laying out free sausage, Vlado wondered if Johnny was just stocking his own fridge. It was a Saturday, the day of the week he normally spent with Stefanie and Janet Ivan, going to the zoo or digging around in fake-Aunt-Vera's garden, but it had been spitting rain all day and they'd been stuck at home staring at each other, so he muttered something about Joe needing something and headed out the house and down the hill. He jingled through the front door—unsurprisingly, no customers were out braving the weather— and headed straight back to Stein's Office where four people were tossing cards around in the inevitable game of pinochle. Three of them he expected; one, he did not.

"Johnny, I think you have my chair."

Obersteen looked at Vlado like he didn't recognize him, then smiled, stood up, and clapped his hands on Vlado's shoulders.

"Hey, it's the sausage impresario. Just keeping it warm for you. Here, you play 'em." His head indicated the just-dealt hand. He pressed Vlado down into the empty chair and pulled up a stool. Everyone around the table had their nose in their cards.

Vlado picked up his hand and considered the possibilities. "So, isn't somebody going to throw something?"

"Oh, right," said Inky, and tossed out a two of clubs, still without meeting Vlado's eyes. The front doorbell jingled.

"I'll get it," said Joe, suddenly alive.

"No, I'll get it," said Inky, but Joe was already out of his chair.

The only sound in the room was the reassuring hum of the compressor and the less reassuring wheeze of Johnny's breathing as he peered over Vlado's shoulder. Bootnose cleaned his teeth with the butt end of a wooden match, eyes closed in profound meditation, while Inky squinted at his cards, folded them, opened them, folded them, reopened them—

"All right, who died?" Vlado peered around the table, but only got a shrug from Inky. Bootnose opened one eye then closed it again. Johnny either coughed or burped, it was hard to tell. They sat there motionless, like gunfighters awaiting the annihilation, until Joe returned and reclaimed his seat.

"Dorothy Penny, here for her sausage," he said brightly, but nobody laughed at what had become a running joke.

"What gives, Joey? I swear, there's no shit on my shoe."

Everyone was quiet, as if they were listening for the door to ring again. Finally, Joe said to the table, "It's really good news, isn't it?" Then his eyes met Vlado's. It was the same look—a mixture of shame and apology—he'd had the night he told Vlado he couldn't leave Croatia with him. Of course, they'd gone anyway, Vlado thought, so whatever it is—

"Raphael's wants to put your sausage on the menu," Johnny said and held up his glass for a toast, but nobody moved.

"Well, that is good news. Right?" Vlado said and a weak murmur of assent went around the table.

"But," Johnny said, and here came the knee, heading for Vlado's gut, "They have a few suggestions—"

"Suggestions?" Vlado said. "Like you should get a nicer suit?"

Johnny opened his arms in a conciliatory gesture.

"'Sweeter,' they said. And maybe more of a 'pop' from the skin. No big thing." A fake laugh. "Like they know shit from sausage, right?"

Vlado thought how both the carving knife and Obersteen's ample gut were within arm's reach. He wondered if Stefani would visit him in jail.

Or would it be Lydia? Or maybe he'd get off clean—assault from aggravation, maybe. But thinking he'd for certain be back on Martina's list and at a loss for words for the Holy Oyster, he let the impulse pass.

"Okay, Johnny, we'll get right on it." He snapped his fingers. "Joe, your pencil." Joe reached for the stub parked behind his ear and flipped open a page of his notebook. "Okay, write this down. Sweeter. S . . . W . . . E . . ."

"I got it."

"And make a note. More 'pop.'"

Johnny gave Vlado a dubious look. "You guys fucking with me?"

Bootnose, who had been quiet up to this moment, cleared his throat. "Don't worry, you'd know it if they were."

Inky chimed in, "Odds are—"

"Odds are we're fucking with you, Johnny." Vlado said. "But in all seriousness, of course we can add something, a little of this, a little of that, to where it might be a kind of thing their crowd will be willing to pay for. I mean, what do we know about what Missouri people like to eat?"

This was all it took to light Johnny back up. "See, it'll be great. Custom made for Raphael's by Johnny's Smokehouse. They can charge seventy-five cents for a dime's worth of ground pork. Do the numbers, Joe."

Joe's pencil had returned to its pride of place. "There aren't any numbers yet, Johnny."

"Here's a number for you," Vlado said. "Eight. As in, eight tomorrow you'll be hitting the streets again, so maybe you should try to get your beauty rest."

"Tomorrow's Sunday. Besides, it's only six o'clock."

"Dinner, then. Gotta keep up your strength."

Bootnose retrieved Johnny's mack from the coat hook and held one sleeve out for him while Inky went to open the front door, and soon all that remained of Obersteen was a whiff of cheap aftershave and wet dog.

"Leave it open," Vlado said.

32

"What the hell is this?" Joe said. His mouth was apparently fuller than he wanted it to be. He and Vlado were sampling the new recipe, sawing into a sausage whose reddened hue might have been from embarrassment.

"Pretty awful, isn't it?" Vlado said with pride.

"Actually, it doesn't taste like much of anything."

"For which we have the sugar to thank. Hell, that could be chicken meat in there for all anybody knows." Vlado shuddered with an inkling of an idea that he filed away for later.

Joe squeezed his thumb down on the remaining link until some gray mush popped out the end. "Nice 'pop,' anyway. They'll probably love it."

"Well, Joey, don't you worry, I'm happy either way." Nothing would give Vlado more pleasure than to have the proprietors of Kansas City's finest give Johnny the heave-ho, but on the other hand, there was a mortgage—*thanks for that, Joey*—and other stuff that was unspooling his wad of bills like a roll of toilet paper. So, either way, win-win. Or was it lose-lose?

As if to wash his hand of the whole deal, Vlado wrote out the instructions, underlining the obscene amount of sugar because who would believe it, and gave it to Inky, who'd apparently been waiting his entire life for this moment. He grabbed a handful of knives and headed to the back like a bulldog off his chain, and soon he was chopping away and singing like Bessie Smith, if Bessie Smith had swallowed a toad . . .

Need a little sugar in my bowl
Need a little sugar in my bowl

The electric grinder crunched into motion and Inky raised his voice over the clatter, swooping up to the high notes . . .

Come on and save your mama's soul

I need a little hot dog on my roll

Fortunately, Vlado had other important tasks at hand. The Stude had developed a little chink-a-chink in second gear which meant a trip to Pinkie's garage, followed by an afternoon of painting the kitchen, or at least being around to make sure Stefani didn't screw it up. He was still stung by the whole thing between Johnny and her, mostly because he wasn't sure what the thing was.

He hollered a goodbye to Joe, then slipped his herringbone topcoat off the hook, buttoned up, and shouldered out the door into another inevitably freezing evening, amazed that anybody could think of February as the shortest month. He'd walked a half block up Sixth before realizing that the coat he was wearing was the same one he'd abandoned in the piano player's hotel room weeks ago. He doubled back to Big Sausage.

"Joey, where did this coat come from?" He flapped the coat open with his hands on the lapels.

"Emery Bird's, I'd guess? Or was it a Bootnose procurement?"

"No, I mean, how did it get here?"

Joe cocked his head at Vlado. "I don't know, how does a coat get anywhere?"

"What I'm saying is, I left it . . . I might have left it . . . I thought it was lost." Once again, he had the crazy thought that the night with the piano lady had just been a dream. There was nobody to say one way or the other.

"Well, it's obviously yours. Sometimes I wonder if I'd recognize you without it. Martina wanted to get you a new one for Christmas, but somehow every December you end up on the list."

The coat was old. The herringbone was fading from brown to gray and the pockets sagged where he stored his hands on his frigid walks to the store, but during the winter months, it was like a second skin. He didn't know what to make of today's blessed reappearance other than be glad for it and try not to dwell on the mystery of it all.

Back on the sidewalk, he reached out of habit into his coat pocket for his gloves, which weren't there, and instead pulled out one of the

Big Sausage business cards Inky had designed; "Vlado Novosel – Meat Manager," it said, along with the address of the store. *Of course, mystery solved.* Then he noticed the back of the card where an address was written in a florid hand, a low number on Grand Avenue across the river. He detected a clove-y scent and, waving it under his nose, something else he couldn't place. He buried the card deep in his wallet, thinking of the piano lady, Helene, and her sad eyes. She'd found him, which made him uneasy, as if he were being watched or followed. But at least he'd gotten his coat back, so he wasn't freezing his ass off. Inside his wallet, the reclaimed business card glowed with a heat all its own.

He rounded the top of Barnett and saw a car down in front of his house that was just pulling away. He knew all his neighbors' cars, and this wasn't one of them, some kind of small pickup, noisy, with a smokey exhaust. *Obersteen drove a pickup, right?* His mind filled with crazy possibilities, just more evidence that he might in fact be nuts, which only increased his anxiousness about all this business going on around him, real or not real.

33

To everyone's surprise, Obersteen turned out to be a formidable salesman. Within a few weeks, he had several prominent restaurants—the Muehlebach, Raphael's, and even the Savoy, with its seafood menu—lined up to serve the mess that Vlado had conjured, which meant they'd be selling what was essentially cheap, ground-up sugar-coated pork scraps for the price of prime steaks. Vlado hated the idea that Stefani might have been right about all this. But why should he care? Johnny was taking all the credit—or as Vlado called it, the blame—for the awful links that Vlado wasn't even making anymore, having farmed the job out to Inky. *Plausible deniability, right?* So, there was no reason for him to think about it at all, just ignore the whole deal, sit back and count the *kuna* and thank you very much, Mr. Ovaltine, now get the fuck out of here.

It was with some reluctance on Vlado's part that he and his sweet petunia and Joe and Martina accepted Johnny's invite to dine at Casanova's House of Italian, a former spaghetti emporium near the Power and Light now gussied up as a "prestigious fine-dining destination." Johnny promised a big surprise but of course they all knew what it was, and Vlado was already trying to figure out how to avoid eating the crap that his, or Johnny's, Missouri clients now apparently held in such high esteem. On the other hand, he couldn't resist the opportunity to observe Stefani and Johnny in the same room. If there was anything going on, he'd see it.

The four of them arrived before Obersteen and entered a hushed, red-hued dining room with amber chandeliers and white-linened tables. A wisp of a man in a dark suit whisked them toward a small stage that held a baby grand piano. He laid down six menus at a quilted leather booth. Vlado eyed the piano with distrust and asked if they might have a table further back, so they were shown to a round-top closer to the bar, where surely the tinkle and rattle of glasses and ice would mask any interfering messages from the stage. The room was nearly full, with waiters dressed like penguins gliding among the tables, pouring, serving, discussing. A low murmur conspired with the plush carpet and soft lights to slow Vlado's thoughts to a manageable velocity.

"Drinks?" he said to the table.

"Maybe we should wait for Johnny," said Stefani. Her voice warbled like a nervous bird. "You know, to be polite." Vlado shrugged and picked up his crystal water glass and took a sip, wiggling his pinkie at her, but she avoided his look. He went to open the long, book-like menu, and her hand jerked at his arm.

"Johnny wants to surprise us."

"Johnny, Johnny, Johnny," Vlado said to the ceiling and made a show of pushing away the menu and folding his hands onto his lap like a naughty schoolboy. He fidgeted in his suit coat and fiddled with his necktie. He inspected his fingernails, patted his breast pocket to verify the presence of cigars, took another sip of water and tried to back his way into the peaceful feeling he'd had moments before, but now there was an itch of annoyance he couldn't scratch. It didn't help that on the stage a man was unloading an accordion from a case. He'd propped up a sign — *Franky Fontana*—and primed a brass spittoon tip jar with a couple of conspicuous bills. Vlado tried to ignore that and listen to what Stefani was saying to Joe, something about the latest thing the brilliant Janet Ivan had done, but his focus blurred, and he drifted off while the voices around him droned like car wheels.

Vlado's reverie was interrupted when a herd of waiters parted like the Red Sea and Obersteen materialized in a fog of cigar smoke, garbed in a well-fitting suit and bowtie, standing there with his arm around . . . well, it was certainly not the surprise Vlado expected, which is often the nature of surprises, but even allowing for that, Vlado desperately wished for a drink to clear his vision. For a long moment there was no sound or movement, then Johnny cleared his throat and said,

"Sorry we're late. I believe you all know Miss Penny."

Miss Penny. Do we all know Miss Penny? Dorothy Penny?

Vlado and Joe immediately tried to stand, nearly knocking the table over, and Johnny waved them back down into their seats. He installed Dorothy Penny next to Martina and lowered himself down on the other side next to Vlado, who leaned away from Johnny's mixed scent of sweat and lavender-y cologne that suggested a roast lamb gone bad. Vlado kicked Joe under the table, overshooting to where Martina gave him a sharp look, followed by a thin smile, a smirk even. Of course, she'd known all about this, no doubt part of some larger to-do he could scarcely guess at.

"Well, it's lovely to see you all," Dorothy said. The silverware and crystal glasses on the table, the elegant China plates, and maybe the room itself, leaned in with a warm glow. She wore a simple navy party dress, with two thin straps holding up the works, and her auburn hair was pinned up in an elegant bun. She plucked up Johnny's napkin, draped it across his lap and followed suit with her own. Everyone else at the table lunged for theirs, and Vlado beckoned desperately for a waiter.

Soon enough, drinks and bread appeared. Johnny, quiet as usual when food was in front of him, buttered up a dinner roll—no surprise—then placed it on Dorothy Penny's plate—big surprise—while Vlado tossed back a shot of the local and refilled his glass from the murky carafe. He heard the first wheezing notes of the accordion and felt like he was on a boat about to capsize, but the sound resolved itself into a not unpleasant melody, lovely actually, a song he recognized, about *amore* something. He didn't know an accordion could even do that. Dorothy Penny had turned from Johnny and was in a deep conference with Martina that he couldn't hear, except for the occasional giggle. Vlado leaned behind Stefani to whisper in Joe's ear, *I guess Dorothy's here for her sausage.* Joe looked straight ahead and bit his lip while Stefani pinched Vlado's thigh harder than he thought he deserved.

Obersteen was working through his third dinner roll and Vlado was looking at the bottom of his third drink when Joe suggested they order.

Johnny leaned back and picked up his menu and solemnly opened it, as if he were Father Oyster addressing the Big Book, while eying everyone at the table. Vlado opened his and scanned down a list of items described in an Italian he didn't understand.

A thin man with dark, baggy eyes arrived at the table. He was no penguin, favoring instead a wide-lapeled pinstriped suit which he wore with the authority it vested in him. "Good evening, Johnny. Miss Penny. And your wonderful-to-look-at-friends," he said and uncorked the first bottle of real wine Vlado had seen in years. Johnny tasted it and glasses were filled.

"Thank you, Mario," said Obersteen. "We'll all be having the *speciale* tonight."

"Ah the *salciccia allegro*. I'm sure you will enjoy." He gathered up the menus and vanished into the carpeted twilight.

"Salsay-shay what?" said Stefani.

"I hope it's not what I think it is," said Martina.

"It's what you think it is," said Joe.

"I swear I know that guy," Vlado said. "Didn't he used to be a blood-sweeper at Armour?" This earned him another pinch from Stefani, and he nosed into his wine, then gave it a tentative sip. He made a face and said, "Johnny, tell your friend Mario this needs more sugar. In fact, have him bring us a bowl of sugar on the side, because what doesn't need more sugar?" He tugged at a passing penguin's coat, "Could I have some sugar for my sugar, please," he said, and gave Stefani an affectionate squeeze.

She squinted at him. "Vlado—"

"Sugar." He smooched her on the cheek.

"So, Dorothy," Joe said quickly. "We haven't seen you around the store lately."

Vlado couldn't hear her reply over the accordion, which was doing some high-dive maneuvers. He eased out of his chair, stumbling a bit, then pulled out his roll of bills and peeled off a dollar. He waved it at the table to the interest of no one then weaved around toward the stage. Franky Fontana, eyes closed, was pumping away in a joyous trance. He wore a pink ruffled tuxedo shirt beneath a white dinner jacket and purple bowtie, like something you'd see on the dessert tray at the Muehlebach, if not for his oiled hair and thin, upturned mustache. Vlado was about to feed the spittoon when he got a closer look.

"Sinovic?"

Matt Sinovic opened his eyes in mid-wheeze and looked at Vlado with annoyance, then with alarm. "Vlado," he whispered, pinching out a painfully high note. "You don't know me," he said and gazed nervously around the room.

"Not with the fake mustache, anyway," Vlado said, resisting the urge to rip it off, honestly amused for the first time that night. He dropped his bill into the spittoon and pulled out another and tucked it halfway into the lapel pocket of Sinovic's jacket. "Ciao, amigo," he said, giving Sinovic a slight slap on the cheek, and returned to the table, where Obersteen was holding forth about God knows what.

He plopped into his seat and interrupted Johnny. "Hey, you'll never guess who's here," he said to the table, but at that moment three stripe-shirted gondoliers sporting white neckerchiefs and ribbon-festooned straw boaters appeared and, with synchronized flamboyance, laid down six plates piled with a colorful array of. . . something, along with two more bottles of wine.

It looked worse than he'd anticipated. Dismembered limbs of eggplant, carrots, turnips, beets, poked out of a smothering overcoat of cheese—*cheese?*—which was bleeding a thin red sauce to the edge of the plate, all some horrible carnage. Vlado used the tip of his knife to peer under the cheese at what looked less like sausages and more like a couple of digits that could have once belonged to Lubo Grisnik's left hand. Joe, to his credit, was carving cleanly into his own dinner and chewing it with a sense of stoic purpose. Johnny stuffed his own face while the ladies nudged things around on their plates with dainty fork movements. Dorothy Penny sawed off the tiniest corner of cheese and sausage and nibbled on it. Vlado wanted to gag on the smell—was it the smell, or something else?—and reached past his wine glass to pour another shot of the homemade, hoping to dull his senses, but it landed in his empty stomach with a bang, and he felt his chest tighten dangerously.

"Joe, your pencil," he said, and without waiting, plucked the stub from behind Joe's ear and scribbled something on a cocktail napkin. It was a song request, which he signed, "From the owner." He wrapped the note around a bill and beckoned for a waiter to deliver it to Sinovic, who had just finished a torchy ballad to a smatter of polite applause. Matt read it and looked across at Vlado, who quickly glanced away. He shrugged and launched into a boisterous rendition of the "Beer Barrel Polka." Back at the table, Vlado began clapping to the beat.

"*Hvartska!* How can we not dance!" He stood and held out a hand to Dorothy Penny, who was too shocked to do anything but take it, and suddenly he was steering her in circles around the table. "Roll out the barrel," he sang, "we'll have a barrel of fun," *and why was everyone not joining in?* He gave Miss Penny a kiss on the cheek and spun her neatly into her chair, then staggered back against the table behind him. He was clapping and singing as he approached Stefani, who was giving him a look of either undying love or disbelief. He reached for her, but her hands were glued to her knife and fork, so he stood there like a fool, feeling the eyes of the room on him. Stefani, the love of his life. His face burned with humiliation, and he fought the urge to just run out the door, but to who? Lydia? Helene? Back to Zagreb?

Stefani narrowed her gaze, then put down her silverware and took his hand.

"*Jebote*," she said, and Vlado pulled her up.

Stefani gripped him tight, and they weaved around the tables, moving as one, everybody else be damned. Joe urged Martina out of her chair and two of them got in step with Vlado and Stefani. They lurched through the room past startled diners who began clapping to the music, until other couples were up as well, and it seemed like they'd all moved from Italy to the more fun side of the Adriatic.

Sinovic did the big finish, and Vlado and his crew returned to the table, flushed and out of breath. Johnny was neither chewing nor smiling, and Dorothy Penny's lips were tightened as if to ask why she was just sitting there with a giant toad while everyone else was having all the fun. Their empty chairs had been pushed tight up to the table—*more room for dancing,* Vlado thought—but then he saw the little man with the dark eyes holding their wraps.

"Another round for the table," Vlado announced, then realized there were two gondoliers, one on either side of him, and his first thought was he didn't know they were so tall, and his second thought was that it was by design. One of them took his arm, but he shrugged it off and pulled out a couple of twenties and slapped them down. The hand returned, gripping him tighter, but Vlado wrenched away, knocking over glasses on the table behind him, then grabbed the guy by his neckerchief and jerked his head down toward Vlado's full dinner plate.

"Here, you eat this crap if you like it." He felt a hand on his shoulder, he turned, and there was the other guy, opening his mouth and saying something Vlado couldn't make out for the buzzing in his ears. It seemed like he had all the time in the world to examine the man's face, his thin, womanly eyebrows, his greased black hair, his skinny lips stretched into some unfortunate grimace, and his jutting chin, something nobody could miss, least of all Vlado, who watched as if it were someone else's fist that flew from the end of his wrist and found its unmissable target. Unfortunately for the gondolier, the fist was powered by a butcher's arm, and he went down like a two-by-four. Everything went quiet, and *well I guess that takes care of that* crossed an errant part of Vlado's brain, but then it was noise everywhere and he felt himself lifted by about a thousand arms and propelled through the restaurant like a battering ram, until he was shoved through the front door and launched like a paper airplane, one that was wingless and too heavy, and which crash-landed on the unyielding pavement with Vlado's thoughts tumbling wildly inside. He heard a door slam, and the sound of a distant siren.

34

Vlado sensed that he was in a strange bed. Somebody else's bed. *Surely not Lydia's,* he thought with excitement and dread and reached his arm out for the body next to him, but his knuckles grazed a cold wall. Then, as his soul seeped back into his body, he wondered if that was an actual ice pick inserted in his forehead and why did his every muscle feel like it had been tenderized with a meat hammer.

"Do you want some of my pancakes?"

Vlado squinted beneath the too-bright fluorescents. Two images became one and he was looking at a thin man, balding, middle aged, sporting a blue plaid suit jacket and a yellow tie that was fatter than it needed to be. He was sitting on another bed and held out a tin plate with a couple of doughy-looking discs frozen under a glaze of syrup.

"You missed breakfast, and they don't come back," the man said. "You can have my juice too."

Vlado pushed himself up and looked around the tiny cell, at the two little beds, the metal sink, the exposed toilet, and memories began to assemble themselves: being shut into the back of the squad car; Martina yelling at a cop and Joe pulling her away; the quick drive to the station, then nothing. Now, somehow, here he was in his slacks, socks, and sleeveless underwear, shivering in the morning cold and accepting a tray of questionable food from a stranger who smelled like he'd gone swimming in a distillery. Vlado muttered a thanks and tried to scrape a pancake up off the plate, but it was glued solid.

"You kind of look like hell," the guy said. Vlado fingered a couple of tender spots on his face that had been bandaged, and one that had not. His fingers came away with a dab of blood.

"Well, you look a little overdressed for the occasion." *Who the hell was this guy?*

"It's all about how you present yourself." He straightened his tie and ran a finger around inside his pressed collar. "They know by now I'm not going to hang myself. You, on the other hand, are a different story." A card materialized that he handed to Vlado.

"Leopold Gorsky, Esq.," Vlado read aloud. "What's the 'Esq' mean"?

"It means if you're ever in any legal trouble, you can give me a call. You aren't by chance in legal trouble now, are you?"

The anxious dread Vlado'd been hauling around lately welled up and thrummed on his bones. He knew he was a stranger here, on the wrong side of the river, and that cell door wasn't going to open itself.

Leopold Gorsky, Esq., stood and called out, "Marvin, we need you! Court's in session." A stout, red-faced guard appeared at the cell door. "My client, Mr. . . . ."

"Novosel," Vlado said.

"My client, Mr. Novosel, will be arranging for bail forthwith. Can you please bring him his things?"

Marvin disappeared and returned with a pillowcase that he squeezed through the breakfast gap. Inside were Vlado's clothes, keys, and his roll of bills. Vlado counted the money to verify it was correct then turned to Gorsky.

"I suppose there's a fee."

Gorsky mentioned a number, and Vlado peeled off a few bills.

"Plus, another ten for the pancakes," Gorsky added. "Just kidding." He took his business card from Vlado, tucked it into the top of Vlado's undershirt and gave his chest a friendly pat.

"You'll be needing that later."

Gorsky pushed something through the bars to Marvin who opened the cell and pointed down the hall. "Sandy'll process your paperwork."

Vlado buttoned up his shirt, slipped into his shoes and pocketed what was left of his cash. Coincidentally, the amount for bail was the same as the amount left in his diminished roll, in exchange for which he received a no-nonsense document that required his appearance in court a month hence.

Outside the police station, he looked for the welcoming committee but saw only a stream of anonymous faces. It was just after 7:30, so of course Joe would be busy opening the store. And Stefani had little Janet Ivan, after all. He jingled the change in his pocket, hoping it was enough to get him on the bus back to the Hill.

The driver knew him and spotted him a nickel and he limped off the bus at Fourth, looking forward to a bath and his sweet petunia's healing touch. He patted his jacket for a cigar, but they were gone. He turned down Barnett, happy to see his little house, his warm love nest where he hoped to put the terrible night out of his mind. Vlado was surprised to find the front door locked. He fumbled with his key, let himself in. The house was cold, the lights were off, and he didn't need to check the rooms to know that no one was there. He stepped back outside and walked through the yard, geraniums be damned, to fake-Aunt-Vera's house and banged on the front door, a couple times more than necessary. It opened and Ivan stood there in his pajamas, a half-smoked cigar dead in his mouth.

"So much busy-ness this morning. A man needs his rest." *Right, because here comes a long day on the couch.*

"Where are they, Ivan?"

Ivan cursed and started to close the door, but Vlado put his foot in the way. Ivan lowered his unshaved face and smoke-stained teeth down to Vlado, who leaned away from his garlicky breath.

"They're finally sleeping," Ivan whispered hoarsely. "Come back later."

Vlado kept his foot in the door.

Ivan pulled his cigar out and gestured back toward Vlado's house. "Go on. You can't win now."

Vlado had the urge to take Ivan's cigar and . . . well, that's the sort of thing that had gotten him in this spot.

Back in his own house, he stood in the bathroom and waited for the tub to fill. He stared at a clearly inferior version of himself in the mirror —doughy face, swollen racoon eyes, a puffed-out lower lip, and skewed, oily hair matted with either dirt or dried blood. Pain shot through his right wrist as he pulled off his clothes and winced into the hot water. He let his head sink back until all that surfaced were his two nose holes. It occurred to him that he could open his submerged mouth and just take a deep breath, and that would be that. Everybody's problem solved. But they'd all be sorry, right? He imagined Joe, and maybe even Martina, sobbing at his funeral. The guys at Morty's toasting to *Vlado Novosel, sausage legend*. Dorothy Penny realizing the opportunity was lost forever. Lydia? Who could say? Stefani wailing and Janet Ivan looking around for her daddy.

Janet Ivan. Unable to shake the image of her accusing stare, Vlado groaned out of the tub, dried, dressed, and shuffled out of the house and down the hill toward St. Margaret's hospital.

35

Vlado hobbled out of St. Margaret's with a couple of stitches above one eye and a plaster cast containing what might have been a broken right wrist. He made his way to the store like a poorly oiled machine, thinking he'd talk it over with Joe, get the lay of the land—but the sign said "Closed" and the door was locked. On a Tuesday morning? Of course, Joe had suffered a hard night too, so let the Hill's crew of freeloaders and cheapskates starve for a day. He didn't want to go by Morty's, not knowing what anybody knew, and unsure of what he knew himself, but Vlado couldn't stand the thought of returning to his empty house. He considered St. John's, and a quiet pew to mull over current events, but the fear of running into Father Oyster-Face, who probably already knew more about the incident than the police, led him to make a left at Quindaro and begin the hike out to Joe's place.

Twenty minutes later, Joe stared at him through the screen door. Vlado smelled coffee and toast, and could have used an egg or three right now, but Joe made no move to let him in.

' "Your car's in the back, if that's what you want," Joe said. His face was blank, and his eyes were puffy.

"Fine, Joey, I'm glad you got home okay. So, you were just going to leave me in there?"

"I was getting to it."

"Getting to it?"

"Yeah, getting to it, after I was done with getting an earful from all concerned. Vlado *this* and Vlado *that*, because you weren't there to clean up your own mess."

"Well, Stefani—"

"Oh, Stefani, right, not happy. Not one bit. Good luck with that one. I've got my own bright-lipped American girl to deal with. And

Obersteen? You have no idea. You think they let him stick around like nothing happened?" Joe seemed weirdly upset. He squeaked open the screen door and beckoned Vlado in toward the kitchen. "For once in your life, just don't say anything."

Martina was fussing at the sink while they sat opposite each other at the kitchen table. Without looking at Vlado, she laid down two coffee cups and took what seemed like forever to fill them. Then she clunked the sugar bowl down in front of Vlado, louder than necessary he thought, and turned from the room, closing the door behind her.

"She knows I don't take sug . . . oh, I get it. Okay. More sugar. Right. Very funny, but maybe that gets at what the real problem is."

"Vlado, just shut up." Joe blew over the top of his lukewarm cup of coffee, then set it down without taking a sip. He took the pencil from behind his ear, wagged it at Vlado to punctuate some unspoken thought, then flung it past Vlado's head at the kitchen window, where it bounced and clattered into the sink. He elbowed onto the table, rested his head on his fingertips, and closed his eyes.

"All right, so what happened, happened. The guy's fine, right? I mean, one punch." Vlado said. "In fact, you should see the other guy." He tilted his chin forward.

"Who knows if the guy's fine? At this point he's whatever he says he is," said Joe. "We're not teenagers, and this is not the crazy world we grew up in. What about Stefani? And your little girl? And Martina? And my boys? And all this?" His head indicated the neat, well-appointed kitchen, but Vlado knew it wasn't just that.

"So, I can apologize, right? Make it up, somehow."

"Apologize to who? You think everybody's lined up to get an 'I'm sorry' now from the rude Croat from the ghetto who didn't like his dinner? Maybe you could buy donuts for everybody. Send Johnny a sausage, two for Dorothy Penny, who we know *likes her sausage*. There, I'm saying it for you, so don't. And Sinovic—"

"What's wrong with Sinovic?"

"He was right behind us on the way out, barely had time to pack up his accordion. These guys were not amused. Not Mario. Not Johnny. I don't know Obersteen very well, but I can't imagine he'd just let this go."

Vlado had never seen Joe this upset. "You were part of this, too," he said.

Joe stared down into his coffee and said, "Go on home, Vlado. We'll talk later, see who rings what bells. I'm sorry." He stood and walked into the living room where Martina had disappeared, closed the door behind him, and Vlado saw his own way out.

At least the Studebaker was undamaged and coughed into action. The rhythmic clug of the V-8 soothed him. He gassed it and steered toward Quindaro, determined to put the whole dreadful night out of his mind. Joe'd get over it, of course he would, he always had before, even the crazy nights in Zagreb. And probably by now Stefani's mom would be driving her nuts and she'd be back home, with Janet Ivan looking for Daddy, dinner in the oven, well, maybe not, but he could fix that. And fucking Obersteen. Definitely pissed, but surely Dorothy Penny could sweet talk him into writing off the evening as a rowdy night with the boys. And nobody died. Joe would have said. Vlado let these thoughts rub together in his head until they generated a spark of his old optimism. He gassed the Studebaker down Minnesota Avenue toward the Hill, thinking how he and Joe could hit the Missouri side again without Johnny, how everything was beautiful and how wrong he was to think that he could lose everything.

Lost in his rumination, he almost continued onto the viaduct and across the river but caught himself in time and whipped a quick right onto Fourth. A woman hoisting two overfilled grocery bags was crossing the street, unaware of the car bearing down on her. Vlado saw the imminent calamity, jerked the wheel lefty-loosey, and the Stude jumped the curb and launched itself down the too-steep hill toward the river, picking up speed, branches snapping against the windshield while Vlado uselessly pumped the brakes and grabbed at the emergency, until the chromed, fendered, straight-eight love of his life bounded through the willows lining the bank and lurched into the murky waters of the Kaw with an enthusiastic spray. The car wedged into the mud and then, lightened by the current, slipped loose and began drifting toward St. Louis. For all its charms, Vlado knew the Stude was no boat and despite his shock, he knew he had to get out of there. He shoved on the door, but it was crunched shut. The window was open, however, and he managed to push himself through and somersault into the frigid water. His feet sank into the silty river bottom which anchored him in the chest-high current. Just beyond, drifting downstream, the Stude's engine was churning and blowing bubbles in the water with cheery persistence, until, with a giant belch, it tipped sideways and disappeared beneath the surface.

Vlado managed to pull one foot loose from the muck and turned to wade back to shore, cursing aloud and unable to believe that someone's idea of a just God had just cast him and his dear Studebaker into the muddy waters of the Kaw. But the current caught him, pulled loose his remaining foot, and swept him slowly but insistently toward the river's main channel. Weighed down by his waterlogged overcoat and plaster cast, by his exhaustion of the past day, and by the hand of fate that seemed determined to crush him with its indifference, Vlado felt his stroking arm weaken until it was all he could do to keep his head above the surface, then hardly that. He took in mouthfuls of the dirty water, choking it out through his nose, his eyes stinging. Something heavy bounced painfully against his right arm, and with a terrific lunge he grabbed onto it with both hands. It was a whitewall tire, most likely the spare that must have shaken loose from the side of his dearly departed. He dug his fingernails into the treads and managed to drag his head up out of the water, suck in a breath, and clutch the whole thing to his chest. The tire sank a few inches but managed to support his weight, and so it was that he and the final remains of his precious automobile drifted together down the Kaw like so much driftwood.

Soon the channel widened into the Missouri, where the cross-current put his makeshift raft into a slow, counter-clockwise spin. Helpless as a fishing bobber that had slipped its line, Vlado gripped the tire and tried not to think about his dangling feet and the giant catfish that patrolled these rivers looking for a quick bite. He steeled his thoughts against the cold while the receding silhouette of St. John's steeple spun into view, a mocking reminder that he was once again moving in the wrong direction. Then the pens and low buildings of the Armour plant, the chill of their carving rooms nothing compared to the icy clutch on his balls that threatened at any moment to drag him into the depths. He rotated past the looming skyscrapers of downtown Kansas City until he was staring straight down the endless stretch of the Missouri. He shivered violently and clutched the tire tighter, willing his heart to stop its crazy drumming, but it pounded even louder while his last stores of warmth ebbed into the river's darkness.

How sad that it would all end like this, another random thing he didn't see coming. Like his flight from Zagreb, his all-of-a-sudden marriage to Stefani, Janet Ivan, the disaster with the piano player. Even Big Sausage, which would have never happened without Joe making it happen. For five minutes he was a big shot with a big car, but now here he was, a tiny and ridiculous speck being dragged unseen down the middle of some fucking river. And just like that, he understood. It had been bigger than him the whole time. All of it. The whole shebang. But that meant he was innocent, right? That nothing was his fault. *The defense rests*, he thought, and his breathing began to slow. His eyes sagged and the water wrapped around him like a blanket, carrying him down the river like Moses in his little basket, and he felt himself warming, relaxing, in sync with the current, sharing its journey to the sea. Vlado had been to sea, had crossed the ocean, knew what lay ahead: a new world, friends and family, a home and respect, and here he was on his way to make it all happen. He felt the happy promise of his future, knew he had to let go of the past, let go of everything, and slid off the tire and into the promising embrace of the wide Missouri.

Vlado opened his eyes with a shock and saw only a murky darkness. He flailed his arms and jerked his head up to gasp at the air. The tire bobbed on out of reach, and the current picked up as it whipped around the tip of a protruding sandbar. The eddy had a firm grip on him, but his legs brushed against something, and he reached down and grasped a submerged branch with a strength he didn't know he had. He kicked his legs and pulled himself toward the sand bank until his feet found the mud and he was able to hoist most of his miserable self out of the water and collapsed face-down onto the gritty oasis.

Vlado lay still until the spinning slowed, then pushed himself upright on shaky legs. The river breeze knifed through his wet clothes, and he felt as if the frigid water was rising back up to reclaim him. He had to get away. The overgrown banks and cliff concealed all but the tip of the Power and Light, which seemed to beckon him onward. He clenched his chattering teeth and slushed his frozen, water-soaked boots, left foot right foot, through the heavy sand toward the shelter of the brush. There he found a narrow path that switch-backed up the hill. He faltered, pulling at tree roots and long tufts of grass that didn't support his weight, falling and getting up, his bones rattling.

He was nettle-stung and out of breath when the bushes finally opened into a clearing that he recognized as the back of the city market. A couple of Mexicans were unloading boxes of lettuce at a warehouse dock like nothing had happened, and—not wanting to be mistaken for a common laborer—Vlado straightened up, buttoned his shirt to the top, and repositioned his hair with his fingers. He took off his soaked overcoat, shook it out like a rug, then squirmed back into it and walked toward the front of the market like a man with a purpose. A mission. Always forward.

Suddenly the day had turned unseasonably warm, and he was sweating, flapping his coat, wondering at the shoppers moving through the market tents in their heavy wraps. He was burning up with heat but shaking from the cold and only knew he had to get to higher ground. He trudged up the hill, boots squeaking, past a row of bars and liquor stores, until he recognized the back of the tow lot on Main Street. Maybe he should drop in and see how that kid was doing, if he had any extra cars. *You see, I lost mine in the river.* He pushed on but was drowning with fatigue and settled heavily onto a bus stop bench. He watched the downtowners shuffling past on the sidewalk, wondering why they were staring at him in such a rude way. Was it that obvious he was from the other side? Well, fuck 'em. *No sausage for you.* A young blonde woman in heels and a tight skirt—no Dorothy Penny, but still—approached him with an understanding smile. She stood in front of him and fished around in her pillbox purse. He waited for her to speak, but she took out a dollar bill and set it gently on his lap, then continued down the street. *Maybe he'd been too hard on these people.*

Encouraged by her show of kindness he stood, unsteady, but determined to continue his mission, the mission that would soon reveal itself, on the next corner, the next day, the next bend of the river. No, not the river, he shivered again. He continued his plod up the hill, looking around now, no idea where he was. The brick and brownstone buildings gave no clue and the streets in every direction seemed to lead to just more of the same. At the next intersection, he looked up at a street sign. Grand Avenue. *Of course,* he thought, *Grand Avenue,* and his thoughts fizzed up like Alka-Seltzer. It was a riddle, for sure, and he stared at it, trying to divine the answer. He checked his memory, checked his watch, checked his pockets and then his wallet, looking for something. He pulled out a water-soaked card with the miraculously still-legible address and apartment number. The lovely pianist had been waiting for fate and the forces of nature to bring him back, and here he was, as promised by a higher order of things, delivered to her by the mighty river. He turned up Grand, repeating her name—Helene—with every destiny-fueled step. He recognized the number on a brown-brick apartment building, where he entered a musty lobby and found the steps. By the time he reached the third floor, he was burning up and out of breath and had to steady himself against the wall. He checked his hair one more time and then knocked politely. He had the sense he was still at sea, weaving back and forth to right the ship, until the door quietly opened, and a woman stood there in the twilight.

"Vlado," said the familiar voice.

Yes, it's Vlado, here at last. He took a step forward, the floor tilted, and he collapsed into her arms. Then they were in a clumsy dance, moving together toward a couch, where she released him, and he fell into darkness.

36

Vlado heard a shrill whistle, which meant his shift had thankfully ended. He could hardly move, as if his veins had been stuffed with ground pork. He reached for his knives to wipe them clean, but they weren't on the table. Then there was no table, and he was lying on his back, wrapped in something soft and warm. He loosened one arm and found a damp cloth draped over his forehead. He opened his eyes to see if he was dead, but if he was, it meant that hell was a dim room with a peeling-paint ceiling. The whistling had stopped, and light footsteps came his way. He jacked himself up with one elbow and saw a woman approaching with a teacup. She drew close and he thought she must be an angel, until the light caught her, and he was staring into the worried face of Lydia Tomasic.

"Looks like you're finally back," Lydia said. She set the cup next to him and pressed the warm back of her hand against his cheek. She had on a terrycloth robe and strands of her black hair straggled out of a sloppy bun. He reached up to touch it, like Thomas seeking proof. *Lydia*. Worry lines stemmed out from her eyes, which were droopy and dark against her pale skin.

He wondered about the time and made the habitual grab for his pocket watch when he realized he was naked beneath the blanket. Lydia read his alarm.

"You would have died in those wet clothes. Don't worry, it's nothing I haven't seen before."

Vlado groped in the empty room of his memory. "So, we didn't—"

"No, we didn't." She smiled slightly. "I mean, if you need to ask . . ."

She propped some pillows behind Vlado's back and blew over the cup of tea before placing it into his shaky hands. He sipped, and the warm liquid massaged his frozen innards. His brain unreeled the recent events:

the surreal hike up from the river, the deathly chill of the water, his car, gone. He stared at Lydia, confused.

"Why are you here?" he asked. *Was this even real?*

"Who else would you be expecting? The question is how is it that *you* are here, looking like you crawled up out of a sewer? Anything to impress a girl, right?" She broke out a smile, which warmed Vlado as much as the tea.

"You told me I'd never find you," he said.

"You wouldn't have, without some help." She fingered the card with the address that lay in evidence on the table next to the tea saucer. "Don't hurt yourself thinking about it, Vlado. I saw your coat at the Lo-Ball—I mean, who wouldn't recognize that ratty old thing. I was just going to return it . . . probably a bad move, and a worse move to scribble on the card, judging from the look on your face."

"You were at the Lo-Ball?" he asked.

"Yes, I spend my nights at random bars waiting for you to show up." At that moment, Vlado would have believed anything, but she went on. "I waitress there on weekends. In fact, I saw you the night you came in with Joe and Martina and your precious Stefani. I begged off with a headache, but I heard later you'd caused some sort of commotion."

"Then Helene must have brought the coat back to the bar."

"Helene? The piano player?" There was dead silence and Vlado knew she was following the logical paths toward an unfortunate conclusion. He waited for the explosion, but Lydia gave him a look that was more hurt than anger.

"You know, Vlado, I moved over here so I wouldn't feel like a damn fool every time I saw you. And yes, you found me, congratulations. I'm sorry I'm not who you're looking for. Am never who you're looking for, except for one reason. Here, is this what you want?" She opened her robe and revealed a flash of modest white breasts, then turned from him and shrugged the rest of the robe off her shoulders. Leaving it crumpled on the floor, she stepped calmly out of the room.

That wasn't what Vlado wanted. Probably. In fact, if there was ever a time that Vlado absolutely didn't know what he wanted, this was it. He clutched his blanket and stood up from the couch and shuffled toward what he hoped was the bathroom. His hopes were realized, and there he found his clothes drying on a rack. He had a long pee, then pulled on his underwear and trousers, not as dry as he might like but close enough, then the rest of it, and buttoned it all up to where he looked like some sort of modern art version of himself. He ducked his head out, saw the coast was clear and minced over to a small galley kitchen with tidy lace curtains that looked out onto an alley fronted by another drab building. He was peering into the refrigerator when Lydia appeared at the door.

"Why are you still here?" She had combed out her hair and put on a modest navy shift and a smatter of makeup.

"I haven't eaten today," said Vlado.

"And I suppose you expect me to stop everything now and fix you something nice, like I'm your dear Stefani."

Vlado was too hungry to argue and reached into the fridge for some eggs and butter and grabbed a saucepan lurking on the back of the tiny apartment stove. He found garlic, green pepper, onion, a spice rack, and a half wheel of cheese. He diced and grated and soon had a pan full of simmering vegetables over which he cracked the eggs and stirred, while Lydia sat silently at the little kitchen table.

"The trick is to put the cheese in at the very end," he said, giving it all a final swish, then scraped it onto two plates which he set on the table. He found forks and napkins and sat opposite Lydia, who was giving him an exasperated look.

Vlado took a bite of the eggs and almost died right then from their velvety splendor. *The one good thing about a chicken.* He gestured to Lydia's plate, and she raised a bite to her lips without taking her eyes off Vlado. She chewed slowly then put down her fork.

"Stop it, Vlado. Just stop it."

"You don't like it?" He didn't think she was angry anymore, but what did he really know about women? Increasingly, he thought, very little.

She clipped a nametag onto her chest and took her plate to the sink. "Just give me a break. Eat your eggs and get out of here, will you? I have to go to work." She grabbed a coat and her purse, hurried out of the kitchen, and slammed the front door. He retrieved her plate from the sink and in a few moments had gobbled up all the eggs and went searching for a bottle of rakija, which he found behind the toaster.

Vlado's various cogs and wheels slowed. He was warm. He'd eaten. Outside, the Missouri river was chewing up everything in its way and carrying it down and spitting it out into the vast ocean, but here he was safely above the high-water mark. The previous night's disastrous dinner seemed like another lifetime and the bizarre sequence of events that followed had rolled out, one after the other, with a spooky inevitability. Like some larger plan he had no say in. And now somehow, here he was in Lydia's apartment. Not like he would have expected. No soft lights or incense, or Lydia in black lingerie.

He moved out of the kitchen and sat down on the couch in the tiny parlor. Faded floral wallpaper hung on the walls, dingy in the dim overhead light. A couple of pictures rested on a small banquette that held a vase of plastic geraniums. The room had a musty smell, or maybe it was him, but either way it was comforting, like the reek of long history. Like grandmothers had lived here. He thought of his real Aunt Vera, remembered her aroma of perspiration, of rising dough, of alcohol and sweat and worry. He sensed his own odor, of mud and mold and damp.

It didn't take much searching to find Lydia's bedroom and her neatly made double bed with the chenille spread. Vlado pulled off his boots —always the gentleman—and burrowed beneath the covers, sinking his head into a poufy pillow that damped out the racket in his brain. He had no more thoughts before the world disappeared of its own accord.

Later, in the timeless dark, Vlado felt a rustling. A body slid between the sheets next to him.

"You stink," was the last thing he heard before he dropped back into a deep sleep.

37

Vlado awakened at first light, still in his clothes, next to Lydia, who was sound asleep and wrapped chastely in a long sleeve cotton nightgown. His heart skipped a beat or two before his memory caught up to the events. *Christ on the cross.* He stole out quietly, trying not to poke any of the beasts that had been stalking him, desperate to get back to the side of the river where things made some sort of sense. It was a manageable walk to the Bottoms where he caught the workmen's trolley that crossed over to the Hill. He gave the river a wary look, then slouched down in his seat to avoid any stray bit of extra gravity. Once he was finally safe on Kansas soil, it was a quick stroll to Barnett, then down the block to whatever awaited.

Stefani burst into tears when Vlado walked through the front door. "It was you after all," she sobbed, grabbed him by his coat lapels and shook him, then punched him hard in the chest. "You can't do that."

Vlado had no idea which of his many transgressions from the last twenty-four hours he couldn't do, but he knew he had to take the initiative.

"Why weren't you here?" he asked. "You all left me over there."

"Always about you, Vlado. We're the ones who were left. Me and Janet. And now here you are, back from the dead, smelling like a damn catfish."

"Where is Janet Ivan?" Somehow, he thought his baby girl might be more reasonable.

"With my mom, who's not happy about it."

"She's never happy about anything." Had he really returned from the great beyond only to be bickering with Stefani? "And you can decide if you're happy to see me or not. Believe me, I want everybody to be happy."

Sadly, Vlado realized he was back on the side of the river where everybody wanted to argue about everything, except, he guessed, for the fact that he needed a bath. He detached himself from Stefani and went to turn on the hot water for the tub, grabbed a cigar—guaranteeing he'd get crap for smoking in the house—and the bottle of rakija to help him not worry about it. He closed the door and locked it, and if Stefani had any further comments, they were lost in the gurgling water. After a while, the holy trinity of booze, bath, and cigar helped Vlado feel as if he was sliding back into his own skin and had at least a fighting chance to piece things together and consider his next move.

He lay there until the water turned cold, then dried himself, listening for clues, but the house was so quiet he could hear Janet Ivan bawling next door. He wasn't ready to take that on, so he shaved, dressed, and hightailed it out the back and down to the store. He felt nervous walking in, as if he might not belong there. Joe's kid Tommy was ringing up an order. "Why aren't you in school?" Vlado said, then walked past the counter toward Stein's Office, to the shocked looks on the faces of his brothers-in-arms, who were lurking around the table like the layabouts they were.

The room held its breath while he stood there spreading his arms out like Jesus on a holy card.

"He is risen," Vlado said.

Inky stood and clapped his hands in slow motion. "Look what they dredged up from the river bottom."

"Did I miss anything?"

Bootnose said, "From what I hear, you didn't miss that guy's face," and laughed like it was the funniest thing anybody had ever said.

Joe suppressed a smile and he said, "You missed a lot." He told him that the woman he'd almost run over had seen the car disappear into the river but didn't know whose it was. Word spread, and that, coupled with Vlado's absence, had everyone assuming the worst. They weren't far off the mark, Vlado thought, when you consider there are few worse things than floating down the Missouri River on a spare tire. A fact he decided not to share.

"So where were you last night?" Inky, with the question Stefani didn't have the nerve to ask.

"Tucked in with Dorothy Penny, what do you think?"

"I think you're full of dick," said Bootnose.

"Well, if anybody asks, I was at Josie's Bed and Bath, where somebody might care that I sacrificed my car so some old lady could take her sweet time crossing the street." Vlado figured nobody would bother to check with the boardinghouse, but he might have a discreet word with Josie later.

"According to Johnny, you broke the guy's jaw," Joe said.

"Too bad, I was aiming for his nose. And wait, you talked to Ovaltine?"

"First of all, for the record, fuck that guy. Secondly, he buttonholed me in my front yard this morning just after you left. He's not happy. *His* reputation. *His* sausage. Jebote. Not to mention you ruined his perfectly good night with Dorothy Penny."

"Maybe we need to let the air out of his spare tire," Bootnose said.

"I'm not sure we have a move now." Joe wasn't smiling, but Vlado was relieved that he said "we."

"Meanwhile, I'm out for a while." Vlado held up his useless right arm.

"We got you," Inky said, and Bootnose muttered a curse.

Joe was quiet then and uncharacteristically sipped at his slivovitz.

"Joey?" Vlado said.

Joe pulled the pencil from his ear and wiggled it nervously between two fingers.

"Apparently your gondolier friend isn't going to let it go. He's suing you, me, Big Sausage, and who knows, Mae Jankovic?"

"But it's not even our sausage, is it? 'Johnny's Smokehouse,' right? Tell him to go stick his thumb up Obersteen's fat ass."

"Except it wasn't the sausage that broke his jaw."

At home, Stefani at least pretended to accept Vlado's version of where he wound up that night. *Was I supposed to come home again to an empty house?* he'd said with enough bitterness that she let it go. So, a truce prevailed, which Vlado honored by putting in his hours at the store then spending most evenings with Janet Ivan while Stefani went next door to gossip with fake-Aunt-Vera. His little girl was changing every day and her endless babbling had condensed into an actual word here and there: *dada, mine,* and *boat, boat, boat* she would repeat, which Vlado was pretty sure meant *jebote* but kept that to himself. He envied her, how she ate and slept and let the complexities of life go on around her. *And cried,* so maybe her life wasn't so simple either. In any case, most evenings they found a shared peace, snuggled into Vlado's saggy lounge chair and listening to whatever was on the radio. Sometimes it was news or the farm report, other times it might be some big band crooner, and Vlado would sing along in a quiet voice close to Janet Ivan's ear.

Vlado got his cast off and within a couple of days he was back into the swing of slicing and chopping and stuffing, as if nothing had happened and he'd been doing this his whole life. Which it seemed like he had. Johnny hadn't been back at the store, and they hadn't heard a word from him. Vlado had Inky stop making the vile "sugar dogs" as he called them, thinking they had enough business without supplying Johnny's Smokehouse with bullshit sausage. So maybe his show of force had been a good thing after all, and they were finally done with that fucker.

38

THE following Monday, Vlado was sweating inside his go-to-funerals-and-weddings-and-baptisms and apparently go-to-court suit, standing before a judge in a musty, wood-paneled room in downtown Kansas City, Missouri. Next to him was Leopold Gorsky, Esq., splendid in his blue plaid sport coat and too-wide yellow tie. Stefani sat behind him in the gallery next to Joe and Martina in a show of either support or recrimination.

Vlado was at first excited to be in a real court room, even though he was the criminal, or would be, if not for his "presumption of innocence." But now his thoughts loitered in the dim light and stuffy air while the judge went on about "aggravated" this and "unprovoked" that, and damages that occurred to the plaintiff, who glared at Vlado from the other table. Surely the metal contraption the guy was wearing around his jaw had to be for show. *Where's your little hat?* Vlado whispered; *Fuck your swan's balls*, the guy answered, and the judge rapped his mallet.

When it was time for Vlado to speak, he stood next to Leo, straightened his tie, and announced in a loud voice, "Not guilty, your honor," without a hint of pleading.

The judge lowered his head to look at Vlado over his half-moons. "Are you saying you didn't do it?"

"Do what?" Vlado said, cleverly avoiding the trick question.

"Did you punch the guy or not?"

Leo took a tiny step forward. "My client asserts his fifth amendment rights."

I'm supposed to say that, Vlado whispered.

The judge took off his glasses, rubbed his eyes, and gave Vlado a tired look. "Fine, there are plenty of people who can tell us what happened.

Why don't the bunch of you go work this out and come back next week. Monday, ten o'clock."

Leo steered Vlado out of the room. Martina and Joe and Stefani followed behind.

"Let's see what he has to say." Leo indicated the prosecuting attorney, a mousey guy in a baggy brown suit lingering by the courtroom door. Leo went over and the two of them found a corner in the hall and began a discussion Vlado couldn't hear. The attorney said something, and Leo laughed, then the other guy laughed and scribbled on a piece of paper, folded it, and stuck it into Leo's vest pocket. They shook hands, and the prosecutor disappeared back into the courtroom.

Leo returned and took the cousins' elbows and walked them down the hall. He spoke in a low voice.

"We caught a break. Me and Mikey go way back, and I explained the situation. He made us an offer—all in and done—which, considering everything, might be cutting us a break." He showed them a number with four digits. Vlado looked desperately for a decimal point, then stared in horror at Joe, then Leo.

"The fuck is this?"

"It's money. Your money, admittedly," Leo said. "But it's not all that bad, really, when you think of the expenses. The plaintiff with the jaw, the restaurant owner, the judge, the prosecutor—"

"Wait, the who?"

"What do you think, Vlado? Those guys don't work for free."

Joe said, "It doesn't matter, Leo. We don't have that kind of money."

"You're making money, right? What about your business?"

"Well, that's the thing, we put it all back into the store. We're expanding and have a big monthly nut, what with the loan and all."

"What secures the loan?" Leo asked. Joe scratched his head with the eraser end of his pencil then stared at it as if he'd never seen one before.

"My house," he finally said.

"The one you live in?" Leo asked, like Joe might be some real estate investor.

"The one I live in. With my wife and two boys."

This hung in the air for a moment, until Leo said, "I get it. I'll see what I can do."

Back on the street, Vlado told Stefani to ride home with Joe and Martina.

"I'm going to go by Katz, check on a few things."

"We could all go," Stefani said brightly. "I'm famished."

"Maybe you should get back to our little pumpkin before your mom decides to float her down the river in a basket." If that was a joke it was too true to be funny. "I'll be home soon, promise."

He kissed her decisively on the cheek and turned down the street toward the used Model T that sulked at the curb a block away. It was the only thing he could afford after the chintzy insurance payoff for the Studebaker, and Vlado cringed every time he heard the tinny squeak of the door opening and the crunch of the springs poking up in the thinly padded seat. The jalopy started up with the usual bang and puff of tarry smoke, and soon he was pulling in front of the big, black kitty-cat sign that promised everyone their hearts' desire. Or at least a decent breakfast any time of day.

Inside he went straight to the flower stand—another Mike and Ike innovation—and after a brief look around, grabbed a handful of purple irises, like the ones he remembered from the dinner table at real Aunt Vera's a lifetime ago. He handed them to the girl to arrange into something nice. She rewarded him with a *how sweet are you* smile, clueless about the miles of hard road that lay ahead of her in a world inhabited by specimens of humanity such as himself. He returned to the car with the bouquet, and only then did his resolve start to waver. He'd destroyed the card with the address and now almost hoped he couldn't find the building, but there it was on Grand Avenue, a brown brick monument to his stupidity with an open parking space in the front that might as well have read "Reserved for Assholes."

He walked slowly up the three flights, wondering what he was going to say, or if he'd even have a chance. He squared himself up at the door, smoothed his hair and straightened his tie, then loosened it and unbuttoned his top button, took off his topcoat, put it back on, checked the shine on his shoes, then went to knock, but his right hand hung back with a mind of its own. He put his ear to the door but there was no sound. He set the flowers down carefully and pulled out one of his cards and a pen. He couldn't decide whether to write "I'm sorry" or "Thank you," then figured she could decide for herself and set the card on top of the flowers. But the hardened criminal in him warned him to not leave any incriminating evidence, so he pocketed the card, left the flowers, and stepped quietly back down the stairs. As he was leaving the lobby, he heard a door squeak open, and got the hell out of there.

39

Apparently, Leo didn't have an actual office other than cell number three at the city jail, so later that afternoon he, Vlado, and Joe squeezed into a back booth at Morty's, as far as they could get from the tamburas ratcheting out of the Majestic. Leo got right to it.

"It looks like you guys have a guardian angel. This Johnny guy has agreed to make it all go away. He's going to pay everybody off—I mean, settle all the damages. The charges will be dropped and everybody's happy."

"Joe and I will be happy?" Vlado asked. Like he knew anymore what counted as happiness.

Leo tugged on his sagging neck skin. "It depends. How do you feel about having a new partner?"

"You want to be our partner?" Vlado was lost.

"I think he means Johnny," Joe said, and the chilly hand that had been gripping Vlado's insides since that morning in court gave a sharp twist.

Morty appeared with a bottle, a jar of eggs, and a plate of sorry-looking anchovies. "Today's special," he shrugged. "My treat, they're no good tomorrow."

The stink of the fish threatened to unleash Vlado's innards, and he reached for a shot to force everything back down.

"How much of a partner?" Joe asked, which Vlado thought was a dumb question because it wasn't going to happen.

"He asked for a half, but I told him to go piss up a rope," said Leo. "We penciled in twenty percent."

"No!" Vlado slammed down his empty glass. "Fuck that guy. If I have to go to jail, so be it."

"It's up to you, of course," Leo said, "but if the courts are forced to go through the whole rigmarole, it might in fact be jail, lots of jail, and then some. You could end up with more partners than you might like, and," he looked at Joe, "someone else living in your house. I'm telling you, it's the other side of the river, the fix is in, and I can only do so much."

"What if I just don't show up?"

"That bridge goes both ways."

Vlado felt the thing that was not a heart attack surge in him, and he stood and reached for his coat. "I'm going to the store to make sure Inky hasn't burned the place down. Do whatever you want, Joey. What do I know about all this, except I fucked everything up?"

Outside, it was an insultingly beautiful afternoon. While Vlado had his head up the world's collective ass, spring had quietly slipped in, painting the tree tips a pale green and spreading a warm humidity across the Hill. Red geraniums and rocking chairs had sprouted on porches, where the grandmother brigade would soon be installed, drinking beer, crocheting, and eyeing the streets for sinners. As he trudged toward the knives and corpses waiting in Stein's Office, Vlado pulled his cap low and thought how if he heard so much as a single bird singing, he was going to climb up the goddam tree and strangle it.

"So where did you get the money, anyway?" Vlado asked Johnny. They were in Joe's back yard—Joe, Vlado, Obersteen, and Leo—to sign the papers. It was a clear day, but high anvil clouds indicated a coming storm. The wind was still, and Vlado was sweating in the late afternoon humidity.

"No, see, that's the whole beautiful deal. I'll worry about all that," Johnny said. "You go ahead and do your magical thing and know that certain other things are being taken care of. You'll see, Vlado, I'll be good for the bottom line."

"Are there some 'other things' we don't know about?"

"It doesn't matter. That's for me to worry about. Let's just say, everyone over there gets a little taste of your sausage."

Vlado wondered if the entire workings of the universe might come down to one extended dick joke, then realized that thought was a dick joke in itself. It was hopeless.

"And one other thing, Vlado. The Ovaltine business kind of hurts my feelings, you know?"

Vlado gave Joe a disbelieving look, then stared back at Obersteen.

"Ovaltine? Obersteen? Oh, I get it. That's pretty good, who came up with that?"

Obersteen poured himself another shot and tossed it back. His face paled, his eyelids drooped, and he put a hand over his heart like he was going to say the pledge of allegiance. He swallowed a burp.

"I don't get why you don't like me, Vlado. I mean, sure, I'm not a slick guy like you—"

"You're slick enough, Johnny." Vlado had the image of Obersteen eating a Junior's giant corned beef with the rendered fat running down his chin and over his fingers. He put a fraternal hand on Johnny's shoulder. "Slick, like a greased pig."

"It's a Croatian expression," Joe said. "You know, like the bee's knees, or cat's pajamas."

"No, I get it. I'm not an idiot."

Leo laid down a stack of papers and pushed them towards Joe along with an ink pen. "I read these, so you don't have to," he said. "Just sign, and we're done."

Joe scribbled in the noted spaces. "I, Josip, take you, Ovaltine, I mean Obersteen, sorry, in sickness and in health . . ."

Vlado felt a laugh trying to surface, but it drowned somewhere in the back of his throat.

The new partnership got off to an unpleasant start when Obersteen insisted on being there every Thursday night when the four brothers-in-arms looked at the books over a few hands of pinochle and shots of whatever was stashed in Stein's Office and figured on what to do next. Sometimes Leo would show up and deal a round of poker, usually to his own benefit. Johnny would sit there with a pleased-with-himself look and scarf up whatever snacks Joe had grilled, laughing like a lunatic at Inky's cornball jokes they'd all heard a zillion times. Between that, Joe's seeming indifference, and Vlado's nagging desire to give Johnny a kick where it hurts, the room seemed too complicated, and Vlado would excuse himself to go poke at something in the smoker or straighten up the shelves in the front before his annoyance could spin into something darker.

Vlado was sleeping less and less, thanks to the cold front that had settled into his happy home. He tried to be nice to Stefani—cook her lambchops, diaper the baby, forego Morty's—to make up for whatever he had to make up for, but his anger at her betrayal kept pulling him up short. Worst of all, he knew Stefani thought he should be grateful, that bringing Johnny aboard was good for business. Vlado was less sure of that than ever, but still, Stefani acted like her feelings had been hurt. It didn't make any sense. He tried to make it all add up, but his thoughts shifted in his brain like loose cargo.

Maybe he'd made the wrong choices all along he thought, toward the end of one especially tiring day. He was using a cleaver to chop the pork spareribs off from the rest of the infrastructure, each *thwack* powered by a smack of regret: *thwack* for marrying Stefani, *thwack* for not kicking Obersteen's ass from day one, *thwack* for messing with Lydia, *thwack, thwack, thwack,* for all the things on Martina's list, all the sins Father Oyster could see that he didn't, *thwack* for driving his fancy Studebaker into the river, for dallying around with the pianist, for punching the gondolier, and for every other damn thing he'd randomly chosen without looking past his own nose. His left hand got a grip on the rib rack while his right hand lifted the cleaver higher than it needed to be. He closed his eyes. The blade would find its way to one bone or another, and since when was it ever his choice?

A hand grabbed his upraised arm, and he opened his eyes to see Joe prying the cleaver from his fingers.

40

After splitting a bucket of beer with Joe at McGowan's, Vlado only felt a little better about the whole deal, mostly uncertain about what the whole deal was. He found his way home and climbed the front steps, wiggling his full set of fingers, and paused at the front door, trying to sense the weather on the other side. He was surprised to find the house quiet and, upon further investigation, the kitchen dark but for a single candle flickering in the center of the Formica table. Stefani sat there, silent as a saint, her face haloed in the ambient light. His first thought was that he was in some new trouble—had he paid the electric bill?—but for once, she didn't look bothered. In fact, she was wearing a thin-lipped smile, which was flanked by hoop earrings, underscored by her favorite pearls, and topped with an arrangement of hair that had taken more than a minute or two. Her eyes were lashy, and her round cheeks shone apple-pink in the candle's glow. Vlado sat down, terrified on one hand, but feeling a smidge of desire on the other.

Stefani finally spoke. "I'm sorry about your car."

"Me too." *Just now she was sorry for his car?*

She took his hands in hers and lightly stroked his palms with her fingertips. Vlado couldn't remember the last time he'd been touched like that. It had been weeks since they'd had sex, and in general, their bedroom escapades had devolved into sweaty wrestling matches where each of them got what they wanted and see you later.

"And I'm sorry about this whole Johnny business."

"That dickhea—"

"Ssh." She touched his lips lightly then grazed her fingertips along his cheek, into his hair, to the back of his head, then pulled him across the table and kissed him like she meant it. She pulled his hands to her breasts, which were almost escaping from the satiny blouse she wore instead of one of her shapeless housedresses. She stood, and he saw that's all she was wearing and wondered how long she'd been sitting there half naked waiting for him but decided to stop wondering when she led him into the bedroom.

They were entwined under the covers, and Vlado felt Stefani's body grip onto his. She had him in a kind of scissor hold, which wasn't unpleasant, and had her arms around him with one hand firmly gripping the back of his neck, holding his head while she kissed him soundly, until she let him go and Vlado sank back into his pillow. She climbed on top of him and rested her elbows on his shoulders, all her fragrant beauty sagging down in front of him. She gave him the no-nonsense look she'd used on him so many times, a sort of magic talisman that commanded his attention like a dog told to sit.

"I figured out the problem," she said.

Problem? A new problem? *What else had he done?*

"I'm sorry," he said, just in case.

"Don't start with that business. I don't like it when you're sorry, Vlado, it's too pathetic. I don't want you to be sorry about anything." She reached down and gave him a little squeeze that somewhat reduced his sorrow, which he wasn't so committed to anyway. Stefani went on. "We should be looking into the future, with happy thoughts, and new plans." She took his hand and placed it on her belly, and a bolt of fear shot through Vlado.

"Are you pregnant?" he said and rolled out from under her. They'd been careful, but you never know. She pushed him back down on the bed, then turned away from him, and wrapped her loose blouse around her.

"No, I'm not pregnant. But would it be so bad if I was?"

Vlado's head sagged back. He felt like a failed husband. And a failed father. He already had one precious daughter who never saw him, and now Stefani wanted another, and where would it stop, all these orphans crying in their cribs while their daddy worked day and night. Janet Ivan was continually surprising him with Croatian words, which she had to be getting from grandma, and where was Stefani every day and who would take care of another baby? But still, the idea of a little boy, a tiny Vladimir. Not a Vladimir, necessarily, something more American, like Steve or Bob or Vinnie. No, not Vinnie. Ah, he was doomed.

Stefani shrugged out of her blouse and turned back to him, sliding under the sheets and relaxing her body into his. Her thumb and finger massaged his earlobe while she whispered in his ear. "Come on, it'll be fun," she said, and he was out of arguments. He looked toward the nightstand where he kept his trusty latex Trojans inside an old Rio Tan box, but it was gone.

"I guess it doesn't hurt to be good Catholics for a change," he said, and reached for her.

41

CATHOLICISM had never been so much fun for Vlado, who was enjoying wanton sex without a rubber and without the guilt of extramarital activity. In short, he was screwing his wife almost daily in his efforts to be the best Catholic ever. What a religion! He wondered if confession worked both ways, if you could go in and tell the priest about all the great things you're doing, maybe bank it away as a down payment against future sins. He and Stefani suddenly had more important things than to brood about Obersteen. In fact, Vlado looked more favorably on the whole deal, trying not to picture his roll of bills unspooling in the face of another mouth to feed.

As it turned out, the new partnership with Johnny didn't change much of anything. Joe and Vlado explained that if he wanted to be a partner, he had to be more than just a salesman, because that's what he already was before. He didn't have any butchering or sausage-making skills, so by a vote of two to one they appointed him Head Sanitary Engineer, responsible for maintaining the standards required of a respectable food-manufacturing operation, *and here's your mop*. As a result, Johnny made himself scarce, spending his days hawking the Johnny's Smokehouse brand of goods to Missouri restaurants like before. So Inky went back to making the dreaded sugar dogs, and Vlado decided to get his mind past the whole muddle.

By late spring, the kerfuffle from across the river was far back in the rearview, and a breeze of optimism and renewal wafted down the streets of Strawberry Hill. At Big Sausage, the regulars—Mae, Dorothy, Tereza, the Altar Society girls, and even Martina on occasion— would perch on stools and crates at the end of the counter, pouring beer into mason jars and teacups and chirping about the past, future, and circumference of life on the Hill and the relative virtues of the world within and beyond. They unanimously loved the handsome (Mae thought) new president, Franklin Roosevelt, who promised better times; moreover, it looked like Prohibition was on its way out, which didn't necessarily please Morty, who'd carved out his niche of iffy transactions, but Vlado liked the idea of finally being able to drink something other than the modified gasoline Morty sold.

Easter came and went with a flurry of smoked hams, *budla*, and nutbreads flying out the door of Big Sausage. Joe stole a couple of apprentice butchers from Armour to help with the demand for smoked sausage and freshies that was increasing thanks to word-of-mouth beyond the Hill and the bit of extra money that was appearing in people's paychecks. Johnny's restaurant sales across the river were solid—*let them eat whatever the hell they want*, Vlado thought as he fingered his roll of bills. Bootnose had hired a couple of guys on his own to help with the increasing need for pigs and cows and to drive the Boyko Meats truck that still supplied the clueless Katz brothers. Joe wielded his pencil like a carving knife, while Vlado sweated it out in the back, slicing up animals and shouting orders to the high school kids who manned the front counter for the after-work rush.

Vlado could finally look back on his near-death river voyage and his frigid, hallucinatory climb to higher ground without shuddering, and the whole chain of events settled into a ludicrous story that he would tell his grandkids someday, exaggerating the hell out of everything. *There I was, floating down the Missouri River, riding on a car tire and watching while the air slowly bubbled out of it . . .* Okay, so not so exaggerated. He'd never tell anyone about his imaginary affair with the piano player, both relieved and embarrassed about how he'd lost his nerve in the hotel room. Or about his chaste night with a new version of Lydia that he couldn't get a handle on. Lydia. A picture of her, looking small, and even frail, without the makeup and saucy attitude, would nag its way into his mind on occasion. But there'd been no word from her since the flowers. He hadn't expected any. *Because she was no dummy.*

42

About a month into the new regime with Stefani, Vlado slunk into work late one morning, Stefani having surprised him with an early awakening that was worth the cost of the extra sleep he could have used. Thanks to her surprising new agility, they'd been going at it as if they were trying to start a new Habsburg dynasty of short, chubby, bullheaded Croatians.

"Where have you been?" Joe looked more tired than he should have for having loaded the display case alone, swept the aisles, stacked the morning's produce . . . well.

Vlado held out his hands in a gesture of helplessness. "'Sow your seed in the morning, and at evening let not your hands be idle'," he said, quoting the Bible verse his real Aunt Vera had crowed to get him out of bed and off to school.

Joe didn't reply and returned to needlessly polishing the glass front of the display case. Vlado stopped his hand.

"Joey, what is it?"

Joe pitched the rag into the back where it landed in a tub of pork trimmings.

"It's Martina."

"What, is she sick?"

"No, worse than that." He sat down heavily behind the display case and chinged the cash register. "She's pregnant."

"How did that happen?"

"Funny thing, that's exactly what she asked me when she found out. I'm thinking we all need to take a field trip out to Starr's farm and learn how all this shit works."

Vlado imagined how cows might do it, shuddered against the horrifying images that surfaced, and resolved once again never to get within ten miles of that loathsome place. And chickens, he wondered . . . *Christ on the cross.*

The front door jingled, and Dorothy Penny poked her perfect head in and gave a quick look around the store.

"Don't worry, Dorothy, he's not here," said Vlado, referring to Johnny and her reluctance to cross paths with him again. Fortunately, he only showed up twice a week, each time right at opening, to load his cooler before setting off in his ratty pickup for the forbidden city.

Dorothy straightened up, smoothed her skirt, and approached the counter, behind which Vlado and Joe stood at rapt attention. She perused the display then looked up at Vlado. At Joe. At Vlado again. She squinted at them.

"What's going on with you two?"

"Nothing," the cousins said at the same time, and Vlado could see her wheels turning.

"She's pregnant, isn't she?"

"Who, Stefani?" Vlado jumped in to try to save Joe. "Definitely not Stefani," he said, not really saving Joe after all, whose silence and reddening face told the whole story.

"I see. Well, since everyone else is having *sausage* these days, I guess I'll have some too," Dorothy said brightly, and Vlado mentally kicked himself. *Of course she was onto the joke.*

Joe wrapped up three smoked rings, Dorothy paid and turned to leave.

"Um, Dorothy . . ." Joe said. "We're not telling . . . you know . . ."

She looked back at him and drew a thumb and finger zipper-like across her perfect lips and glided out the door.

"She's certainly going to make a big deal about it," said Joe, when Dorothy was out of sight.

"Think about it, Joey. She's Martina's best friend, right? So, she won't say a thing."

Joe thought on that for a moment, then said, "Goddammit, she already knew, didn't she?"

Vlado stared at his cousin in rapt appreciation of this display of genius. He shook his head. "She's going to make somebody miserable someday, don't you think?"

"Too bad it's not going to be Ovaltine."

"Well, if that's what you want, we can always fix him up with Mae."

Joe stared off into the distance, perhaps looking back on a different fork in the river. "Let's try to not upset Martina when she's in such a delicate way," he said, tying on his apron, and heading back for his knives.

"Not so fast." Vlado followed him with the rakija bottle and two growlers, and they faced each other across the carving table.

"Don't even say it. It's just one damn annihilation after another, isn't it?" Joe said.

Vlado laughed, grabbed a chunk of Joe's cheek, and gave it a rough shake. "My little Jozo's going to be a daddy."

"Again."

"Again."

They drained their glasses and got to work, each with their own private thoughts about sowing seeds and idle hands.

After a while, Vlado was pretty sure everybody knew about Martina's coming blessed event, but no one dared mention it, except for Stefani, who added it to her own litany of unfairnesses that she wielded with a Martina-like expertise. As if there were a limited supply of babies being doled out only to the worthiest. Vlado tried to tell her they should just enjoy the process, however long it took, and eventually the score would be three to two, and keep in mind Joe and Martina had an eight-year head start. But secretly he was worried about the whole deal. Amidst all the craziness and rumination and doubts and temptations and overall cyclone of thoughts and experiences that threatened to derail him on any single day, at the center of it all, calm and happy in the eye of the storm, was his little girl. Who had already laid claim to the entirety of his heart, and how could there be room for one more?

By mid-August, Martina's layers of bloomers and baggy housedresses could no longer hide the obvious. She and the ladies were at Big Sausage, huddled close to the display case to leach a bit of cool air. Vlado wasn't in the mood to hear all the usual chatter and moved back to detach some pork jowls from a mercifully silent corpse, but it was no use.

"What's a good name for a baby these days?" asked Mae Jankovic, the first to broach the taboo subject.

Martina had no reply, being of the generation that would never utter the word "pregnant", and in the silence, Vlado could hear her embarrassment.

"Maybe something modern, like Howard or Clarence," said Tereza.

"Or Franklin. Maybe he'll be president someday," added Mae.

Dorothy Penny laughed. "Fine, as long as it's not Herbert."

"What about the gospels?" Tereza asked, fingering her scapula. "Luka. Or Marko."

"But what if it's a girl?" Mrs. Divac asked.

Martina found her tongue. "It goddam better be a girl. I've had it with those two criminals." She swallowed the last of her beer, slammed down the mason jar, and steamed out the door like a battleship, banging it behind her, to the distress of the poor bell that had to bear witness to it all.

Vlado headed out the back and ran around to catch up with her.

"Marti," he said, but she kept on, and he reached an arm to her shoulder and slowed her to a stop. Her face was bright red.

"*Mali vrag*, how did this even happen?" she said—always the same dumb question, but this time Vlado got it. He was astonished to see her eyes soften with tears. "Once again, my husband will be running around across the river, you and him dancing and carrying on like I'm not stuck at home . . ." She couldn't continue. Vlado produced a handkerchief.

"You know, Marti, how I never knew my mother. But sometimes when I think about her, I imagine she might have been somebody like you, believe it or not. Somebody who would give her life for her child. And she did, I guess. But not that you'll have to or anything." He wasn't very good at this, but he pushed on. "But without things like that," he almost touched her belly then jerked his hand back, "none of this would be happening." Vlado, suddenly the philosopher, waved one arm out as if to embrace their entire little kingdom. He knew Martina loved her boys like Stefani loved Janet Ivan. He also knew he'd had the benefit of more years of wild singlehood than Martina, who had first become pregnant at twenty-four, right when she and her new husband should have been lighting up the town.

"Come on, I'll give you a ride home." He steered her toward Barnett where his jalopy was parked.

She wiped away a tear and fluffed out the baggy dress that only she thought concealed her coming event. "Fine, but try to stay out of the goddam river."

They drove in silence for a while and then Vlado pulled up to Lesac's Florist on Minnesota Avenue. He left Martina in the car and returned with a potted red geranium which he set on her lap.

"Here," he said. "The ones in your yard always look a little ratty this time of year."

43

Now that Martina was out of the closet, she wasted no time ensuring she got the service she deserved. Joe complained to Vlado about having to rub her feet every night, and how there'd be hell to pay if a leg of lamb didn't appear on Sundays. But it was Stefani who was the most aggrieved. She complained to Vlado about seeing Martina parade down the avenue in a now-tight housedress and colorful babushka, "as if she's about to give birth to the human race." *And what about me?*

Soon thereafter, Stefani got her period for the third time since they'd initiated the new master plan, and by this point, even Vlado was mystified. *Wouldn't you make a baby every time?* Otherwise, why be so worried about the condoms and all? He'd appreciated Stefani's ever-ready willingness to step up to the plate, but he only had so much to offer on a daily basis.

One night, he begged off. "It was a long one today"—and a long evening at Morty's as well.

Stefani pulled her robe closed, then sat next to him on the bed with a curious expression.

"I've been thinking. Maybe you should see someone."

See someone? Like someone else? Since when was Stefani so modern? And who would he see? Lydia? Surely, she was off limits. Who, then?

"Mom's rheumatism doctor knows somebody." Mrs. Lovick suffered from a smorgasbord of ailments that had led her to weekly visits with a variety of medical specialists who kept her stocked up with ointments, potions, and advice, the latter of which she shared liberally with Stefani, until the two of them had become experts on most common problems and kept Vlado supplied with a bitter green liquid designed to keep away his fake heart attacks. But why would her doctor know someone for Vlado to have sex with, and how would that help anything? He knew how to do it, and in a way that she liked, which had been proved repeatedly, especially in the past three months.

"So, what exactly do you want me to do?" Once again he was in the tug of some current he didn't understand.

"Vlado, it's not like I think you have some problem," she said, implying he had some problem, "but why not have a professional check out your, um, equipment." She was blushing, and Vlado was even more confused. He'd never paid for sex and especially couldn't imagine doing so now.

"Mom says there are tests they can do right there in the doctor's office. It doesn't hurt, and if there's a problem with, you know, maybe they can fix it."

Tests? Fix it? Jebote. Vlado didn't know whether to feel relieved, disappointed, or angry as the picture became clear.

"You think it's my fault? That you can't have a baby? That something's broken?"

"Vlado, we already know I can have a baby, and if you don't quiet down, she's going to be reminding us again."

"Okay, you give me a name and I'll go see him."

Dr. Dubrowski's office was hidden behind a rickety storefront tucked between a church and a liquor store on a neglected block way out on Quindaro, a discrete distance from the Hill, but Vlado still looked both ways for witnesses before he exited his Ford and made for the front door. Inside, a girl who looked too young to be dealing with things like this took his information, oblivious to his embarrassment, and directed him to a seat in the mercifully empty reception room. He sat with his hands folded in his lap, as if he were in trouble outside the principal's office, thinking how weird were the things you could get in trouble for these days.

Soon the girl looked around the room and said "Mr. Novosel?" as if his presence was a new idea, and then led him down the hall to an examination room. He hadn't been alone long enough to start fidgeting when Dr. Dubrowski bounded in and gave Vlado an assessing look.

"Mr. Novosel, Novosel, Novosel . . . is that Croatian? We got a Serb on our bowling team. Nice guy." He read off his chart. "Mm hmm, problems conceiving, mm hmm, no performance problems, etc., etc. Are there?"

"Are there what?"

"Performance problems."

"No performance problems, unless by performance you mean making a baby."

"Two separate things," he said. He urged Vlado onto a scale, then measured his blood pressure, thumped on his chest and back, probed with his stethoscope, and produced a tape measure with which he measured the circumference of Vlado's head. He opened a small black notebook and scribbled a number.

"For my private research," he said and tucked the notebook into his desk drawer. "But as to your problem, let's just have a look at your little buggers and see what's going on." He buzzed in the girl from the desk, who handed Vlado a lidded jar about the size of Stefani's Vaseline and led him down the hall and into a room not much bigger than a closet. There was a single chair, and a table that held a stack of magazines and a lamp covered with a pink scarf. When the nurse closed the door behind her, he squinted in the puffy light at the magazines—*High-Jinks* and *Whiz Bang*, with their racy cartoons, and the more interesting *Artists and Models* which celebrated the female form, quite rightly so, as the artistic masterpiece God intended it to be. He lingered on a picture of a plump woman in a skimpy bra and panties posed on what appeared to be a giant clam shell, darkened eyes looming out of a mess of black curls and a demure expression which made him think of the Mary Pickford movies he'd snuck into as a boy in Zagreb. Pretty tame stuff when compared with the collection of postcards Morty kept behind the bar that showed the real deal—no underwear, and action to boot—and that's what Vlado decided to concentrate on as he performed the less-than-Catholic task before him.

Afterwards, he waited in the examination room for some time until Dubrowski returned with a puzzled look on his face.

"You seem to be a healthy young man," he said.

"As a horse," Vlado said—except for the fact that he was given to fake heart attacks and a rattling brain. And the occasional problem with gravity.

"Two problems. Not many swimmers, and the few that are there aren't swimming."

"What does that mean?" Why were they talking about swimming?

Dubrowski leaned forward and placed two fingers on either side of Vlado's neck and probed around. "Do you remember these ever being swollen?"

Immediately Vlado thought back to the only time he'd ever been really sick, when he was living with his Aunt Vera in Zagreb just after his father died. He had a fever, his neck was stiff, and his cheeks puffed out like a squirrel with a mouthful of nuts. And that wasn't all that was inflated, he thought with a sinking feeling, remembering the long week of lying in bed with a cold washcloth draped around his testicles, which felt like they could burst like a ripe tomato.

"Mumps," said the doctor after Vlado confessed to his past. "You were one of the unlucky ones. You had no way of knowing, but you've been riding a horse with no shoes your whole life. The good news is it doesn't affect your virility. The bad news is you will never father a child." He shrugged, "Although that depends, not everyone thinks it's bad news."

The doctor was still talking, but all Vlado could hear was a ringing in his ears and a pounding heartbeat that said he had to get out of there. Without a word he walked out of the room, out of the office, and made for his car, where he sat behind the wheel, trying to breathe, trying to think, trying not to think, wishing he were somewhere else, someone else, anything else.

44

The Ford rattled in and out of the potholes on its way back to the Hill and Vlado's thoughts rattled along with it. He once again made that fateful turn at the top of Fourth Street, slower this time—but who knows, maybe driving right back into the river was his best move. He looked down at the brown water of the Kaw pretending to mind its own murky business, then above, to the Power and Light that poked up between the surrounding low-rises like a rude middle finger. To his right, the tower of St. John the Baptist echoed the sentiment. So, apparently the whole world agreed that he was fucked. Certainly, Father Oyster knew, had tried to tell him. So had Stefani, for fuck's sake. He thought of Lydia's glib comment way back when about him being "on the hook." No way she could have known. Was it that obvious he was being played?

But despite this embarrassing turn of events, Vlado didn't feel like he was "on the hook" for anything. Stefani had never lied to him. It had been his decision not to see the writing on the wall. Maybe not a well-thought-out decision, but still. And what if he hadn't married Stefani? Had chosen instead to believe it was Johnny's kid? He'd probably still be chopping bones across the river, free to be as much of an idiot as he wished in his spare time. Janet Ivan would have been born a child of God and safely installed somewhere else with a different fake daddy.

Vlado parked and strode up the stars and through the front door before he could think twice and opt for Morty's instead. As usual, he had no plan or idea of what to say. Stefani was in the kitchen feeding Janet Ivan her lunch, everything normal and in place as if the universe hadn't just exploded. He hadn't told her about his impending visit to Dr. Dubrowski and stood there dumbly.

"What are you doing home?" Stefani asked, *and why wouldn't she want him there*, but of course, it was the middle of a workday.

"I had a thing I had to do . . . So, how are you?" *How are you?*

She blew a strand of hair away from her nose. "I'm fine, Vlado. Why wouldn't I be? You want something to eat?" She gestured to the mess of chopped weenies and mashed potatoes Janet Ivan was scooping into her mouth with more enthusiasm than accuracy.

Between bites, Janet gurgled in her chair. "Boat, boat, boat," she said and reached out to Vlado.

He peered at her fat fingers. Her thick lips. He'd seen it all along, hadn't he? He wiped off her hands and pulled her out of her highchair and clutched her close to him, sniffed up what was left of her baby smell, mitigated by what might have been a small deposit in her diapers. It was a human stink, just like his own, and he buried his nose in the familiar crook of her neck. He carried her past Stefani and out the back door into their tiny yard. She wiggled her fingers and burbled nonsense syllables like a water fountain while Vlado toured her around the yard. He pointed to a sparrow eyeing them from the fig tree.

"Bird," he said.

"Boat, boat," she replied happily.

He set her down, held her two hands up and walked her ahead to the pebble-lined fishpond, where swarming goldfish popped their noses up in hopes of a treat.

"Fishies!" Vlado said.

"Boat, boat, boat."

He swung her onto his shoulders, held her feet, and bounced her along to the apple tree where the fruit had swollen behind spent blossoms.

"Apple," he said.

"Boat."

"Apple."

"Boat." She giggled.

He spun her back down and gave her a stern look. "Dada says 'apple.'"

She returned Vlado's stare, all serious, considering her options. "Boat," she said, and she meant it.

Vlado let out a long breath.

"*Jebote*," he said, finally keeping up his end of the conversation. And she was right. Fuck it all. He remembered how his Aunt Vera had never treated him as anything other than her own. What the hell did it matter, anyway? She was his, and always would be. *Or was it the other way around?* He held her up in front of him and stared into whatever this thing was that was Janet Ivan. "Our secret, sweet potato," he said and gave her a raspberry kiss on her cheek.

"Baba," she giggled, and yanked on his ears until he winced.

Back inside, he tried to look cheerful for Stefani. "Sometimes I just miss my little girl," he said, answering the question she'd forgotten by now. He handed her the precious bundle that was Janet Ivan and headed out the door before he could say something stupid and blow up the whole fucking thing.

45

Vlado approached the store from the alley, not wanting to talk to anybody, because all he could say was what's on his mind—and that's exactly what he couldn't say. The truth? It was whatever they agreed on, right? Stefani and Johnny either were clueless or pretended to be. He knew what Leo would say, that "possession is nine-tenths of the law," not that he was going to tell Leo. Or anybody, although he considered spilling the beans to Father Oyster in the privacy of the confessional, just to see him endure the private hell of not being able to share the juiciest piece of gossip on the Hill.

When Vlado came in the back door, he could see past Stein's Office to the front counter where Joe was speaking with a stranger. The man was medium height and wiry, middle aged, with a grey Fuller brush mustache, thick eyebrows, and a hawkish nose. He wore a tailored black suit topped with a black homburg and gripped a silver-headed cane that he used to punctuate his words, maybe not in the friendliest way. Vlado peeked around from the carvery and saw Joe shrug and splay out his hands. The stranger handed Joe a card, told him "You can call me Artie," and they shook hands. The man turned as if to leave, then spun back toward Joe, took his cane in both hands, and swung the claw head into the display case. The glass shattered with a horrendous noise. Vlado rushed in, but the man was already out the door, where he hopped into a waiting car that sped away.

Joe stood frozen and white-faced. A quick inspection showed he was intact but for a shard of glass that had winged into his left forearm. Vlado plucked it out and stanched the bleeding with his hanky while he steered his cousin into a chair and produced the bottle of rakija that was never far out of reach. He poured some over Joe's cut, took a swig himself and offered the bottle to Joe.

"It won't help."

"Drink, and then tell me." He pressed it in Joe's hand. Joe took a gulp then coughed most of it out.

"That fucker," Joe said.

"Yeah, who was that guy?"

"No, I mean that fucker, *Johnny*." Joe took a deep breath and some color returned to his face. He gazed dolefully at his prized display case, broken glass scattered over its carefully curated contents.

"Okay, what the hell?" Vlado locked the front door, flipped the sign to "Closed," and pulled a chair up close to Joe. He used a rag to brush little bits of glass off Joe's white tunic.

Joe was visibly embarrassed. "I'm just glad nobody was here. I knew the guy was trouble when he walked in. He was asking for Obersteen, and I don't know, for some reason I said, 'Who?' 'Obersteen,' he repeated, and I said, 'Oh yeah, the fat guy, they call him Ovaltine, right?' and he actually smiled. And I said, 'He's that Smokehouse Johnny guy, right?' The guy says, 'We seen him coming in and out of this place,' and I say 'Yeah, he's always trying to sell us his crappy sausage, when we already have the real deal right here.' I reach down to pull out a link and the guy says, 'Hold it,' and pokes the end of his cane right under my chin, and right then I know we're in some kind of trouble."

Vlado took the card out of Joe's shaking hand. It said *Artemis Flannagan*, with a phone number. "Whoever the hell he is, he's not from around here."

"He said he had a message for Johnny. I thought, 'Okay, so what is it,' then he took his cane and dammit—"

"Well, whatever the message is, it looks like it's pretty urgent, and we need to deliver it forthwith." They stared at each other silently until they arrived at the same thought.

"I'll call Bootnose," said Vlado.

They swept up the glass, saved what meat they could, and were taping cardboard over the display when the Boyko Meats hearse groaned into the alley. Bootnose hopped out and opened the back with a flourish. A coffin slid halfway out. *What had he actually told Bootnose?* Vlado mentally measured the coffin and decided it was too small, but was still relieved to see the living and breathing Obersteen pry himself out of the passenger side. He was spilling out of a sleeveless T-shirt, and two pale tree trunks protruded from the bottom of a pair of plaid shorts. He walked toward them with an annoyed look, rubbing his neck.

Vlado could see some red marks near Johnny's throat. He shot Bootnose a look and pointed to his own throat.

"What? I had to help him squeeze into the truck. I mean, look at the guy."

Before Johnny could speak, Bootnose put his hand on his shoulder and gave him a rough shake. "We had a nice ride together. Maybe next time we'll go by Starr's farm, and I'll show you how we slaughter the hogs. I'll even let you ride in the back, my little *bubica*." Johnny flinched as Bootnose gave him a light slap on the cheek. "Grab a hold," he told him, indicating the coffin, and the four of them marched it into Stein's Office with a funereal solemnity.

Johnny was breathing heavily from the effort. Vlado said, "So I bet you really feel like a partner now, doing some actual work for a change."

"Well, if you think—"

"Johnny, just shut the fuck up," said Joe. "Drop it here." They did and followed Joe into the front of the store.

Obersteen eyed the broken display. "What is this? Was there an accident?"

"Not an accident. A message," Vlado said. "You know, how a dog leaves a message on the sidewalk, and then somebody who has nothing to do with the dog's business steps in it."

Obersteen looked mystified.

Joe added. "Like we're some goddam answering service."

"So, who was that guy?" Vlado asked. Obersteen was starting to look more worried than confused. "Somebody here looking for you. Who left you this message." His head indicated the damages. "Tall, older gentleman, well-dressed, looked like he might have been a fighter once. Bushy gray mustache."

Obersteen paled and muttered something inaudible.

"What?" said Vlado, wishing for a moment he had his own cane to crack over Johnny's fat head.

"I said 'Artie.' Was it Artie?"

Vlado handed him the man's card, and Johnny muttered a despairing curse.

"Well, what does this Artie guy want with us?"

"No, you don't understand, Joe, it's got nothing to do with you. They don't know anything about you. It's me." He bit his bottom lip and looked around as if he was searching for a table to hide under. "Turns out I'm a little behind."

46

They pulled up chairs in Stein's Office and Johnny tried to explain. Apparently, there was a price of admission to the restaurant circuit across the river, which meant tucking the occasional fiver, or twenty even, into the appropriate pocket. No big deal, the product got on the menu, everybody happy.

"It's been a good thing, right, Vlado?"

Vlado's roll of bills hadn't gotten any fatter in recent months, and his bank account was still a long way from the price of a new Studebaker.

"I don't know, Johnny. I don't feel any richer."

Obersteen bit his lip and blinked several times.

"Okay." He let out a long breath. "The truth is, I haven't exactly been *selling* them the sausage. But here's the thing. I give them the stuff, which you admittedly don't even like, and then they charge me a little to sell it in their fancy restaurants."

Vlado saw the expression on Joe's face and could imagine his pencil exploding behind his ear. "*You're* paying *them*?" Joe's face was bright red and Vlado looked around for any knives that might be within reach. No point in everybody going to jail.

"Well, I was, but it was out of my own share, I want you to know. At least, until it ran out."

Johnny went on about how everything was fine until he was accosted by a guy at Harvey's, over at Union Station, when he was making a delivery.

"Tall, distinguished looking, mustache, nice suit. Sound familiar? He seemed to know me and said he'd be taking care of the gratuities now. I asked if I should talk to him instead of Billy, my regular guy, and he said, 'From now on, you talk to me instead of everybody.' I told him I needed to check with Billy, and he said, 'Okay then, follow me,' and I dragged the cooler after him down along the tracks. He asked me what was in there and I told him, and he was suddenly happy. We stopped, he opened the cooler, unzipped his pants, and pissed all over it. Swear to God, I'm standing there watching this and am about to pee in my own pants."

Despite the unfortunate image, Vlado wondered how his—make that Inky's—vile sugar-dogs could be even more revolting.

"He zipped up, closed the cooler, and acted like nothing happened. He wrote a number down and told me, 'This much every Monday, here, nine sharp.'" It was a big number. But at least I thought it would take care of the whole deal, so maybe this was the efficient way to do it. I told him I didn't have that much on hand, and he held out his arms and said that Big Tommy wouldn't be happy to hear that."

"Big Tommy? Who the hell is Big Tommy?" Vlado had a bad feeling.

"How the fuck do I know? But I'm sure there's a reason they don't call him Little Tommy. Anyhow, he tells me that any business requires a certain amount of investment and that he could probably get Big Tommy to extend some credit until we really hit. It wasn't necessarily at the preferred interest rates, but at least I didn't have to put up any collateral and I'd still be getting the product in the restaurants."

"Collateral?" Vlado was steaming. "You're the goddam collateral. And us too."

"Why didn't you tell us?" Joe asked. "We could have gone to Poochie."

"Joe, I know you think I'm some idiot, but I promised you wouldn't have to worry about this. I'm just trying to be a good partner and keep up my end of the deal."

"Yeah, maybe this is the end of the deal right here," said Vlado. He was more disappointed than angry. Embarrassed, even. *Ovaltine. Possibly the father of his child, acting like some dummy across the river and now getting everybody's ass kicked.* He wanted to say, what about *your* little girl, what kind of example is *this*, but he stuffed that thought deep into the churning pit of his stomach.

Bootnose leaned back in his chair. He cracked open the cooler door and a chilly fog rolled out. "If you need a place to hide, we got you covered."

"Better yet," Vlado said, "forget the restaurants, fuck those Missouri assholes. No sausage for them." *What could possibly be worth this kind of complication?*

"Yeah, well, I tried that, but apparently there's no going back. The guy explained to me in a very nice way that he had a family to support and had come to rely on the income. He was sure I'd understand. And as a show of good faith, he gave me another week. Which, to be honest, was two weeks ago." His eyes drifted shut in a moment of confession. "And I still gotta pay the interest on the money I borrowed. Plus, the money itself. Obviously. But like I said, there's no shit on your shoes. They only know Smokehouse Johnny, no connection to Big Sausage, except apparently that I show up here to try to sell you stuff, which was good thinking on your part, Joe."

Joe, Vlado, and Bootnose looked at each other and apparently realized the same thing with the same urgency.

"You can't be here now," said Joe.

Vlado stood. "We gotta get you out without anybody seeing. What if somebody's watching?"

"Maybe we should empty this." Bootnose patted the coffin next to him and Johnny shrunk back in his chair.

"Not that I wouldn't," Vlado said, "But he'd never fit unless we rearranged a few things."

Joe shrugged. "At least that's something we know how to do." Vlado thought back to Bootnose's night watchman gag and how that pig face didn't look so different from Johnny's.

"Right, Joey, I think I should call my apprentice," said Vlado.

"Inky?"

"Yeah, he can take care of this for us."

Johnny turned an even whiter shade of pale, and Bootnose couldn't keep a straight face any longer. He cracked up and emitted a loud fart.

"And that's my last word on the subject," he said and walked away from the table, snorting and shaking his head.

Vlado smiled. "You're in luck, Johnny. We can't afford to be seen taking you home in one of our meat trucks."

A short time later, Inky arrived in his rusted-out roadster, parallel-parked at the store's front door, and after a quick look up and down the street, they squeezed Obersteen's hopefully anonymous bulk into the passenger's side.

Vlado told him, "Strict orders, Johnny. Stay home and especially stay away from here, or next time your friend Artemis decides to leave you a message, we'll tell him where to deliver it."

The car rattled off and Vlado put his hand on Joe's shoulder. "It's been a long fucking day."

47

After a week, Vlado stopped looking over his shoulder every time he walked to Big Sausage, thinking they'd convinced the powers-that-be they had nothing to do with Obersteen. But what about Johnny? He still owed the money, and now he had no way to make it up. As Leo'd said, that bridge goes both ways.

Vlado tried to put that worry out of his head when he went home, hoping to leave it all on the table and enjoy the evenings with his giggly daughter and adoring—for lack of a more accurate word—wife. But all he was hearing from her was *Marti this* and *Marti that*, and why won't you go see the doctor. So, on that pretense, he took off one afternoon and went down to Kaw point and sat in his rowboat for a while, drank a beer, ate a sardine sandwich, and stared into the muddy, slow-moving current, which was taking its sweet time getting to the Gulf of Mexico. He didn't know what to tell Stefani. If he was honest about his visit to Dubrowski, it would make it seem that she'd deceived him. But she hadn't, and did she even know who the father was? If he lied to her, they could continue their shared pretense, if that's what it was, but then what happens when there's no new baby? And hovering over all this was the sense that once again, thanks to Obersteen, Big Sausage itself was in danger of getting chopped up in its own grinder. Maybe him along with it. And Joe as well, the whole thing unravelling. He thought back on all that stuff about the disappearing piano notes, and lost melodies, his dream about Johnny, the pianist who made him feel the loneliness that was possible. Everything that seemed so strange at the time was now coming true, bit by bit. Hell, he wouldn't be surprised to hear that Starr had got himself an elephant. But it was too much to keep all in his brain at once, and he was glad when the first gusts and a few drops of rain from an encroaching thunderhead urged him out of the boat and towards home.

Vlado found Stefani in the kitchen, humming to herself and adding unidentifiable animal parts to a strange-smelling concoction on the stove. Janet Ivan was babbling away in the next room. He gave Stefani a hug from behind and smooched the back of her neck. He didn't know what he'd decided until he heard himself speak.

"Good news," he said, "we're still in business. The doc says don't worry, it'll happen."

Stefani turned and gave him a deep look.

"What, are you pregnant?" Vlado said.

She gave him a solid punch in the chest. "No. I'm just so relieved. That we can do it. That we can have our own new little baby." She took his hand and led him out of the kitchen. "It's time for Janet Ivan to go to bed."

Vlado wasn't proud of this, but what could he say at this point that wouldn't blow up his entire life? She'd have to know eventually, but he could only solve one goddam thing at a time. And right now, it was how to get out of the tangled mess Obersteen had brought to their door. Somewhere across the river, restaurants weren't getting their product and a scary guy named Artie wasn't getting his expected cut, and some Big Tommy guy who'd lent money to Obersteen was probably itching to give him a manicure with a pair of pliers. *Do they do that?*

Inky came up with the idea. Since there was no such thing as Johnny's Smokehouse, they'd have to create one. They were at Morty's on Sunday morning, and as usual, Inky seemed way too happy for the time or circumstances. "It's like shooting at cans. You know, nobody gets hurt. Except for the can."

"Meaning we're the cans?" Vlado was lost.

"No, there aren't any cans. Forget the cans. What we need is a red catfish."

"Joey?"

"I think he's saying we need to give them something to shoot at. Although hopefully it won't come to that. And Inky, it's red herring, not catfish."

"Red herring? That can't be right. Seriously, Joe, who'd ever eat something like that?"

Vlado and Joe hadn't seen Stritchie in a while, but Vlado was pretty sure he'd never heard him whistle before, which he was doing when they met at McGowan's. They tucked into a booth well downstream from the large guys in matching jerseys yelling at each other about football. Or something. Stritchie placed his fedora on an empty chair and smoothed back the sides of his hair, which held a few new streaks of grey. He looked a little fuller in the face and if Vlado didn't know any better, he'd say that the new wrinkles on the edges of Stritchie's eyes were smile lines. Maybe they were. What did they know about Stritchie?

"You boys are looking well," Stritchie said and held three fingers up toward the bar. They followed the holy trinity of drink, food, then business, waiting until Stritchie was wiping his mouth and gassing out a series of tiny belches for Joe to begin his pitch. *Business is good. We need more space.*

"It's been a good two years, right?" Stritchie said. "I get the rent. Mae gets her sausage."

Mae? Jankovic? In fact, they hadn't seen Mae around the store much lately. Who knows what she did in her spare time? She had to be twenty years younger than Stritchie, but why not?

"Yeah, I'm glad everyone's getting fed," said Vlado. "Even across the river, between you and us, we're selling to some pretty fancy restaurants. But here's the thing. As soon as you have a successful business, somebody else sees what you're doing, and wants to get in on the action."

"Competition. It's the American way."

"Exactly. But what if we were our own competition?"

Joe picked it up. "You know how in the Bottoms they take the same junk and put it in different packages and pretend there's a difference between Swift and Armour? The idea is we open a new sausage place under a new name, and sell stuff that's just as good as ours, because, of course, it is ours."

Stritchie laughed out loud, a first in Vlado's memory. "Nice to see you boys have been learning something. So, what do you want?"

Vlado said, "We figure there's a lot of stuff up and down Quindaro that's laying around unused. Maybe you own something you want to unload cheap. And here we are to help." He took a deep sip of beer and peered over the top of his glass at Stritchie, who gave him the *you're full of shit* look he'd anticipated.

"Nothing out there, but I do have an old mechanic's garage down south in Armourdale. Turns out anybody can fix a car if they have a half-inch wrench, so I had to bump the guy because no rent, and frankly I'm tired of dealing with it. I've got better things to do. You want it, it's yours."

"As long as it's in a safe neighborhood," Vlado said. "We'll have a lot of expensive, specialized machinery in there."

Stritchie spread his hands. "Not my problem, that's the whole point, right? Get some good insurance."

"Can we afford this?" Joe asked.

Stritchie flashed a disconcerting new-Stritchie smile. "I'll make sure. Let's go see it today, and if you like it, we'll drop by Poochie's and draw up the financials."

There wasn't much to like about the place, a free-standing building with a single garage bay in an industrial neighborhood south of Kansas Avenue. The bay would hold any amount of gear, and an adjoining stucco box fronted by a plate glass window could house the "office." A mulchy smell wafted off the Kaw, a few blocks to the south, and the walls of the garage shook a little as a freight train rumbled past a hundred yards away. Most of the surrounding buildings, small warehouses and silos, were shuttered; theirs was the only car visible on the street.

"We'll give you a dollar a month," Vlado told Stritchie.

He laughed. "Believe me, it won't be much more than that, and one less thing I have to worry about. We'll meet Poochie at Morty's. I'm craving anchovies."

Poochie arranged the paperwork, Stritchie got his anchovies, and Vlado and Joe received the keys to their new sausage emporium. They made one more stop, at Ratko Horvat's insurance office. Vlado'd never liked Ratko, who was a pushy loudmouth, and whose lovely wife, Myrna, seemed to have a bad habit of falling down and bruising her face. Nobody was able to put the finger on Ratko, and the Big Sausage ladies had made efforts to include Myrna in their down-the-counter chit-chats, but she always seemed to have something else to do. In any case, Vlado took a great satisfaction in signing the fire insurance policy, thinking if something should accidentally happen—and who knows?—he couldn't think of a better person to take the fall.

The next day, they took Inky and Bootnose over to show them the new place. They walked around to the front and Bootnose gave the garage door a kick, its clangorous rattle echoing through the empty bay. They opened the office to the smell of mold and excrement. Spiderwebs laced the corners of the tiny space. Everything looked grimy and gray through the grease-smeared windows.

"The only thing missing is Ovaltine," Bootnose said, opening his arms to appreciate the rank beauty of it all.

Inky was inspecting the shelves. "I didn't know rat shit ever got this big." He swiped a single finger along the surface of a beam that crumbled into dust. "Termites."

Vlado and Joe grinned at each other. "It's perfect," Vlado said. "We'll hang the big sign right on the window."

48

The next day was Sunday, and after a rich dinner of roast lamb that Joe had cooked for their two families, he and Vlado sat in the living room taking turns spinning records on Joe's little Victrola. Martina and Stefani were cleaning up in the kitchen, where Vlado heard more laughter than clanking of dishes. Tom and Donald were running Janet Ivan around in the back yard, and for the moment, all seemed calm and bright.

Joe slid a disc out of its sleeve, positioned it on the Victrola, and dropped the needle. "I bet you don't even remember this one."

Vlado recognized it immediately, the banjo—*ban-yo* as they'd called it in Zagreb—with its happy-tambura sound, if that was even possible. He'd first heard it when they were fifteen and Joe worked as a stock boy at Meister Fromin's department store off Illic Square. Sometimes Vlado would show up at the end of Joe's shift and Fromin, a grandfatherly guy from Austria, would invite the two of them back into the office for the tiniest glass of wine and maybe a listen to some of the new records that were arriving from America. Vlado recalled asking Fromin to explain the title of one song, "Junk Man Rag."

"Ah, it's an American phrase," he replied. "*Junk Man*. Like a tinker, but with worthless stuff. And *Rag*, I don't know, some kind of music, we'll see."

Vlado had been thrilled by the plinky sound that nonetheless filled up the room like an entire orchestra and the up and down and sideways movement of the beat, which skipped instead of marched, and now, listening to Joe playing the song again, he felt the same joyous sense that anything could happen.

The kitchen door opened, and Martina and Stefani, giggling in their aprons, danced into the room, turkey-trotting around the furniture. Joe and Vlado clapped along. When the song ended, Joe reset the needle and they were all up out of their chairs.

Soon they were out of breath, seated, and passing the bottle. Stefani's face was flushed, and Martina showed a weary smile as she rested one hand on her precious belly. Joe bit the tip off a Rio Tan and offered one to Vlado. He couldn't understand how Joe did it. Here in Joe's world, for this time and this day, there were no gangsters, lost loves, war, hunger, or even worse, dreaded secrets between husbands and wives. For Joe, all that could resume tomorrow when he was back open for business. Vlado, meanwhile, was swatting away buzzing thoughts in his head—the whole worrisome thing with Johnny, Janet Ivan, his dead swimmers, and Stefani's dumb willingness to believe him. And somewhere behind that, an image of Lydia looking hurt and the piano player, looking for God knows what. After listening to "Junk Man Rag," he thought back to Zagreb, and the last time they saw Fromin's department store: broken windows, a boarded-up doorway, red paint splashed all around the entrance. They never saw Fromin again.

But today . . . now. No, he couldn't let it go.

Martina got a sick look on her face and left the room. Stefani gave Vlado a smug-ish smile. He wanted to reassure her that soon she too would be fat and puking, but who was it who'd said, "When you find yourself in a hole, stop digging"?

49

The digging resumed the next morning when the cousins summoned Inky and Bootnose to the store and explained the plan.

"Go to Starr's and see if you can borrow his flatbed," Joe told them. "Here's a list of the kind of things we need. I don't know, try the junkyards, or look down some of those alleys behind Quindaro or below the viaduct where people toss stuff. It doesn't have to be pretty, and it doesn't have to work."

"And if you use the Boyko truck, take off the sign," added Vlado. "Don't answer any questions, and we'll see you at the 'undisclosed location' just after sunset. And Inky, for Chrissake, lose the apron and the bowtie."

The streets below Kansas Avenue were deathly quiet at the end of the day, when the last bit of sunlight glowed on the cross of distant St. John's, either a blessing or a warning. Or maybe just an ever-watchful eye. The one always looking over Vlado's shoulder waiting for him to fuck up. He was happy to have his thoughts interrupted by the sound of grinding gears and the sight of Inky and Bootnose in the cab of Starr's flatbed, navigating down the tight alley to the rear of the undisclosed location. Joe opened the back of the bay and the four of them hurried in a motley collection of rusted sinks, dented galvanized steel watering troughs, sagging chairs, a moldy-smelling couch, some doors that they positioned on sawhorses as tables, as well as a potbellied stove, a bag of cans, random scraps of plywood, a few hoes and rakes, a coil of hose, and . . .

"A sewing machine?" Vlado stared at Inky.

"Oh, that's for Tereza. It goes back on the truck."

They spent a few hours organizing their treasures into some sort of reasonable facsimile of a sausage shop until Joe and Vlado inspected it from the front and found it convincing.

"It'll be even better when Inky washes the windows," Bootnose said.

"Me?" said Inky.

"Who do you think's gonna do it, the cleaning lady?"

"Leave it," said Vlado, who was happy to let the grease preempt a clear view of what lay within. "Now let's go, we've already been here too long." He pulled the chain on the single overhead light, and they felt their way out the back to their respective vehicles.

"Ha, Starr won't even know it was missing," Bootnose said to Inky, and they climbed into the flatbed. *Jebote. These guys.* Vlado was just happy they worked for him. Sort of.

Soon they'd gone their separate ways, leaving the night as quiet as they'd found it.

50

The party was on. It just so happened that the two-year anniversary of Big Sausage coincided roughly with Stritchie's birthday. The planned celebration would be too big for Morty's or Big Sausage, so Vlado and Joe booked the Croatian Catholic club, a gymnasium-sized venue with a stage, kitchen, and bowling alleys even, next to St. John's. Vlado usually avoided the place, never at ease with the grand saint's day celebrations and National Day parties, where the cacophony of jabbering Croatians and tortured accordions had him yearning for the peace and quiet of his rowboat. He hated bowling, and it didn't help that the Club observed the letter of the 18th Amendment, as if somehow God himself was the killjoy Vlado had always suspected he was.

The key was that everybody had to be there. Everybody. Especially Stritchie. And Obersteen. And anybody associated with Big Sausage. It was a momentous occasion for everyone on the Hill to be seen together, and most importantly, to see each other and say, "Here we are, as one, raising our glasses and celebrating our life and presence." Here on Strawberry Hill.

And not in Armourdale.

Joe had wanted to do the meeting, but Vlado knew he'd screw it up. Besides, Artie would recognize Joe from the store. Johnny had told them when he was expected at Union Station, but as the day approached, Vlado's gut started to do the jitterbug. Union Station was a grand and opulent place, where well-heeled travelers came and went, and politicians arrived on their trains to great fanfare. Just off the cavernous hallways, Harvey's offered fancy cocktails and fancy dining, where the legendary Harvey girls in their black and white garb served up large plates of oysters and steaks, always ready to listen to your jokes or light your cigar, and who knows what else.

Vlado wasn't so dumb to think all these people got rich by working twelve hours a day at some shit job. He'd been to Harvey's once, but didn't like the sense that there was something going on above and around him that he didn't understand. He recalled with dread how three months earlier the *Star* had reported in gory detail about a shoot-out right there in the parking lot between special agents and the notorious gangster Baby Face Malone. There had been actual machine guns, and a lot of police and hoodlums died in the melee, which had been dubbed the "Kansas City Massacre" by the ambitious press. To say the least, Vlado was nervous about the upcoming meet-up, so he called on his pinochle buddy Lubo Grisnik.

"It's a business meeting," he explained to Lubo as they sat at the far end of the bar at Morty's. Lubo, despite his six-and-a-half-foot hulking presence, was the nicest guy in the world who would do anything for anybody, and Vlado had to choke back a wriggle of guilt for preying on his good nature.

Morty had left them a bottle to be responsible for, and Vlado observed his responsibilities by keeping Lubo's glass full, and his own as well because, to be honest, who in their right mind would go through something like this?

"Admittedly, it's an unusual situation," Vlado explained. "And I know you're a meat cutter and not a businessman, so you just do what you know how to do."

"I should bring a knife?"

"No, what do you think this is? It's business, I'm saying, you don't have to do anything but stand there. I'll do the actual business-ing. I'll pick you up at six tomorrow night. Dress like you're going to a funeral."

They headed across the viaduct just before sunset in the anonymity of Inky's borrowed pickup. Despite a brisk cross-breeze off the Kaw, Vlado was sweating like crazy under his straw boater. The downtown buildings grew larger, and so did his thoughts about Lydia. He pictured her as he'd last seen her, a grey-and-white presence so different from the *seks lonac* he'd once lusted after. And behind her, the piano player blinking in a lavender darkness. And here he was again, crossing the great divide, dry at least, but heading towards some other unknown thing outside the sanctuary of his precious Hill.

Lubo was quiet and seemingly lost in his own thoughts. He was wearing a dark wool suit, overcoat, and serious-looking fedora. He had his elbow on the windowsill and was slowly flexing the five fingers on his right hand, and the three on his left, a gesture Vlado often saw with the career meat cutters.

"I could never tell if it's the cold or the fact you're doing the same damn thing over and over," Vlado said. "And what do those assholes care."

Lubo shrugged. "Sometimes I stick them in a bowl of ice at night. But you know, you gotta eat." Lubo's wife was a plain, quiet, God-fearing woman whom you'd rarely see gabbing in any of the front yards along Barnett St. He had a thirteen-year-old girl who was a notorious troublemaker, and her nine-year-old brother who was quiet like his mother. Maybe a little slow, the word was. But a sweet kid.

Across the river, they turned right onto Broadway and rattled south towards the train station, where Johnny had been delivering sausage to Harvey's restaurant. Vlado pulled in and nervously scanned around for bad guys, as if he could tell, then parked in a loading zone like he had business there. Which he did, right? Lubo dragged the Smokehouse Johnny ice chest out of the trunk, and they rolled it past the grand archways of the elegant station to the tracks on the west side of the building, as Obersteen had instructed.

Vlado figured the less he told Lubo the better, and that seemed fine with Lubo. "We're going to meet a guy, or I am anyway, and he and I will have a conversation. Your job is to say nothing. I'll tell him you don't speak English. Whatever happens, you just stand there, and maybe flex your fingers like you were doing. Make sure he notices your two missing fingers. You know, like you still got eight left, so don't fuck with me."

Lubo stared quizzically at his left hand as if he were seeing it for the first time.

They rounded the end of the building and stopped at the furthest reach of a platform where a train was pulling in just feet away from them. They leaned away from the steam blowing out of the side of the engine, which was dragging a half dozen cars, shiny steel with wide polished-clean windows. The train screeched and slowed, and Vlado could see inside where gentlemen in tailored suits sat across from prim ladies with fancy hairdos and little flowered hats. They were all smiling and sipping from teacups or martini glasses and gesturing past the boys toward the grandiose station and the wonderful possibilities that surely awaited their every next moment. So different from the steers that bellowed shoulder-to-shoulder in the stinky boxcars that unloaded daily at the Armour plant.

"Where's the big guy?"

The voice startled Vlado, and he turned and saw the gentleman in his black suit, homburg and brushy mustache, who seemed to have materialized out of the train's trail of steam and smoke. He tapped the claw end of his cane on the cooler and asked, "What's this? And where the fuck is the fat guy?"

"The fat guy?" Vlado said. "You mean Ovaltine?"

"I'm not here to make jokes. And who's this?" His head indicated Lubo.

"That's my driver. He's from Lithuania. He doesn't speak." *Lithuania?*

He tapped the cooler again. "I wasn't looking for any more sausage."

"It's not what you think it is," said Vlado. He headed further down the track with the cooler, accompanied by his new best friend with the threatening cane. Lubo remained behind, a large and hopefully ominous silhouette.

Vlado wished that everything he'd rehearsed was on notecards that he could just read off of. Instead, he heard himself say "We got a problem with Obersteen," which didn't have the calming effect he'd hoped for.

"No, *I've* got a problem with your Ovaltine guy." Artie replied.

"No, not our guy. Okay, hear me out. Open the cooler."

Artie used the tip of his cane to angle open the lid, then reached in for the small clutch of bills that was its only content. He thumbed through the rubber-banded twenties and gave Vlado a sour look.

"He owes a lot more than this."

"No, that's not from him, it's from us. Think of it as a down payment. Seed money, is that what they call it?"

"I'm listening."

"Thing is, this guy used to work for us, sold our stuff to the fancy restaurants, you know all about that. But he stole our recipes and now has his own place, in some undisclosed location, and he's trying to cut us out of the action. You know the feeling? All I know is we heard him whining about this tough guy who's trying to shake him down across the river. I'm not pointing any fingers, but here you are, obviously a tough guy, in Missouri, who clearly has a hard on for Johnny's Smokehouse, and here I am to see if we can find something that works for both of us."

"I'm thinking your fat friend doesn't have much of a choice."

"That's what we'd like to think. But for sure, he's not going to pay you any money, he thinks you're just some ignorant *paison*."

"Well, when I find that fucker—"

"We found him. He just opened a wholesale place in Armourdale, down in the oxbow."

They left the cooler behind and strolled down the gravel next to the tracks and stopped at a point where anything they might say would be masked by the puffing engines and clanking rail cars.

"How do you know so much?" Artie asked.

"I'll be the first to admit we don't understand anything about what's going on in Missouri, and the fact that we're even here would be the proof of that. But we do know what's going on in our own backyard. You know the saying, 'Telegraph, telephone, tell a Croatian'?" Artie gave him a dim look. "Okay, let me make it simple. You're not going to get a dime out of Obersteen. So, when you decide to deliver a final message to this guy, we just want to make sure it goes to the right place."

"And where would that be?"

"His new joint doesn't look like much, but he's sunk everything he has into it and is cranking out product at a rate that's going to undercut us and bypass you with other so-called distributors. But we don't want anybody to get hurt. Including you. Not that I give a shit but hey, it's only sausage. So, you have to wait until the place is empty, which is tough, because even after he closes, he's got one or two guys with shotguns who sit around and drink beer and blast at rats all night, because, you know."

"What do I know?"

"Well, it's a butcher shop, with meat scraps all over and . . . never mind, you don't need to know, except that they're there."

Artie laughed. "We know a little about shooting rats ourselves."

"That's fine," said Vlado. "Who am I to tell you how to conduct your business? But think about what you're really after. You gotta figure Johnny had to get a fire insurance policy in order to close the loan. So, if anything were to happen to the place, you and he can have a frank discussion about who the beneficiary should be, in terms of settling debts and whatnot. Then we can all go out and come back in again. You know, start fresh. Without the fat guy."

Vlado couldn't tell if Artie was mulling over the idea or considering whether to give Vlado a good whack with the head of his cane. Vlado turned around to where he could see Lubo in the distance. He was flexing his left hand and had buried his right hand significantly into the pocket of his overcoat. Genius. Vlado put his own hands in his pockets so Artie couldn't see them shaking.

"Okay, mister businessman, what do you have in mind?"

"Here it is. There's going to be a big party on the Hill, and everybody will be there. All the Croats, Johnny, his crew, even the local cops. And fire department," he added, giving Artie a knowing look, he hoped, if that was even possible. He felt a smidge of confidence, as if Joe were there next to him, whispering in his ear.

"When?"

"Soon. You decide if you're in. Then we'll let you know the date of the party, and on that day, we'll give you the address in Armourdale. Nobody will be there, so nobody gets hurt, right?"

Artie combed two fingers down through his bushy mustache. "When's the party?"

"This Sunday."

Artie wrote a phone number on a card and gave it to Vlado, who stared at it and said, "You'll hear from us in the late afternoon."

Artie lightly tapped the head of his cane to Vlado's chest. "You go on now, you and your 'driver,' and I'll enjoy a cigar here for a few minutes."

Vlado let out a long breath and celebrated the thought that he wasn't going to die, at least not right then, and turned to head back to Lubo.

"And funny boy," he heard and looked around at Artie. "Don't fuck this up."

Vlado wanted to say the same thing, but what were the odds in this fucked up world that anything would go as planned. When he came to the Smokehouse cooler, he gave it a hard kick and it tumbled off the platform onto the tracks. He reached Lubo and clapped him on the shoulder.

"You did great, big guy. Come on, I'm gonna buy you the largest steak you've ever seen." He took his arm, and together they entered the giant archways and made their way into the bustling interior of Harvey's.

51

That night, after he'd delivered Lubo home and sworn him to secrecy, Vlado entered a quiet house, everyone thankfully asleep. He poured himself a shot and wandered around the dark living room, a hundred tamburas trilling in his head.

"Come to bed," Stefani said, appeared out of the darkness, in a droopy nightgown with her hair down. "You've been pacing around out here and it's driving me crazy, whatever it is." She drew close to where he could see her soft features, could feel her trust and contentment. Her comfortable world, their little girl, with another one soon to be on the way. Right? Well. She placed a warm palm on his cheek and leaned up close to him. She smelled of sleep and sauerkraut, and Vlado let his head drop onto her neck for a deeper whiff.

"Whatever it is, it'll still be there tomorrow. Come on." She hooked his arm and led him into the bedroom. They undressed and climbed under the sheets, and she spooned up to his back and draped an arm over his chest. He cradled back into her and felt the tamburas quiet and the rattling in his brain settle.

The next morning Vlado awoke before sunrise. He shook Stefani, who moaned a protest.

"Come on, get up, we've got a party to plan."

She gave him a bleary look. "Why are you so happy all of a sudden?"

"Happy? Who's happy? Not me, that's for sure, because we still need a dozen more nutbreads by Sunday." He grinned at her. "I'm taking Janet Ivan to the store today while you and Marti get to chopping walnuts."

Then he was up, showering, shaving, dressing, and soon had the kitchen filled with the aroma of eggs and sausage. After everyone was fed, he kissed Stefani, hoisted Janet Ivan onto his shoulders and headed out the back door toward Big Sausage. Autumn had arrived, and the crisp bite in the air reminded him that time was passing; again he thought of the disappearing piano notes and all the events that had brought him to this moment, never to return. But today was a new song, with the bungalows along Barnett draped in a golden glow that promised a beautiful, blue-sky day. Janet Ivan beat time on the top of his head while she explained the meaning of life to him in her gurgling Ukrainian, and he quickened his step, veering left and right like a happy junk man.

Joe was just opening the store when they arrived.

"All hands on deck," Vlado proclaimed and plopped Janet Ivan into an empty A&P box. "He bought it, Joey. Hook, line, and sinker. Lubo did great. And hey, look, I'm not dead."

"Not yet, anyway."

"Well, in a hundred years—"

"Don't say it."

Vlado could see Joe was in a mood. "What's the matter, rough night with Martina?"

"She knows something's up and it's killing her that she doesn't know what. And liable to kill me too."

"Well, you gotta keep a lid on it. Because if Martina knows . . . In any case, it's too late to back out now."

Throughout the day, Vlado and his cohort of butchers relentlessly sawed at the pig corpses that Inky and Bootnose dragged out of the hearse: they spent hours grinding up scraps and shoulders for sausage, separating ribs and necks and cheeks out to be simmered with sauerkraut, salting bellies for bacon, and popping whole heads into boiling vats. They tossed the skins into the deep fryer and sliced the meatier chops thin and stacked them in the cooler for the orphans. At one point, Vlado held a tail between his fingers and thoughtfully inspected it, not for the first time, before pitching it into the trash.

Vlado had left Janet Ivan with Joe at the smoker all afternoon. Joe liked to show her how to feed in sticks of hickory, just enough wood to keep a thin, blue line of smoke wisping out the top without overheating the reddening kobasas hanging inside. To get the temperature just right you had to pay attention to the wind, the heat of the day, the position of the sun, "and the amount of beer in your glass," as Vlado'd once said. Vlado went outside to check on Joe's progress and found him sitting in a chair with Janet Ivan snoozing on his lap, his head back and his eyes closed. Vlado nudged the chair with the tip of his boot and Joe squinted open one eye.

"Don't bother us, we're cooking."

52

Early on Sunday morning, a slightly rusted Ford Model-T, a car like most any other car, rolled down an alley in Armourdale and parked behind a beat-up garage south of Kansas Avenue. A man got out, anonymous in a low fedora, grey scarf, grey overcoat, and grey gloves, as if he were part of the swirl of the fog that liked to hang around the Kaw that time of day. From the trunk of the car he removed two large buckets, which he lugged with some difficulty to the back door and into the garage bay. Inside, rusty sinks were propped against one wall, metal shelving sagged against another, and a couple of tables centered the room. A broad assortment of wooden and metal detritus was arranged about as if this were a junkyard and the owner was taking inventory. The man split the disgusting contents of one bucket—a mix of chicken skin, bones, feet, fat, heads, and every other damn part of the loathsome bird except the little bit that might be edible if you were starving—between one sink and one table. He reached into the other bucket, filled with the same awful stuff, and strewed it around, tossing gobs of fat into the corners, and one fistful against the wall for good measure. He noticed that a five-gallon lug of motor oil had leaked across the floor and made a mental note to speak with the management about a possible fire hazard. In the adjoining office was a painted wooden sign that he took out the front door and hung on a nail above the plate-glass window. *Smokehouse Johnny*. Hello, here I am!

He peeled off the slimy gloves, tossed them in the trunk, and climbed back into the car. The Ford made an alarming noise when it started up, but he figured no one was around and puttered out of the alley thinking there was nothing more he could do. It would happen or not.

The bells of St. John's rang the noontime hour, Morty gave last call, and after an annihilation toast, Joe and Vlado headed up to the Croatian Catholic Club to oversee the setup. Thanks to the Altar Society ladies, or their husbands, the upstairs gymnasium floor was already lined with tables and chairs and the walls were festooned with colorful, crocheted afghans for the auction. A broad empty space in front of the stage was reserved for dancing. Downstairs, next to the bowling alleys, Inky and Bootnose were stacking ribs and rings of sausage by the grills behind the bar. Morty arrived and wheeled in a fifteen-gallon tank of "lemonade" which together they hoisted onto a table, and they all tested the spigot to make sure it worked.

Vlado peered through his glass. "I've never had grape skins in my lemonade, but you're the genius." He swallowed it back, and the sourness jolted him more than the alcohol. "Maybe needs more sugar?"

"Don't start," said Joe. He pulled Vlado aside. "When are you going to make the call?"

"After it's rolling and everybody's here. Especially Obersteen."

They'd released Johnny from house arrest and told him they'd smoothed it all over and insisted on seeing him at the party. Come casual, but you know, put on a shirt.

A line already snaked down the sidewalk when they opened at five o'clock. Joe and Vlado had invited the entire Hill: the Irish, Germans, Slovenians even, and everybody else who you'd see every day at the grocery store or bars or getting a haircut or chatting in their front yards with passersby. Nobody gave a shit that it was the second anniversary of Big Sausage. Or Stritchie's birthday. It was a party, a big one, and an end in itself. No one objected to the twenty-five-cent admission charge, which would go to the orphans, and soon a steady stream of friends and strangers were pouring themselves "lemonade" and going up the stairs to the gymnasium to fill their plates with sausage, sauerkraut, boiled ribs, sarma, steamed potatoes and coleslaw, and plenty of sliced povitica. The smell of garlic and smoke and humans combined with the locker-room odor to create an aroma that, for better or worse, you'd never smell anywhere else in the world.

Matt Sinovic had put on his Franky Fontaine mustache, greased back his hair, and was weaving along the lines of tables playing Italian arias while a saxophone and tambura ensemble tuned up on stage. Martina, Mae, and Dorothy Penny sat at the front end of the tables with Father Oyster. Dorothy was putting sausage on his plate while Martina massaged her more-impressive-than-usual belly and poked at her potatoes. There was Junior's daughter with her little one, Dinko and Hugo and the rest of the Armour guys, Poochie and Mrs. Poochie with their girls, as well as a bunch of folks Vlado only vaguely knew from McGowan's, and from the Serbian parish, and another half roomful of people he didn't recognize if only because they had their faces mostly down into their plates. Vlado was too nervous to eat. He scanned the room, feeling a little queasy about the fact that only he and Joe knew the real reason everybody was there.

Joe appeared at his elbow and poured a little something into Vlado's lemonade.

"You know, Joey, if our business plan of giving away free food holds up, we're going to be rich beyond our wildest dreams."

At that moment, Stritchie strode into the room. He looked around until he saw Mae at the front table and went straight there, while Mae got up to fetch him a plate of food.

Vlado nudged Joe. "Mae Jankovic. Fucking Stritchie."

"He deserves everything he gets," Joe said.

Vlado spied Obersteen carrying a plate toward where Stefani was shoving chunks of kobasa into Janet Ivan. Next to her were fake-Aunt-Vera, then Ivan, and an empty chair that Obersteen settled into. Vlado watched Johnny and Janet dig in. They each took a rib with their left hand and chewed on it. Johnny used his fork to shovel in a mouthful of sauerkraut, and Janet Ivan did the same with her fingers. Vlado was standing next to Joe, watching them chew in time with each other, with the same intoxicated expressions. He saw the same dark rings under their eyes, their pug noses, and chubby cheeks. He looked around, convinced everyone was watching this.

Joe gave Vlado a worried look, like he knew what he was thinking.
"It's obvious, isn't it?" Vlado said. "You can see it, right?"
Joe nodded.
"Do you think anybody else can see it?"
Joe looked at Vlado. "Everybody knows, Vlado."
"Everybody knows? Everybody knows what?"
"Everybody knows that you're her daddy."

With Obersteen finally present and accounted for, the time had come for Janet Ivan's daddy to make the call. "Here we go, Jozo," Vlado said and went downstairs and asked for the bar phone. His shaking hand misdialed the number. He tried again, and when the familiar voice answered, Vlado told him, "425 South Orville," and hung up quickly. He pulled out his watch. 6:45. He wound it and returned it to his pocket, where it felt heavier than usual.

He refilled his lemonade and heard the opening notes of the tamburitzans echoing down the stairs and felt the rhythmic thumping on the ceiling that said the dancing had begun. He'd had enough of people for one day, so he settled into a bar stool and enhanced his lemonade with a squirt from his flask.

Everybody knows you're her daddy. So, biology be damned. Janet Ivan was his, and everybody knew it. Like everybody knew Jesus was the son of God. Like everybody knew that tomorrow would be another day. Until the annihilation, life would go on, a bigger thing than could be determined by one person.

But one person could certainly fuck it up. Like Johnny, with his greedy involvement with forces bigger than he could handle. And like Vlado himself, having thoughtlessly broken Lydia's heart, who apparently had loved him in spite of himself. And now here he was, "fixing" everything by deceiving Poochie and Stritchie and in fact the entire Hill, the insurance business, and some dangerous characters from across the river. And he'd put Lubo at risk without thinking twice. How could he ever confess this to Father Oyster? Who surely would know anyway, the same way that everybody knew everything. *Forward, always forward,* Vlado liked to think, but maybe that wasn't always the best. Like the time when his fist cracked a guy's jaw. Or, years ago in Zagreb, when he shattered a kid's knee with a pool cue. And then there was the night with the piano player, when he was either smart enough or scared enough to let it go.

The realization suddenly struck him that he was being as foolish as Johnny, and he recognized the sick feeling in his gut as future regret for what they were about to do. Who was he kidding, outside of deceiving all his neighbors? Even if they pulled this off, there'd be no end to it. One problem solved by creating a hundred more. Vlado and Joe would be just as deep in the murk as those assholes across the river muscling each other. What were they thinking? Maybe that was the problem, too much thinking, something he wasn't so great at.

Vlado checked his watch—7:05. He bounded up the stairs where he found Joe bringing Martina another plate. He pulled him aside.

"Joey, I made the call."

"Okay. Then I guess it's on."

"No. I'm not gonna do it."

"Are they not coming?"

"Oh, they'll be there all right. But we have to stop them."

"What do you mean?"

"Joey, I've been doing this wrong the whole way. One thing after another. I should have never changed the recipe for those idiots. We never should have gone into business with Johnny, and now, look, here we are. Fucking around with forces we have no idea about. We're stepping in deeper and deeper, until it's going to suck us under." Vlado had been to the river, *had been in the river,* knew about currents and other things beyond his control. He'd always known what it meant to be the victim of somebody else's circumstances. But now the victims could be everyone he knew and loved—Janet Ivan was burrowing her gaze into him from across the room—and the circumstances were his.

"Grab your coat, Joey."

53

Outside the Catholic Club, the street was dark and quiet, but for the muffled boom of stomping feet leaking out of the gym. As well as some laughter. Then silence, followed by the chaos of over a hundred people singing what could only be "Happy Birthday."

"Stritchie's hating that," Vlado said to Joe.

"At least he has an alibi."

They hustled down Barnett toward Vlado's Ford along a curb lined with vehicles. Even police cars, because how could there be any crime when everyone, including the police, was at the club misbehaving under the protection of St. John the Baptist? Vlado wondered if his little Model-T could even make it in time, and what they would do when they got there. Without really thinking about it, he jiggled the door handle of one of the cop cars, and it opened right up. He saw the key dangling in the ignition and scanned the empty street.

"Joey, get in."

Vlado hopped in the driver's side and engaged the starter, surprised at the smooth purr of the engine, and with a nostalgic thought of his mighty Studebaker, pulled into the street. He gunned it around the bottom of Barnett then south toward Armourdale, whipping past stop signs and bouncing recklessly over potholes and the occasional curb. Despite the wild ride, his queasiness disappeared and he felt a space open in his chest where a stony weight had been lodged since the beginning of all this. He directed a hopeful smile at his cousin, but Joe wasn't having it.

"So now we're car thieves too," Joe said.

"Just make sure this stays off Martina's list, along with the rest of today's hopefully venial sins."

"And what are we supposed to do when we get there?"

"Well, first . . . I don't know. Let's see what happens. At least we have a big fucking car that says 'Police Department' all over it."

"And hats." Joe took one of the two hats on the seat and popped it onto his head where it sank down to his ears. Vlado donned the other one.

"Those fuckers don't know who they're dealing with."

"Let's hope not."

They soon crossed Kansas Ave. Vlado slowed onto the top of Orville Street, then crept down towards the ill-fated service station. There was no sign of any activity, and he coasted to the front of the building, which seemed to be undisturbed.

"Get the sign," he told Joe, who bolted out of the car and jerked on the Smokehouse Johnny marquis until it pulled off the nail and crashed down. He tossed it into the brush on the side of the garage and hurried back to the cruiser, and before he'd closed the door, Vlado was peeling out of there.

They went left and left, then up a narrow street to the top of a ridge where they had a view of the locale. Vlado stopped the car and turned off the lights. They sat in silence for a while until Joe spoke.

"I don't know. It seemed like the numbers worked out . . ."

"That's your job, Joe. But the thing I forgot is, it's not just numbers."

"Maybe it's my fault," Joe said. "That night at dinner. I could have thrown a punch too, and maybe we'd be done with that fucker."

Vlado smiled at the idea of his cousin ever throwing a punch. "You know that question about which is mightier, a pencil or a punch in the nose? Maybe it's neither one."

Joe continued, "What I really mean is—"

"Forget it, Joey. You were right to be pissed at me, acting like I was some kid in a Zagreb bar. It's the annihilation, and there's no getting around it. We made this mess, and we can clean it up. Look at how we stuck it to the Huns."

Joe laughed, "You mean by getting the hell out of Croatia?"

"Exactly."

On the street below, two black Fords appeared out of the darkness and cruised with their lights off toward the Johnny's Smokehouse building. They stopped, and four dark figures got out. A flashlight's beam bobbled toward the trunk of the second car. *Now what?*

"At least we have a bigger flashlight," Joe said, indicating the searchlight mounted outside the passenger door.

"Here's what let's do. Flip it on, then pan it slowly down the street, and when you hit the cars, switch it off."

Joe angled the light up Orville, switched it on, and trolled the narrow beam down the street until it shone on the men. Before they could turn around, he shut it off. He repeated the trick and the men ducked behind their cars. Joe tried it a third time, but then there were only the two cars with nobody in sight.

"What about this?" Joe said, fingering a crank mounted under the dashboard.

"Do it."

Joe gave it a slow turn, which generated a low moan like one of Starr's cows, before it rose to a wailing pitch.

"Straighten your hat, Joe. Here we go." Vlado gave the car an audible amount of gas, turned on his headlights, and accelerated down the hill. He was in no hurry to reach what would have been the scene of the crime *because what then?* so he made a squealing turn down another dark lane, and another, crisscrossing back and forth across Orville, while Joe waved his searchlight around and cranked the siren like a baby with a new toy.

Vlado ran out of cross streets and had no choice but to turn onto Orville. The cars were still there, a couple blocks away, the men nowhere in sight. He stopped the car, imagining them hiding in the bushes on either side of the road. Joe held the spotlight on the back of the cars while Vlado slowly rolled ahead. He couldn't imagine what he would do when he got there. Maybe jump out and say "Boo;" they'd all have a good laugh, and he'd invite them back to the party, because wouldn't you rather be eating sausage than freezing your ass off in Armourdale, up to no good?

He stopped about fifty feet away. There was no movement, and they couldn't tell if the men were inside or not. Joe jiggled the searchlight. Vlado flashed the headlights. He thought about fishing, how you had to give the bait the right motion.

"Turn it off, Joey." They peered in the darkness, trying to see any movement, but nothing. "Okay, open your door."

"I'm not going out there," said Joe.

"Just open the damn door." Joe did, and Vlado opened his. "Now slam it shut and slouch down." They shut their doors and ducked behind the dash.

Everything was dead silent as Vlado counted the imaginary steps it would take to reach the cars. Then a horn honked, engines started up, and the two Fords lurched onto the street and sped eastward up a hill. Vlado waited to allow the imaginary policemen to return to their cruiser, then flipped on his headlights and gunned the engine. Joe cranked the siren and off they went in pursuit, in no hurry whatsoever. He was not surprised to see them whip onto the Kansas Avenue Bridge and scurry back to the Missouri side, where he and Joe had no jurisdiction.

Vlado pulled the car into a dark space behind the Catholic Club, and they scurried back up the street. They walked casually into the bar, as if they'd just gone out to smell the flowers, then up the stairs to what was left of the party. The tables were littered with empty plates and overturned glasses, and a dense fog of cigar smoke hazed the air. A couple of guys from McGowan's were trying to start up a crowd rendition of Danny Boy, but they were drowned out by an accordion quintet on the stage playing a polka at half speed, while a few couples staggered against each other on the dance floor. In one corner, Lubo's nine-year-old son was passed out on the floor, and somebody had placed a pink carnation in his mouth. *Okay, so who doesn't like lemonade?* He looked around for Martina or Stefani, scanning the tables with their slumped-over occupants, thinking that at least the party had been a wild success.

"Vlado!" It was Stefani, pushing her way toward him through a choppy sea of overturned chairs. She wasn't happy. "We've been looking all over."

"We're right here, what's the big deal?" The last thing he needed now was drama from Stefani. Mostly he wanted a drink and a chance to put his dreadful experience behind him.

"It's Martina," she said. "They just left for the hospital. Come on, we gotta go."

"They?" said Joe.

"Yeah, Inky took her. It's the baby."

"Oh, is the baby finally coming?" Vlado said. "That's all I've ever heard about for the last month. Finally."

Joe gave him a hard look. "Vlado, it's too early. It's way too soon."

Jebote. How would he know?

"Come on, then," Vlado said. The three of them hustled out of the club and down Barnett to Vlado's car, past two cops who were staring in confusion at an empty parking space.

54

Vlado had forgotten to wind his watch and could only guess where they lingered in the unaccountable time between late night and dawn. There was no telling in the windowless hallway where he, Inky, Stefani, and Joe had been sitting in folding chairs for hours, waiting for news from the other side of the double doors, doors that so often were the entry to, or exit from, the world itself.

Joe had been pacing and returned to his seat. Vlado offered him his flask, but Joe waved it off.

"This is a good place, Joey," Vlado said, "You have two great kids already to prove it. Not to mention my little Janet Ivan. It's what they do here, like how we make sausage. Whatever it is, they'll work it out. And you know Martina, always wanting to be the first with everything."

Vlado thought that if he was the kind of guy who prayed, now would be the time, then wondered if that thought itself was a sort of prayer. It was complicated. Fortunately for all of them, Stefani was clacking away at her beads, and Vlado wished he might have something like that to do with his hands. And his brain. Joe stared at the floor, his face ashen.

Such a thin line, Vlado thought. Breathing or not. Waking in the morning, or not. Above the water or below. He thought about his own birth. Who had been there worrying? What had his mother thought as her own life ebbed away in favor of his? He watched Stefani sitting opposite him, eyes closed, mouthing her Hail Marys, thought of her not being there, of Janet Ivan disappearing. Of Joe without Martina, without his boys. And this new baby, straddling the line at that moment. He imagined himself gone from the earth, the feeling of being left out, of missing the party that would still be going on without him. His gut seized with panic, with regret, with some deeper thing he couldn't name.

"Where are the boys?" Vlado asked Joe.

"With their Aunt Sophie. They don't know what's happening."

"Ha. They hate her cooking."

"None of the Vukovic girls could ever cook worth a damn."

"At least you got the best one," Vlado said.

"Yeah, well she makes a decent neck bone soup, if I remind her about the salt."

Just then the double doors squeaked open, and a young-ish guy in a too-big white coat strode toward them. He was staring at a clipboard and didn't look happy. Vlado and Joe stood. The young man's eyes met Joe's.

"The baby has been successfully delivered," he said, and Vlado exhaled.

Joe looked confused. "Thank God. Right?"

"Please, Mr. Marevic, have a seat." His lips tightened and he frowned down at Joe. "Your wife was bleeding badly. She's unconscious now, and it's possible there's an infection." He rapped the clipboard with the backs of his fingernails. "We're giving her a heavy dose of antibacterials, blood, and saline. Hopefully we'll know more by tomorrow. When she wakes up. But I can't promise that."

"You can't promise you'll know more, or that she'll wake up?" asked Vlado.

"We're giving her the best care possible," he said, *not answering the fucking question.*

"What about the baby?" Joe asked.

"Well first of all, congratulations, it's a boy," he said, but his tone was not congratulatory. "Unfortunately, he arrived prematurely. We've done all we can, but it's up to him now."

"How is it up to him?" Joe's face reddened. "How could anything be up to him? Goddamit, he's not even supposed to be here."

The doctor gave Joe a tired look. "It's not as bad as it used to be. We know better what to do. Keep him warm. More oxygen. Come on." He led them through the doors and down toward a small room with a wide window.

Vlado stared through the glass at a crib that held something too tiny to be a human being.

"Fortunately, he's big for his age, if you will," the doctor said. "Almost four pounds. That gives him a better shot."

A nurse was positioning a tent over the little thing's head— "Oxygen," said the doctor—but Vlado could still make out its bitsy fingers. They were wiggling, playing an invisible baby piano.

Vlado put his arm around his cousin. "He's going to make it, Joey. What's his name?"

55

They weren't allowed to see Martina, so Stefani left with Inky to check on Janet Ivan and to rescue Joe's boys from Aunt Sophie. Vlado and Joe found the hospital cafeteria, where they settled into folding chairs at a small table, nursing stale coffee under bright fluorescents that interrogated Vlado's thoughts.

Finally, Vlado spoke. "About the other thing. The original deal with Johnny. I thought you wanted to do it."

"No, I thought you wanted to."

"I guess we both wanted it to happen."

"It was fucked up."

"It wasn't us."

"It wasn't you. All I thought about was the numbers."

"We're screwed, aren't we, Joey."

"I'm too tired to think about it."

They pondered on this. Vlado poured a little something into their coffee and they did a silent toast. He wandered over to the coffee bar and paid for two packages of Twinkies and some corn chips and brought them back to the table. Joe was slumped in his seat, eyes closed. Vlado took his herringbone coat and draped it over Joe, then sat down and opened his Twinkies, took a bite of its creamy sweetness and tried to ignore the fact that some large guy named Artemus was wandering around with his cane-of-attrition, looking for money he didn't have.

Someone was gently shaking Vlado's shoulder. He jerked awake in his chair, covered with his coat, stiff and confused, and saw that Joe was gone. Before he could speak, Stefani took his hands.

"Don't worry, he's with Martina. She's going to be fine."

Stefani helped him straighten up and nudged him a hot coffee. After a few moments, Vlado's memory filled the empty spaces.

"What about the baby?" He said, his worries bubbling up.

"The baby? You mean Patrick Vladimir Marevic?"

Vlado almost spit up his coffee.

"Just like Joe to give him an Irish name," he choked out.

"Unfair for him to steal all the good ones. What will we name ours?"

Vlado was seized with panic. "You're not—"

"No. But it doesn't mean we can't think about names."

Vlado daily regretted the fact that Stefani wasn't pregnant, but what if one day she turned out to be, and what would he do about that? He pushed the thought away, ashamed to imagine what that would mean. How was he ever going to get fucking Obersteen out of his head?

A nurse directed them to room 41, where Vlado peered through a tiny window and saw Joe sitting next to Martina's bed. She lay with her eyes closed, covered to her neck with blankets. Her hair, usually knotted in a tidy bun, splayed out over the pillow, as if she was done with it all. *Was she breathing?* Joe saw Vlado and came out to meet him.

"She's not as bad as she looks," Joe said and closed the door behind him. "They gave her something to make her sleep, and she'll be here a few days. She knows the baby's okay, which is the most important thing."

Vlado could feel Joe's relief calming his own anxiousness.

"The baby? You mean 'Patrick Vladimir Marevic'?"

Joe blushed a little. "I wanted to tell you myself."

"It's a terrible idea. I can't even say the whole thing without taking a breath in the middle. Plus, it'll be an impossible name to live up to."

"Hopefully he'll be up for the challenge."

"Not him, Joey. Me."

56

With Martina in the hospital, Stefani and Janet Ivan moved over to Joe's for a few days to take care of the boys. Vlado was glad they were away from the Hill, as he had no idea what to expect from their new pals from across the river. The garage on Orville remained unmolested, and Vlado could only guess at the stench inside from the chicken guts. They hadn't seen Obersteen since the party, which was fine with Vlado, who secretly hoped . . . well, no need for another sin to confess. Meanwhile, they'd closed Big Sausage for re-stocking, their locust-like neighbors having chewed through their entire inventory as if it was their last supper.

Tuesday morning, Bootnose and Inky sat in Stein's Office watching Vlado work the bone saw while Joe stuffed casings and twisted them up for the smoker. Nobody was talking and the slivovitz stayed stowed away in the cooler.

"What are you staring at?" Vlado asked Bootnose, who exchanged looks with Inky.

"Something's up with you guys," said Inky.

Vlado stared at his bone saw. "Like what?" Out of the corner of his eye he could see Bootnose squinting at him, maybe painfully, as if giving birth to a new thought.

"You said Martina and the baby would be okay," Bootnose said, eliminating for himself one option.

"And everybody loved the party, right?" Inky offered.

"But what was that crap Sinovic was playing?" Bootnose asked.

"It was romantic," Vlado said. "And there was poor Dorothy Penny, sitting by her lonesome waiting for someone to dance with her."

Bootnose grunted a curse, leaned back in his chair, and crossed one dirty boot over the other on the end of Vlado's carving table. Vlado thought how his saw was uniquely suited for slicing through leather, skin, and of course the bone that lay beneath it all.

"So?" said Bootnose.

"So what?" Vlado replied.

"So, what is it? The big secret. Something."

"You guys haven't said two words all day," added Inky.

"Maybe it's better you don't know," said Vlado, accidentally admitting there was something after all. "It's business, that's all."

Inky wasn't having it. "If it's business, then it's our business too."

Joe spoke to Vlado in Croatian. *Maybe we should tell them part of it. Not the police car and everything, but they need to be keeping their eyes open.*

Then the whole world is going to know.

Nah, they won't want to admit to it. I'll just tell them about the new place like it's a possibility but that some rough characters are opposed to the idea.

"Okay, knock it off, you two," said Inky.

"Right. Well. Here it is." The right words were just past Joe's grasp. "We didn't want to tell you until it was all a go, and then there was the thing with Martina—"

"Joe's trying to say we messed up. I couldn't go through with it. Anyhow, Inky, it was a great idea to dummy up a competing butcher shop, and that was the plan until—"

"Wait," Joe said.

"Wait what?"

"What you said. *That was the plan.* Why can't that actually *be* the plan? But no pretending. We take the space, use Poochie's loan to hire out, remodel, make more sausage . . ."

"But we were going to pay off Artie with that. And with no insurance money, how do we pay off Poochie? Aren't those the numbers you ran?"

"Right, but that just leaves us where we were months ago, all this nonsense for nothing. But what if we make a go of this new place? Forget that crap you have Inky making. And forget all those bullshit restaurants. Soon there will be bars, real bars, again, full of hungry drinkers, and you can only eat so many pickled eggs. We'll sell the shit out of

Vlado's Original Kobasa to hungry Missourians who have never tasted anything so wonderful."

"What about Artie? And the Big Tommy guy? I only hope they don't know it was us the other night."

Joe smiled. "Since when is it *my* job to talk *you* into some crazy deal? If it's going to be the annihilation, we might as well know."

Vlado looked at Joe with a heart full of admiration. "Well, if you're gonna go that far, who am I to say no? Yeah, we're already renting the place. Inky'll clean up the inside. We can do just sausage, no grocery, mostly wholesale so no fancy deal. Why not? In a hundred years we'll all be dead anyway."

Bootnose and Inky wore confused looks, listening to all this quietly. Inky was the first to speak.

"Who the hell is Big Tommy?"

57

Vlado and Joe agreed Morty's would be the safest place. Vlado warned Morty in advance and secured a booth in the back of the room, with instructions that only Morty could approach them. They were already in position when Artie arrived at the front door and Morty pointed him their way.

Artie stood next to the table. He nodded to Vlado, then looked at Joe and gave him a thin-lipped smile.

"I should have known it was you guys all along." He settled in opposite them. "But it doesn't change a thing." He pointed the head of his cane at Joe. "It just means you're on the hook too." He angled the cane on the seat next to him, within easy reach.

"Hey, first things first," Joe said, and beckoned to Morty who hurried over. "Do up a plate for three and, what? Some beer?" He looked at Artie, who shook his head and pulled a flask from his pocket. "Okay, just one bucket, and a bottle of Martell's."

"Martell's," Morty snorted. He returned shortly with the beer and his own murky version of brandy. He poured three growlers and left the carafe.

"Go ahead." Vlado nudged a glass toward Artie. "See how the other half lives."

Artie held up a glass and peered suspiciously into it. The cousins raised theirs and they all tossed it back.

"The only thing worse than that is one more," said Vlado, refilling the glasses.

This fell on an empty stomach and thankfully Morty showed up with a plate—pickled eggs, ham, budla, green onions and sauerkraut, and sliced disks of a garlicky-smelling sausage. Vlado picked out an egg and nudged the plate toward Artie, who speared some sausage and sauerkraut. They munched for a bit in silence, until Vlado spoke.

"Okay. So, you can kill us if you want. Probably not here, because look around. But every night I walk home up Sixth Street, and how easy would it be for a couple of guys in a car with a gun . . ."

Artie nodded, probably thinking how they could do just that.

"But I'm sure they'd screw it up like they did the other night," Vlado said.

"There were cops."

"Not our cops. We had them all at the party, you can ask anyone. And now you're coming for your money after not keeping up your end of the deal." Vlado tried to keep the quaver out of his voice. "You have a choice. We can pay you all the money Obersteen owes you, but then we don't have the money to pay back the loan, which we took out to make this whole deal happen. So, thanks to your chicken shit flunkies, there goes our business. You can come at us for more skim, but it won't do any good, because there'll be nothing to skim. And just to reiterate, it's not our fault your guys fucked up and left us in a hole."

Artie took another bite of sausage and sipped his beer. "You think I don't know what 'reiterate' means? Go fuck yourself. So, what's my other option?"

Joe said, "We're prepared to offer you a job."

"Your job can kiss my ass."

"You're here asking us for money, so we figured you might need one," Vlado said.

"I'm not asking." He ran one thumb along the silver head of his cane.

Joe reached for his pencil and began to scribble. "Let's not quibble about what to call it. Put it this way; we're willing to give the Artemis Distribution Company exclusive across-the-river rights to Big Sausage kobasa." He showed him a number. "We pay you a fair commission, just another version of what you had to muscle out of people before, but now it's on the up and up and everybody sleeps at night."

"That's a percentage of nothing," he said. "Your boy Johnny was not selling as much of your crap sausage as you think he was, which is what brought us to this point." He spoke as if he were explaining simple addition to a five-year-old. "Maybe I should talk to what's-his-name, Morty, about this stuff instead." He picked up the last disk of kobasa, popped it into his mouth, and chewed slowly, with an oddly happy look on his face.

Vlado looked at Joe, who could barely suppress a smile.

"I see we're all thinking the same thing," Joe said. He reached beside him and hoisted up the large package of kobasa wrapped in white butcher paper and plopped it on the table in front of Artie. "Take this home with you. Then get back to us. And a nice nutbread for your girlfriend." He produced a bag containing one of Martina's finest and positioned it next to the sausage.

"Have a party," Vlado said. "Invite your friends. Then we'll talk. Unfortunately, you know where to find us."

58

THE store reopened on Monday. The cousins spent a tense week carving and stuffing and selling to their cheerfully clueless customers who didn't realize this could all soon become a thing of the past. Friday afternoon was busy, with the Ladies' Vigilance Society parked as usual on their apple crates still jabbering about the party, while Inky stocked the shelves and Mrs. Divac wandered the aisles looking for God knows what. Vlado and Joe heard the squeak of brakes and the door jingle. They came out from the back to see two men in dark suits standing inside and flanking the entrance. A third man, stout and thick-featured with a ruddy complexion, dressed in a gray suit and matching homburg that seemed too formal for the occasion, walked in. He positioned himself in the middle of the room and peered around. The ladies quieted, and Inky stood there motionless, holding a can of carrots. The man strode past him and approached the counter. Vlado thought he looked familiar but couldn't place him. But whoever he was, he wasn't from around here.

"I just wanted to have a look-see," the man said in an engaging baritone. He pinched a piece of nutbread and chewed, surveying the room like he owned it. Over on the apple boxes, Mae Jankovic straightened up and fingered a curl that had escaped from her bun. The man turned toward Joe and Vlado. Up close, Vlado could see that he was probably about sixty, with fleshy cheeks.

"You the owners?"

No, we're just a couple of yahoos filling in while the owners are away, you know, on their own nefarious business, so hey, what do we know?

"Nice place you got here," he said, without waiting for an answer. Vlado listened for a tinge of sarcasm in his voice, but the guy seemed to be enjoying himself more than the occasion would have called for. He scanned the meat display and pointed to the smoked sausage.

"I'll take six of those. And wrap up another six for your buddy Stritchie." He leaned in and gave a dramatic whisper, "Tell him it's from Big Tommy." He smiled at a joke that apparently only he understood. Joe wrapped up the kobasa and the two guys from the door came up and grabbed them. The big guy reached toward Vlado, who flinched, but it was only to straighten Vlado's bow tie.

"You fellas are doing a good job. Keep it up," he said, then tipped his hat to the ladies and strode toward the door flanked by his two henchmen. He laughed and asked the guy on his left, "Am I really that big?" The door closed and they drove off, while everybody in the store stared at each other as if they shared a collective sense that something had happened, but they weren't sure what.

Vlado and Joe were in Stritchie's office, feeling a little sheepish about delivering him six rings of sausage like it was some big event, but who the hell was that guy?

Stritchie listened quietly to their story. "And then the guy said, 'You fellas are doing a good job, keep it up'?"

"Something like that," Vlado said.

"Exactly that," said Joe.

"Fucking Pendergast. He told me the same thing twenty years ago. He tells it to everybody. If they're lucky. But the guy knows his way around a fork, and you can count on him to make a deal. He just gave you his blessing, and whatever your deal is you're good to go."

"Pendergast? Tom Pendergast?" Vlado said. He'd heard so many stories about the mythical crime boss that he scarcely believed he actually existed.

"He likes to be called T. J. You don't know, but he set me up with all this way back when he was funneling cheap labor to the plants. Which meant jobs for you guys. People think he's a crook, and maybe he is if you apply the law. But he's got his own law, and people seem to be happy about it." He presented evidence for this by pouring them each a shot of something you'd never find at Morty's, which they tossed back.

"And don't worry, you're not going to see that clown with the cane again. Pendergast just wants people to get along, do nice things for each other. That was just some tough guy wannabe who's right now probably floating at the bottom of the Missouri." He must have seen the look on Vlado's face. "I'm kidding. Pendergast doesn't do stupid shit like that. He loves everybody."

"I'll drink to that," said Vlado, but Stritchie made no move to pour. Instead, he stood, which meant they were finished.

"So, when are you going to start fixing up that dump on Orville? I'll be your first customer. Go make some money so I can up the rent. And Vlado, no offense, but this stuff gives me heartburn. Why don't you take it over to Mae?"

Vlado and Joe sat in the front of the Model-T, stunned about what had just happened. Vlado felt like a condemned man who'd just received a call from the governor. The chronically sour feeling in his stomach had vanished and the world had gone from the black-and-white of his inner thoughts to a full-color rendition of a beautiful, blue-sky day. The air was crisp and dry, and just breathing in and out was a whole new pleasure.

"So, what now, mister happy man?" Joe said.

"I don't know. Are we supposed to just go over to Mae's and say 'Look, a present from your lover boy Stritchie'?"

Joe laughed. "Sure, why not?"

"You could give it to her, Joey. Give her the sausage."

"Yeah, well, let's not forget it's Stritchie's sausage."

"Tough luck for you."

The following Monday, a truck labeled ACME Meats grumbled up the alley behind Big Sausage. A couple of young guys in eight-piece Irish caps, work shirts, and suspenders hopped out and met Vlado at the back door. One was shuffling through papers on a clipboard.

"Big Sausage, right? We got an order for fifty units of . . . what is this?" He showed Vlado an invoice.

"This stuff." Vlado indicated the back of the display case, where Joe was already pulling out rings and wrapping them.

Vlado laughed. "Once you get used to the smell, you'll never eat corned beef again." He wrapped up a ring for each of them, adding in a handful of freshies. "Maybe wait until after you're done smooching with Colleen."

"Your balls," said one of them, and they both laughed.

"Here's the thing," Joe said. "You caught us a little short, so we got twenty-five, and the rest will be ready Thursday."

"Then I guess we'll just pay you half today."

"No need," said Vlado. "First batch is on the house."

The lads loaded the rings into the back of the van, and Joe gave Vlado a dim look.

"*Don't worry Jozo, this plan has never failed us before. Like T.J. says, it's about doing nice things for people.*"

"*T.J.? Vrag, your new best friend?*"

"*We're still here, aren't we?*"

The boys were in the truck and about to pull off when the driver said, "Hey, here. This is for you." He handed a bottle out the window to Vlado. "The good stuff's gonna be legal soon, so we gotta get rid of the old inventory."

They drove off, leaving Vlado to look at the bottle, marveling at its clarity. He gave the cork a twist and found three glasses, then a fourth when he heard Boyko Meats rumbling down the alley. Bootnose stomped in and Vlado poured.

"I've got this," said Inky. He adjusted his tie and cleared his throat. He held his glass up and stared into it.

"Well?" said Vlado.

"Okay, okay." He pitched his voice into a high register and announced, "May the best day of your past be the worst day of your future."

Vlado gave Inky a perplexed look.

"What the fuck is that?" said Bootnose.

Inky shrugged. "I don't know, some dumb thing McGowan's always saying. I think it means *zivjeli*."

They all drank, and Vlado almost cried from the smooth burn of the gin. He looked at the four empty glasses in front of him.

"Fine, one more, but we gotta save the rest for Morty."

59

The baby was still at the hospital, but Martina was home, cranky and bedridden, and according to Joe, mercifully clueless about all the monkey business down in Armourdale. Vlado was still putting off telling Stefani about the new venture. He and the boys had been down at the Orville location every night after work, cleaning and painting and setting up the new cooler, and he'd been coming home later than usual. Smelling of turpentine. Certainly, she knew something was up, and he figured he better spill the beans before Inky blabbed it all to Tereza. Maybe just mention something during the height of passion. A kiss, a squeeze, and, *Honey we're putting all our money into a service station in Armourdale.* Or wait till afterwards, even better.

That night, Vlado left Orville early, hoping to catch Stefani at a reasonable hour. He stopped by Big Sausage for a plate of sarma and a bottle of Lubo's homemade wine he'd been saving for an occasion. Why shouldn't it be a celebration? He entered the house quietly, listened, and heard Stefani singing softly behind Janet Ivan's closed door. This seemed like a good sign, and he went into the kitchen to warm the sarma and open the wine. He was pulling out two glasses when Stefani appeared silently in the doorway.

"What are you doing here?" she asked.

"Lovely to see you too." He held up the bottle. "I thought I'd come home early and see if we could—"

"I mean what are you doing here in general? Why are you here at all?" She remained in the doorway, arms crossed.

"Okay, I get it. I haven't been around much, but now I have something to tell you that I should have told you before, but I was worried how you might take it."

"I was wondering if you ever planned on telling me?" She looked ready to cry. *So she already knows? Fucking Inky.*

"Come on, Stef, it's not that big a deal."

"What could possibly be a bigger deal?" Her voice welled up, which meant any subsequent tear would be over his dead body. "What if I were to tell you I was pregnant?"

"Pregnant? Are you pregnant?"

"No, but what if I said I was? What would you think?"

"What do you think I would think?"

"It doesn't matter, Vlado. I'm not pregnant. And it looks like I'm never going to be again. So, what do you think about that?"

Vlado felt his boat taking on water.

"You already know about that, then."

"Dr. Dubrowski is like a son to my mother."

"So that makes him what, my half-brother-in-law?"

"You can joke, Vlado, but—"

"I get it. You know. And I was going to tell you. But I've been more busy than you can imagine. And I knew this would be a whole big thing. Which apparently it is."

The trick with Stefani was to stay on the offensive, one step further down the road to his own demise. *Jebote.* Then he noticed she was shaking and helped her into a kitchen chair. He offered to pour some wine, but she shook her head.

"I'm sorry, Vlado. I really thought it was you. Was yours. Janet Ivan . . . I wasn't trying to . . . it was just the one time."

Vlado waited for her to continue, but apparently that was it. He'd known, of course, in the abstract, but now it was a reality backed by a confession. He tried not to imagine the crime scene.

"I knew about Lydia. I was angry. No, I was hurt. Or stupid."

"Stef, I don't really want to hear—"

"You can just fucking well listen. Because you had a part in all this. I'm at Morty's, without you as usual, and I've got this slob of a guy buying me drinks but at least he's listening to my woes and before you know it, I'm thinking why are you the only one who gets to do whatever you want? But it was horrible. I was so drunk all I remember is how bad he smelled. It was over quick, and he left right after. Thankfully, I guess. But somehow that made it worse."

Vlado thought about Lydia, how he'd gotten right out of there first thing in the morning.

"Then later, when I found out, I was, you know, I couldn't stand the thought that it might be Johnny's. Like I could just erase that one night. I mean, what's the point of even being Catholic if every mistake you make follows you your whole goddam life?"

Hearing her actually say Johnny's name was more of a punch to the gut than he would have thought. Vlado remembered the confusion when this all started and how it had hurt his head to think too much about it. And how nervous he'd been. And angry, because why wouldn't Stefani want to marry him? You couldn't wait around for the truth, there was no way to be sure of anything. So he'd blundered on, and now here they were, like nothing he'd ever imagined.

"No," he said abruptly, as if the one word could make it all go away.

"Admit it, Vlado, you only married me because you thought I had your baby in there."

Maybe she was right. Without a baby coming, would he have been so desperate for her? Who knows why you do anything except it seems like the right thing at the time? If there'd been no war in Croatia, would he and Joe have left and found themselves in this new world of their own making? He could have gone chasing after Lydia. Or stayed the night with the piano player. Or drowned in the fucking river. But he didn't, and here he was in the kitchen—their kitchen. Suddenly he was aware of his own workmanlike odor, mixed with the sour cabbage and the hint that a nutbread had been baked here recently, and a whiff of angry perspiration from across the table. No, she wasn't angry, he realized, but something different. Disrespected by Johnny. And by him. She was *ashamed*, he suddenly realized. When all along the shame should be his.

He stared at Stefani, sexy even in her ratty nightgown, but that wasn't it. Not the sex. Something more that he didn't think about. Like air or light, things you don't notice until they're not there. Or might not be.

"Look, Stef, you told me right up front it wasn't mine. I could have believed you and never got on that bus to Paola. But deep down, you wanted me to be the father. And that's what I wanted. So here we are. Where we should be."

She bit her lip and her blue eyes glistened.

"Stef, don't cry. Please. It's more than I can stand."

A single tear inched down one cheek.

"I don't care what anybody says," he said. "That's our little girl sleeping in there. Come on, let's go to bed. We'll figure it out tomorrow."

60

Joe had been spending more time with Martina, so the next morning, Vlado rose before dawn, left his sleeping girls, and headed out to open the store. If there were birds and weather and trees and happy sounds of the Hill awakening, he had no idea. With each step a single thought pounded into his head. *Stefani should have been angry with him.* How could she think any of this was *her* fault?

He unlocked the door and stepped into the reassuring atmosphere of grease and smoke. Inky and Bootnose would be down at Orville all day—they were hoping to get things cranked up by next week—which meant Vlado would have some merciful time to himself before Joe arrived. He walked back to Stein's Office and opened the cooler, where he stood in the doorway with his eyes closed and let the cold air waft around him, hoping to chill the buzzing in his head he'd felt since his talk with Stefani. He sensed there was something he hadn't taken into account, but the niggling thought was hidden behind a fireworks display of regret and self-accusation.

He took down the rings of sausage in the cooler and strung them up in the smoker outside, then filled the firebox with kindling and got a small flame going. He tossed on a couple of logs, closed the lid to dampen the fire, and soon a thin blue line of smoke wafted from the chimney. For a long time, he watched the smoke curl into the brightening sky. He didn't know how long he'd been standing there when he heard the front door jingle. Vlado went in to see who wanted what and found himself face-to-face with Obersteen.

"I hear how you fucked up the whole plan," Johnny said. Vlado hadn't seen him since the party, and now here he was, like a knee to the chest. Obersteen's look of nonchalance immediately irritated Vlado. If anybody should be worried about something, it was Johnny boy.

"What are you talking about? Nothing's fucked up."

"I ran into Inky down at the so-called undisclosed location."

"Well, okay, so there's a new plan now."

"Yeah, he told me about that too. Nice work. Good for the partnership." Johnny's thick lips stretched into a smile that seemed like a personalized invitation for Vlado's fist.

"There is no partnership, Johnny. You screwed the pooch on this one and should be grateful we bailed you out."

"I knew you'd take that attitude. But hey, you don't want me around, I'm happy to be, what is it, a silent partner? Which is to say, I have better things to do than hang around this grease pit. As long as I get my share, I promise you'll never see me."

Better things? A dangerous thought was surfacing in Vlado's head. "Better things like what?" he asked, and suddenly Obersteen was at a loss for words. Why had Obersteen been at his house with Stefani that day? An old friend visiting? He knew now they were more than "old friends," unless Janet Ivan was a result of an immaculate conception. What was really going on between those two? Suddenly the unfortunate conclusion he'd been resisting popped to the surface of his mind. His cheeks burned. *What kind of a fool Stefani had taken him for?*

The back door opened and then Joe was standing next to him.

"I thought I smelled something," Joe said to Obersteen.

"Okay, so we'll just skip the pleasantries? Fine. I'm here because I'm your partner and want to congratulate you guys on a job well done. We're all going to make a lot of money."

"There is no 'we,' Johnny, unless you mean Vlado and me."

"Hey, a deal is a deal. And besides, you're going to need me to make sure you don't screw up this next phase of the operation."

"And how the fuck would that happen?" asked Vlado.

"It's like this," Johnny said. "Somebody's eventually going to get wind of what you guys tried to do."

"Us guys? What about you?"

"Me? I was at a party when it all went down. And for that matter, where were you?"

"So how is anybody going to get wind?" Joe asked.

"Who knows how it might get out? But what if someone comes sniffing around asking questions? What am I supposed to do, lie?"

Joe must have sensed Vlado's agitation, because he lightly stepped on Vlado's foot.

Johnny went on. "I mean, bottom line, who wants to get accused of attempted insurance fraud?"

Vlado leaned in toward Johnny. "Are you threatening us?"

"Threatening? Come on, I'm just trying to look out for the business. *Our* business." The smug smile was back, and Vlado wondered if a knife or a tenderizing hammer would best accomplish the business he had in mind.

Joe switched to Croatian. *I know what you're thinking, Vlado, but don't do anything stupid right now. We can always do that later. As it stands, he's got us, and we're going to have to take our time and figure something out.*

I could solve all this right here, Joey.

We'll be in for a lot worse than insurance fraud.

How come you always make so much fucking sense?

"You know, you guys sound like a couple of monkeys when you jabber on like that. Hopefully you're talking about how we can put all this behind us and move forward."

Joe's head indicated the door. "I don't think there's anything more to be said for now. We'll be in touch."

Johnny tightened his lips and gave them a reptilian gaze. "I'm sure we will." He popped on his fedora and turned toward the door, almost knocking over Mrs. Divac.

Joe sighed at her. "Sorry. No tomatoes."

Vlado didn't hear her response because he was already heading out the back. Time to get things straight with Stefani, once and for all.

61

Vlado strode with a sense of purpose, a man with a mission—an ever-shifting mission, apparently—which meant he had no idea what to do but was determined to do it anyway. How many people knew about Stefani's affair with Johnny? It was going on right under his nose. Well, not exactly that; he hadn't been around much. But what, was he supposed to hang around the house all day to make sure his dear wife didn't . . . *Jebote*. He thought back to their wedding day, the party at Joe's, where he had to shrug away the idea that everyone was laughing at him. And now, despite all he'd done, everything he and Joe had built, his house, a little family all his own, he was still and again some clown on Strawberry Hill, just another stupid Croat who couldn't see past his own perpetually out-of-joint nose.

He pumped up the hill towards Barnett, the rude sunlight stinging his eyes and his thoughts hammering like the pistons in his dearly departed Studebaker. He was about to turn down his street when he spied a silhouette of someone sitting on a bench on the bluffs overlooking the Kaw. He recognized the yellow topcoat he'd given Stefani for Christmas.

She sat there clutching her large handbag and didn't look up when Vlado approached. He edged down next to her, ready to have it out, then not ready at all. She continued to gaze over the river, and not knowing what to say, Vlado did likewise. After a dry couple of months, the Kaw's water levels had receded, with long sandbars fingering into the remains of the muddy channel. Stefani pointed to something out in the middle that glinted in the bright sunlight.

"Is that your car?"

Vlado squinted, and sure enough, he could see part of a fender and a headlight poking out of the muddy water, giving him an accusing stare.

He stared back and felt his anger sag and a wave of melancholy wash over him. Stefani turned toward him.

"I've been out here all morning." Her green eyes were dull and her expression flat. "I haven't been honest with you."

So here it was. She'd beat him to the punch, ready to confess and end it all, and what could he do but sit here and take it?

"That day Johnny came by to visit me. You've probably figured out by now that it was more than just an old friend stopping by."

Yes, it had only taken him all night and all morning to put two and two together until he came up with four. Brilliant. *Okay, let me have it.*

"That day. I was so surprised to see him I didn't say anything when he just walked right in and closed the door behind him. He brought flowers, which seemed weird. We sat on the couch, and I asked him why he was here. He told me then that he was sorry, that the whole time in Topeka all he could think about was me. He kept scootching closer. I just wanted him to go. Then he said he loved me. That he could make me happy, and what was I doing with a loser like you. Janet Ivan was playing there on the floor, and he'd give her a look, then me, and smile in a creepy way. I just kept talking to get him to shut up. I told him how you took care of me, of Janet, that you were doing a great business, selling all this sausage to Katz. I should have chased him out, but I couldn't, like he's somehow stuck inside of all this."

"Did he—?"

"He didn't touch me, but it felt like he had." Vlado could feel her agitation, which spoke to the truth of her words. "I'm sorry, Vlado, I should have told you. But I knew how you'd be, and with everything going so well; maybe Johnny would just get the message and disappear. Then suddenly he's all in your business, and it's my fault." Vlado could see she'd been crying before, but now it seemed like she'd used it all up.

"Did he ever come back?"

"I don't know. Yes. A few times, but I didn't answer the door. Once he peered through the front window and saw me. Then I heard him walk to the stoop and then nothing for a while, no knocking or anything. Like he was just standing there. I felt like I couldn't move or breathe, until finally I heard him walk off and the sound of that ratty old pickup of his."

Vlado thought how he'd seen Obersteen's truck parked at the top of the street, for no reason he could figure, and wondered how many other things he didn't see because he was too damn busy with whatever else he thought was more important. *Jebote.*

"Ever since, when I see him," Stefani went on, "like when we're all together, he gives me this look, like we have some secret arrangement. It's awful."

Vlado said, "So that night at the restaurant when you were all 'Johnny this, Johnny that'—"

"I was—"

"Nervous. Now I get it."

He reached for her hand and gave it a squeeze, and the answering pressure told him everything he needed to know. He stared at the tip of his car in the river, then past that, downstream, to Kaw Point, where the Missouri ate up anything the Kaw had to offer. The thoughts that had been spiraling all morning wound down to a stop, and a new idea formed in his head.

"I know how to fix this," he said.

"No, Vlado, I knew you'd jump all over this, but you'll just make things worse. I don't want you in jail."

"Ha, nobody's going to jail. Stefani, I swear, I know how to fix this. But I need your help."

She gave him a resigned look.

"And you're not going to like it."

62

Thunderstorms had been hammering the upstream farmland all afternoon, and by now the river shrugged up against the banks on its way toward Kaw Point, where a bulky figure stumbled down the hill in the light of the half moon. He held a bottle in one hand and a coarse army blanket in the other, and he cursed at the roots snagging his feet and the willows slapping at his face. Vlado knew this because he and Joe were crouched in the bushes just off the narrow path watching Johnny Obersteen, aka Ovaltine, lurch toward his special appointment. Convincing Stefani had been surprisingly easy—"Tell him he's all you've been able to think about"—and here was Johnny, as promised, like a fat catfish mouthing the bait.

They let Johnny get a ways down the trail, then followed him to where the bushes opened into a small clearing that sloped down to the water, surrounded on three sides by a copse of elms. Vlado thought back to Zagreb, when he and Joe would hole up in Vlado's secret spot on the Sava River, where they had a goatskin of booze and a ratty mattress stashed beneath a weeping willow. It was a few years before the mattress got any use, and mostly they'd smoke and drink and imagine building a raft that could take them all the way to the Danube.

The cousins got as close as they could, shielded by the last line of trees. Vlado swigged from his flask and passed it to Joe.

"*The worst batch ever,*" he whispered to Joe, which is what they used to say every time they purloined some homemade wine from Aunt Vera's unguarded barrel.

Joe gave the customary reply. *"It'll put hair on your balls."*

Past the meadow, the land curved outward and narrowed to where a single gas lamp marked the grand confluence of the Kansas and Missouri Rivers. Its dim glow conspired with the half-moon to cast their surroundings in a shadowy twilight. Far upriver, silent heat lightning illuminated a bank of thunderheads. Obersteen dropped the bottle and spread the blanket into a neat square, straightened one edge, then stepped back as if to take it all in. He looked all around then stuck his hands in his jacket pockets and faced the river, shifting his weight from one leg to another and occasionally glancing back at the bushes behind him.

Let's give him a little time to worry about it, Vlado whispered.

Fine, I like listening to the birds, Joe whispered back.

And there were the birds, doing their regular nighttime chit-chat, flitting from moment to moment with a song in their heart and a willingness to fly off to wherever the breeze might lead. Vlado thought if he were a bird, what would his song be: the ratchety tamburitzans, maybe, or Sinovic's accordion with its polkas and arias. "Night and Day" dancing off the pianist's fingertips, the confident strut of the "Junk Man Rag," the brash big bands at the Starlight, or Hot Lips Page blasting out of Joe's Victrola. It all seemed like part of the same song, all of it in time or in tune with the jingle of the Big Sausage bell and the clang of the smoker door and the murmur of the swelling Kaw and the Armour whistle and the chatter of the ladies at the counter who testified to the interweaving destinies of God's good people. Some grand symphony. Vlado felt like he was being pulled out of himself, like that first night at the Lo-Ball when he followed the piano notes over the edge, but this time he stayed anchored in the moment with the certainty that whatever happened next had been ordained since the beginning of time. *As it was in the beginning, is now, and ever shall be*—is that how it went? *Jebote.*

He heard a not quite birdlike whistle from off to his right. *Inky.*

Vlado nudged Joe. *Come on, junk man, let's do this.*

Joe clicked on a flashlight and the cousins strode into the clearing as if they were on a Sunday afternoon stroll, approaching Johnny until Vlado could make out the confused look on his face.

"What are you guys doing here?" He squinted against the light.

Vlado gave him a surprised look. "Johnny. Are you having a picnic?"

Obersteen looked nervously past them up the trail.

"Never mind," said Vlado, "Whoever she is, it's none of our business. Hey, I mean, good for you. Right, Joey? Ovaltine's going to get some, and we should put aside our differences and pay our respects to Don Juan here. As for us, Johnny, I got a little boat over there and we're going fishing."

"Fishing? At night?" Johnny looked at them like they were nuts.

"You never went night fishing? It's amazing what you can catch with the right bait. Sometimes they jump right into the boat."

He and Joe stood and took in the evening air. Joe looked out over the water, pointed to something far away, then let his arm drop.

"It's a nice night," he said.

"A little cool," said Vlado. He slowly buttoned up his sweater.

"Might be warmer tomorrow." Joe licked a finger and stuck it in the air.

Vlado paused to give it some careful consideration. "Or maybe cooler, huh?"

Obersteen kept glancing up the trail and Vlado could almost hear the squeak of his piano strings tightening. *Say it, say it!*

"Why don't you guys show me your boat," Obersteen said then, fulfilling the words of the prophets.

"What about your, um, friend?" Joe said.

"It's okay, I'm early. Come on, let's have a look."

"I don't know, Joey," said Vlado, "then he'll know our secret fishing spot."

"I'm thinking maybe we can trust him."

"Yeah, I swear, I don't even fish." Johnny's voice pitched upward.

Vlado shrugged. "Okay, then." He pointed his flashlight at a gap in the willows and led them on a muddy path that kept wanting to dip into the swollen river, forcing them back through the bushes until they could pick it up again. Johnny was grumbling something about his shoes and swatting at real or imagined spiderwebs when they got to the place where Inky had stashed the little rowboat. It was tied to a half-submerged log, with its bow drifting back and forth, scanning the invisible horizon of water like a divining rod.

"Nice, right?" Vlado dragged off the canvas cover and tossed it to Johnny, who caught it heavily. "Fold that up, will you?"

"Hey, you know what?" said Joe. "Johnny should come with us."

"He should definitely come with us," Vlado agreed. "What do you say?"

Obersteen looked confused, if not a little ridiculous, standing in the mud clutching the tarp to his chest.

"I don't fish. And besides, I've got a thing going, you know, and should probably get back."

Vlado looked at Joe. "You want to tell him?"

"You tell him."

Vlado got so close to Obersteen's face he could see the beads of sweat on his upper lip.

"She's not coming," he said. Johnny started blinking rapidly. "She has other plans. She's always had other plans."

Anything Obersteen might have said was interrupted by a thrashing in the bushes. Inky emerged from the darkness dragging a metal tub followed by Bootnose, who carried a cane pole with no line attached.

"What's he doing here?" Inky asked Vlado in a loud whisper as if Johnny couldn't hear him.

Bootnose said, "I think he wants to go fishing with us." He turned to the confused Johnny. "Hey, I brought you a pole." Bootnose pointed the blunt end of the cane pole at Johnny. He held it like a pool cue, sighted down it and mimed a shot, jabbing him in the ribs.

Obersteen backed toward the water. He dropped the tarp and scanned the four of them. "Okay, I get it, you guys are always fucking with me. Very funny, you got me."

Bootnose got closer and started to prod Johnny in the belly, pushing him further backwards. "Your choice, big boy. You can get in the boat, or you can get in the river."

Vlado laughed and clapped his hands, chanting "Boat, boat, boat, boat," and the other three joined in.

"Okay you motherfuckers, this time I'm calling your bluff." Obersteen turned and grabbed onto the boat's stern and tried to lift one leg over. Inky and Bootnose helped hoist him into the craft, which wobbled and settled deeper into the water. Johnny lurched up to the prow, sat down heavily, and looked back at them, arms folded.

"There, you happy? So, come on, you fuckers, let's go fishing. Right? You're so full of shit."

Vlado reached down to untie the craft while Inky and Bootnose hoisted the tub into the back of the boat.

"What's that?" Obersteen asked.

"Sandwiches and water," replied Inky. "Might be out there a while, if they're not biting."

Then he and Bootnose waded out to either side of the boat and lifted the oars from the locks and handed them back to Joe and Vlado, who used them to push the tiny craft away from the shore and toward the current whipping around the sandbar.

"Wait a minute," Johnny said. The panic of realization quivered in his voice. He tried to stand, but the boat jiggled, and he plopped back down. "Hey, I can't even swim."

"Better stay in the boat, then." Bootnose, the voice of reason.

The craft was taking its sweet time drifting off, and Vlado savored each lingering moment with a satisfaction he never knew was possible.

"We're doing you a favor, Johnny. Tom Pendergast knows about your little scam on Orville," Vlado yelled.

"Mine? That was you fuckers." His words were echoing off the banks.

"I don't know, apparently nobody remembers seeing you at the party."

Obersteen let out a stream of curses but shut up when the tip of the tiny craft caught the current, which spun it north like a compass needle and urged it on toward the point and beyond.

Vlado shouted to him, "Just remember, Johnny, this river only flows one way."

Apparently Obersteen had run out of arguments. The four of them watched the boat grow dim in the swirling mist until it passed Kaw Point, bucked to the right, and disappeared into the clutch of the Mighty Mo'.

Inky beamed his flashlight across the water. "You think he's all right?"

"He'll be fine if he stays in the goddam boat," Joe said.

"I'm sure somebody will pick him up before St. Louis," said Vlado. *At least the asshole had a boat.* "Come on, I know where there's a decent bottle of wine."

Twenty minutes later, the birds in the surrounding elms were stunned into silence, listening to four voices veering recklessly around a familiar melody,

Meet me in St. Louis, Loo-ie . . .

We'll dance the hoochee koochee-ee, Loo-ie . . .

63

"You should have been there to see it," Vlado was telling Stefani. "He looked like the lost captain of the S.S. Go Fuck Yourself."

"Well, I *was* supposed to be there." They were drying the dinner dishes together while Vlado told her the story for the second time, reliving for himself every choice detail.

"I don't think we'll see him again."

Stefani dropped her dishrag and squeezed Vlado from behind and rested her head in the crook of his neck. She held on for a long time, then dropped her arms and quietly left the room. He followed her to the divan in the dark living room, and without turning on a light, sat down next to her. He knew what she was thinking about, and it wasn't Johnny. Or Lydia. He put an arm around her and kissed her softly on the cheek.

"Maybe it's for the best," he said, thinking of Martina. Little Patrick was home from the hospital. The doctors said he'd survive, but there would be problems. "Developmental difficulties," they'd called it. Joe was concerned that Martina refused to leave the house, that she felt too ashamed. He didn't know what to do.

"Think of it," Vlado continued. "Our perfect little girl in the next room dreaming about clouds and ice cream. How could we top that?" He pulled her close. "And we can still do it for fun, right?" He slid his free hand toward her breast, but she took the hand, kissed it, and clutched it to her belly.

"Vlado," she said, "You're a mess."

"But I'm your mess, right?"

She let go of his hand. "It's all a mess. I don't know." She got up and went to the bedroom, leaving Vlado alone in the dark with his confusion. Some things can't be fixed. The cruel rules of nature. Sometimes there was no dealing with God, or whoever was laying down the cards. Soon, exhausted by his thoughts, he slumped back on the couch and drifted into sleep, where he dreamt of babies falling from the sky.

There was no grand feast to mark the opening of the new place on Orville. The joint was still pretty shabby, with peeling paint, oil-soaked floors, and a lingering whiff of chicken guts. But the cooler was humming and they could start slicing up pigs and get some product into the brick smoker Joe had built in the back. On Sunday, after Morty's, the four of them assembled around a card table in the garage bay to figure how to get the ball rolling. At least Joe had procured a nice bottle of slivovitz for the occasion. Prohibition was all but finished, and first-rate booze had started appearing on the shelves. He poured four shots and Inky raised his glass.

"To our founder and fearless leader, the captain of our ship . . ."

Vlado felt himself sit up a little straighter . . .

"—a man whose girth is only exceeded by his appetite . . ."

Vlado's hand drifted to his belly, okay, admittedly happier than it used to be . . .

"—the favorite of the single ladies and an inspiration to us all—"

"And getting thirstier every second." Vlado tipped his glass toward Inky, who grinned at him.

"To the Ovaltine," Inky shouted. He started braying like a goat, and all the glasses met in the middle.

"And to everyone on the bus," Bootnose said happily.

"The bus?" Inky said.

"Yeah, Dorothy Penny says he's driving a bus. In St. Joe," Bootnose said.

"How does she know?"

"I think Mae told her."

"How does Mae know?"

"I don't know. Martina? How does anybody know anything?"

Vlado'd figured Johnny must have eventually washed ashore, but it was still strange to think he was really somewhere, really doing something. As long as it wasn't here.

Joe pulled out his pencil and notebook. He scribbled down a few numbers and stroked his chin in apparent confusion.

"It doesn't add up."

"What doesn't?" Vlado asked, as if he didn't know. Inky and Bootnose leaned in for a look.

"Right here. This percentage." Joe flashed around the number. "Johnny's cut."

"I get it, Joey, what are we supposed to do with that? Who could possibly fill those shoes?"

He and Joe locked eyes, all serious.

"What?" said Inky.

Vlado tried to keep a straight face. "Maybe we need somebody around who can get some actual work done." He and Joe turned towards Inky and Bootnose.

Bootnose looked puzzled. "What do you mean? Don't we do a good enough job?"

Inky said, "You dummy, I think they're making us partners."

"I thought we were already partners."

Vlado suddenly felt a rush of affection for the big guy. "You are, Zoran. You always have been. But now we're going to pay you for it." He raised his glass, as did everyone else. "As it was in the beginning, is now, and ever shall be," he said. The glasses met in the middle, and the deal was sealed. Joe poured another round.

"One thing," Vlado said. "I'm pretty busy, what with running the store and taking care of the little one, not to mention our regular business meetings at Morty's." He walked over to the carving table and returned with a long knife. He stared at it as if it could reveal the mysteries of the universe and ran one thumb lightly along its razor edge. He set it carefully in front of Inky.

"You think you can manage to not stab yourself to death?" he asked. Inky looked confused. "Well, somebody has to run this godforsaken place."

64

That week, Vlado made it home for dinner every night. He boiled oxtails and sauerkraut, fried up lamb chops, and on Saturday, simmered a batch of short ribs with the homemade egg noodles that fake-Aunt-Vera whipped up on a regular basis. Anything but sausage. Janet Ivan was thrilled, and after dinner she sat on the floor of the kitchen with her daddy where they put saucepans on their heads and pretended to be soldiers. Stefani was polite, but remote. Every night she washed the dishes and excused herself to the living room to listen to her stories on the radio, while Vlado put Janet Ivan to bed. By the time Vlado pulled himself under the sheets, Stefani would inevitably be asleep, turned to the wall.

On Sunday morning, he held himself to one drink at Morty's and begged off when the pinochle deck appeared. It would have been a good time to go down to his boat and think things over, but that ship had sailed, as it were. He'd always been able to give Stefani everything she needed, and he was mortified by his inability to do so now. He didn't want to go home and sit in the living room like it was some eternal waiting room for heaven. If there was a heaven. But heaven or not, he knew that if he looked to his left the crossed tower of St. John's would gazing down at him. He turned toward the church, thinking at least he could have a quiet moment with his loud thoughts.

Mass was still going on. Father gave the blessing, and then everyone was singing. Even from the back pew, Vlado could hear Inky's wife Tereza warbling over the top while the few men who were there grumbled like misfiring car engines. Voices meandered around in the middle trying to agree on the right moment to sing "panis angeligus," the whole insurgency urged forward by the bellowing organ. Somewhere around the fifth verse, Father Oyster genuflected and turned toward the door, solemnly dragging one foot after another, followed by four altar boys and a cross bearer, like a rag-tag army shuffling away from the front lines.

Vlado must have fallen asleep, because suddenly he was aware that the church was silent and empty. Except someone was sitting next to him.

"It's unusual to see you here." The Holy Oyster himself.

"Miracles happen," was all Vlado could think to say, and Father Kovac's pinched face attempted a smile.

"Am I interrupting?"

"Yeah, I was trying to think of how to make the rivers run backwards, but now I've lost my train of thought." Vlado sighed. "No, Father, you're not . . . Father? I can't call you that. I already have a father, who died when I was a kid."

"Fine. It's Milenko, then. Or Milo, if you prefer." With that he reached into his neck and detached the white collar from his tunic and set it on the pew. "This thing."

Vlado'd never thought of a priest having a first name. "So, Father Kovac is really just some guy named Milo."

"Yeah, like you're just some guy named Vlado. But we both know it's more than that."

So Kovac knew as well. That there's something beyond all this, which he hated to admit was sort of a Catholic way of thinking.

"She's a lovely girl, Stefanija. You did good."

In spite of you, Vlado first thought, but then why pick another fight when his hands were already full?

"Thank you, Father," he said instead. "Huh, I guess 'Father' works best after all. And maybe I shouldn't be talking to you here, outside the box and all . . ."

"The box. That's good. Even I sometimes think it's silly. Mostly it brings comfort to the ladies. But you don't have to tell me anything, Vlado. Odds are, whatever it is, I already know." Kovac paused and seemed to be considering his words. "I should have been more grateful. The meat deliveries, you know."

"Well, it's not like Stritchie gave us a choice."

"You didn't have to keep doing it."

Vlado wanted to explain to him his whole genius business plan of giving things away, but suddenly it didn't seem like a business plan at all. What choice did he have? He was Croatian, which means everybody eats! Oh well, at least after Stefani left him to find a real man who could crank out a decent brood, he could still hang around as St. Vlad and make all the kiddies happy.

"Anyhow," Kovac gave him a pat on the knee. "It's good to see you here." He stood to leave, and Vlado picked up the white collar.

"Don't forget this."

He stuck it into the folds of his robe. "I think I'll take the rest of the day off." He rustled out of the pew then turned back to Vlado. "And you should do the same," he said, and then Vlado had the church—and for all he knew, the entire world—to himself.

65

Vlado moved listlessly through his week. Big Sausage was strangely quiet not having Inky and Bootnose around. Presumably they had things in hand down at Orville. But either way, he didn't care. He couldn't take on the whole goddam world. Joe was lost in his own thoughts about Martina and little Patrick, and Vlado slogged along, slicing and grinding and trying not to think about anything. *Might as well still be on the line at Armour.*

Thursday night arrived, the first Thursday of the month, which meant the orphans. Vlado and Joe were closing up and getting ready to load the leftover chops and whatnot into Vlado's Model-T, when Joe said he had to go home, something about Martina. Vlado objected.

"I hate doing it alone. Like I'm some servant."

"Trust me, you can do it without me tonight," Joe said, looking like he didn't want to discuss it anymore.

At least Joe helped him wrap it all up in butcher paper and load it into the car. Vlado throttled up the hill to the orphanage where, as usual, Father "Milo" Kovac was waiting at the bottom of the stairs.

To Vlado's surprise, Kovac joined him in pulling the packages out of the trunk and hauling them up to the orphanage kitchen. It took three trips, at the end of which the Oyster was breathing heavily.

"Why don't we have a drink?" Kovac said.

Some deep instinct in Vlado said *get the hell out of there*, but then he figured, why not? He was curious what the Oyster might have in his liquor cabinet, and moreover, figured that maybe his new pal Milo didn't have many drinking buddies. Unless you counted "tea" with the Vigilance Society.

Vlado shrugged. "Lead on."

He anticipated heading back to the rectory, but instead Kovac led him down a hallway of the old mansion and into a sitting room, where softly lit Tiffany lamps cast a yellowish glow on flowery wallpaper and lace-adorned windows. Carved mahogany surrounded a stone hearth where a fire happily blazed, next to which a calico ragdoll lounged on a heart-shaped wooden rocker. Against one wall stood a parlor-sized piano, no doubt the prized possession of the previous owners who had gifted the house to the orphanage. Vlado tried to imagine the family that had lived here, in this manicured perfection—Father with his high collar and necktie, Mother with her spectacles and crocheting, girls in pinafores and boys in short pants and suspenders rolling marbles across the dark-stained floors. He felt like he was standing inside a magazine advertisement for better living. Next to the fireplace, Vlado spied a small table with crystal glasses and a couple of decanters half-filled with a promising golden liquid.

But Kovac hadn't made a move toward the booze. Vlado looked around and saw, against the back wall, a large divan, with scrolling arms and a carved wooden back as elegant as the Habsburg emblem. Seated in the center was a woman with her head lowered. Then she raised her head and looked at him. It was Stefani. So that was Kovac's plan, and there they were, all stuck in a room together. Like the Catholic counseling they'd never had. Vlado kicked himself for being so easily suckered, as if the Holy Oyster was going to give the miracle blessing and all would be fine and dandy. Well, he didn't need a drink that bad.

Then Vlado noticed the small bundle on Stefani's lap. Her eyes never left his as he moved closer, got down on one knee and reached toward the bundle, which was wrapped in a blanket. One end was open, and he was shocked to see a tiny pair of eyes looking up at him. He pulled back the edge of the blanket and there were the little arms with their little hands and littler fingers, which wiggled as he reached out a finger of his own to touch the teeny thing's lips.

He looked up at Stefani in confusion.

"She's two weeks old," she whispered, as if they were in church.

She. It was a girl. Vlado felt the room fall away from him, and he was floating in space, afraid to look down.

Stefani spoke. "She was left here." She scooped up the baby and held her to her chest. "She needs a family."

Not a daddy or mommy, Vlado noted, but a family. Suddenly, Vlado was aware of Father Kovac standing next to him.

"Who's the mother?" Vlado asked.

Kovac displayed his bad-oyster smile. "I've pledged my confidence. But it's nobody you know. I can tell you there's no reason to worry."

Vlado thought hard about his next question.

"Okay then. Who's the father?"

Kovac actually smiled.

"If you say yes, then you are."

Vlado reached a hand out to Stefani, who took it and squeezed till it hurt. He gave it a few shakes, smiled at her, then squinted at Kovac.

"Maybe we should have that drink now."

And Then . . .

The bad news was that Tom "T. J." Pendergast, everyone's new best friend, somehow found himself with plenty of free time to hang out at Big Sausage, chit-chatting with the younger ladies to an embarrassing degree and annoying Vlado with a zillion questions about making sausage and how do you cut up a pig and who sharpens your knives. The good news was that in the previous six months, thanks to their pal T. J., they'd made tons of money providing Vlado's sausage not to the snooty restaurants, but to the scores of little bars and speakeasies and jazz spots where it was both a nice break from the pickled eggs and salty enough to require another beer.

That year it was Vlado's turn to host Easter. On Good Friday he got a lamb and a pig and dug a ditch in the back yard. He filled it with dried grass and wood and lit a fire which he let burn down to coals. He tossed in the whole carcasses, heavily salted and spiced, then covered them with willow leaves, and weighed it all down with bricks, until only tiny wisps of smoke leaked out of the corners of the pit. On Sunday morning, he resurrected them from their shallow grave and humped the charred remains into his little kitchen, where he carved out the tender meat and stored it in a warm oven, surrounded by turnips and potatoes. He and Joe had already set up tables out back, beneath what promised to be a lovely blue sky, like all the Easters Vlado chose to remember. Stefani's lilies were blooming in the front yard, and along Barnett you could see fresh pots of red geraniums appearing on the doorsteps. He waved to the Ramalo sisters on the other side of the street, who were Orthodox and celebrated a different Easter, out on their porch, ready for a day of pretending not to be interested in what was going on at Vlado's.

They'd all agreed that Martina would make the povitica, Dorothy Penny would make the budla, and Mae Jankovic would provide her famous blood sausage, so there would be no fighting. But it turned out Mae was on a last-minute honeymoon with new hubby—*fucking Stritchie*—so they'd have to make do without, which was secretly fine with Vlado, who could think of a dozen better things to do with pig's blood. And as mealtime approached, Dorothy still hadn't shown up with the budla.

Vlado manned one end of the long table, with Joe at the other. Next to Vlado, Stefani sat with six-month-old Mila Jo Novosel on her lap, the new princess of Strawberry Hill, who looked splendid in her white Easter dress and a head full of colored bows. She'd been a heartbreaker right from the start. Vlado would never forget the baptism, and how his new pal Father Milo looked like he was ready to crack a tear or two when Vlado announced the baby's name. Next to them, Janet Ivan sat upright in her big-girl chair and fed bits of lamb to her baby sister, who gurgled in approval and reached out for more. Vlado watched them go back and forth as if they were real siblings, with their matching dark eyes and pudgy fingers and healthy appetites. He suddenly felt a shiver run through him and pushed a terrible thought to the back of his mind.

Joe said the prayer, then dishes went round and the conversation amped up. They were well into food and drink when Bootnose strode into the back yard.

"What'd I miss?" he asked cheerfully and took the empty seat next to Joe. Oddly, he wore a necktie and suitcoat, and his normally unruly shock of black hair was neatly trimmed, oiled, and parted along one side.

Shortly after that, Dorothy Penny appeared in the back yard with the promised loaf of bread sausage. She looked like she'd dropped down from heaven, her flouncy baby blue dress backlit by the late sun, her auburn hair pinned into coils on either side of her head. One coil was loose with a straggle of escaping locks.

"It was supposed to be an appetizer," Vlado said.

"Since when is there a bad time to eat budla?" she replied and planted it in the center of the table. Vlado noticed that a few slices had already been carved off the end. She took the remaining empty seat between

Bootnose and Inky and Tereza, and quietly helped herself to the roasted meat and potatoes. Vlado stared at Bootnose, who was staring into his own plate until he noticed Vlado's gaze.

"What?" Bootnose said.

"Nothing," replied Vlado.

Bootnose and Dorothy both dug into their food and kept their mouths too full to speak.

"They're working so hard to ignore each other you'd think they were an old married couple," Vlado whispered to Stefani.

Martina didn't have much to say. She sat next to Joe with little Patrick, still so impossibly small, resting limply on her lap, covered in a colorful afghan crocheted by fake-Aunt-Vera. Vlado tried to catch her eye, but she was lost in her world of sorrows.

For the next forty-five minutes, anybody sitting on the porch with the Ramalo sisters would have thought there was a barnyard behind Vlado's house, with all the bellowing voices and cackling chatter, Vlado getting increasingly hoarse with each shot of slivovitz.

Soon Stefani brought out the roll cake and nutbread, along with more brandy. Halfway through his dessert, Vlado clanked his spoon against an empty wine bottle and struggled to his feet. He raised a glass.

"You know, I look around this wonderful table on this beautiful day at your lovely faces and I can only think . . . in a hundred years we'll all be dead." A quiet fell around the table. "So, I say, here's to the next hundred years!"

"*Obitelj*," Joe shouted from the other end of the table, which even those born on the Hill knew meant "family," and *obitelj* and *hvala* rang out around the table as the glasses went up. Except for Martina, who stood, folded Patrick Vladimir into her chest and shuffled into the house.

The following Saturday, Vlado and Stefani showed up at Joe's after dinner in Vlado's Model-T. Vlado didn't mind the car much anymore, and in fact enjoyed tinkering with it on Sunday afternoons, when Janet Ivan might hang around and hand him a wrench or give him advice on how to clean the sparkplugs. That afternoon the two of them had washed it and buffed the finish to a high sheen—at least the parts that weren't rusting.

"Is she ready?" he asked Joe, who nudged open the door, tying his necktie probably for the umpteenth time.

"Maybe. Who knows? Are you joining the circus?" he asked Vlado, who was decked in a green bowtie, straw boater, and red-and-white checked vest, with red suspenders holding up his baggy, pleated pants. Next to him was Stefani, who anybody would agree looked spectacular in her low-dipping green smock, long string of pearls, and pigtails poking out from under a pink flowered bucket hat.

They entered the living room where Martina sagged on the divan. She wore a coral beaded dress that Vlado remembered from better times. Her hair was down, her dark eyes smudged.

"Come on, *bebo*, let's work on this," Stefani said, taking Martina's arm and leading her toward the bedroom.

Soon they re-emerged with the situation vastly improved. Martina's hair was piled into a spiraling bun exposing dangly emerald earrings and a pearl choker. Stefani had powdered over the black circles under Martina's eyes, lined the lids, and blushed her cheeks. Joe seemed to brighten a bit.

There was a knock on the door, and Joe let in Junior's daughter Emily.

"Where's that little peanut?" she said, and Vlado indicated the bedroom.

"Enough dilly-dally, the band is waiting," said Vlado, and Joe took Martina's arm.

The two ladies squeezed into the back of the Model-T while Joe and Vlado manned the front, and then they were squeaking up Twenty-First Street on their way to the viaduct. In Vlado's vest were the tickets for the Pla Mor Ballroom, courtesy of their pal T. J.

"V. I. P., Joey," Vlado had told him. "It means Very Important People."

Once downtown, they pulled onto Main where lines of honking cars shooed pedestrians back onto the sidewalks. Vlado recalled that first time he and Joe crossed over to hawk their sausage, when he had been terrified of breathing the same air as Lydia. But that was a world ago, and tonight, when he thought of her apartment one block over on Grand, he felt only a bit of wistfulness that he swallowed back. He looked again in his rearview at Stefani, with her pink cheeks and bright red lips, and gave his own horn a few toots.

At the Pla Mor, they were ushered in ahead of the line and seated at a four-top near the stage where Moten's musicians were lubing up their horns and adjusting their music stands. Scores of tables ringed the cavernous room, plush curtains draped the arching windows, and flashes of light bounced off the spinning mirror ball and cast a roving glow across the vast dance floor. At the far end of the stage, a thin man in a striped suit and flowered tie was adjusting a mute on his trumpet. *That sure as hell has to be Hot Lips Page,* Vlado thought.

A skimpily dressed cocktail girl appeared and laid down a round of "V. I. P." cocktails.

"See Joey? Very important, right?"

Joe picked up his glass.

"To the annih—"

"Don't say it," Vlado interrupted. He raised his own. "To our lovely sweet petunias."

They were taking their first sip of some wondrous concoction, which said to Vlado that better days were here, when they were distracted by an electronic howl from the stage. A short man in a gray suit fumbled with a microphone. He tapped it, cleared his throat, and the room quieted.

"Ladies and gentlemen, the Pla Mor ballroom and Ladies' Auxiliary Democratic Club are proud to present Kansas City's own Bennie Moten Orchestra, featuring William "Count" Basie on the grand piano."

Vlado recognized the Count from pictures in the *Star* but here in person, centering himself at the piano, he seemed to glow brighter than the rest. He launched into a solo chorus of a swing tune that Vlado knew from the radio, "Moten's Blues," and it seemed as if the whole room was leaning into the stage. The band surged in, and the sinuous groove was off and running, with clipped horn blasts sparring with the slippery beat, then Hot Lips Page soaring over the top, twisting the melody into new shapes and pushing his horn into the stratosphere. A few couples got up and stepped into various versions of the Lindy Hop, a swirling dance perfectly matched to the new swinging beat.

Vlado stood and went over to Martina and grabbed her hand, not looking back as he dragged her to the dance floor. Vlado didn't know the steps that well, but at least enough to push Martina back and forth, who was going along with it but not bringing much to the party. Eventually Joe cut in, so Vlado went for Stefani and the two of them jitterbugged up close to the stage where they were swallowed in the music's embrace.

After a few numbers, Vlado and Stefani returned to the table, winded, where Joe and Martina were well into their next round of drinks. Vlado was doing his best to catch up when a third round appeared and it was clear they were in for the long haul. Martina seemed lost in her own thoughts, but Joe's eyes were glassy, and he looked happy.

The band finished their tune, the applause swelled, and Count Basie strode to the microphone.

"My friends, I now want to introduce you to a dear associate, who will surely entertain you with her accomplishments on the eighty-eight keys. Please welcome the lovely Miss Helene Delacroix."

Vlado jerked his head toward the stage, unbelieving, and watched Helene Delacroix—*his Helene*—make her way to the piano. She stood tall and elegant, her head wrapped in a multi-colored turban with long golden necklaces hanging down from her thin neck and draping over a burgundy gown that almost reached the floor. She squared up on the piano bench and seemed lost in thought. Her smooth skin glowed shiny in the stage lights and there was a flashing in her eyes Vlado didn't remember. He washed down half of his drink, which did nothing to ease a dizzying sense of unreality.

Joey, he whispered, and Joe looked at the stage, then back at Vlado with a worried expression. Vlado continued to stare in disbelief until Helene herself seemed to come out of a trance, looked to the drummer and shouted out "three, four," and the entire band thundered in with an up-and-down rhythm that sounded like an old-time marching beat from the "Junk Man Rag" era. Bands rarely played ragtime anymore, but immediately the crowd abandoned their tables and surged to the floor, everybody bobbing up and down in the revered Turkey Trot. Helene pounded out a stride rhythm with her left hand and bounced huge, syncopated chords off the top at a frightful tempo, while the horns slid left and right, and the marching beat nailed everything to the floor. Vlado watched her ruby lips spread into a broad smile while her eyes drifted shut. His heart was bursting from his chest, beating wildly to the rhythm of a thousand different feelings.

Joe got up, stumbled against the table, and made his way to Vlado.

"Come on, junk man," he said and tugged Vlado out of his chair.

Vlado laughed. "But who's going to lead?"

"Not me, I'm too drunk," Joe said, and they both cracked up as Vlado took his hand and waist, Joe assumed the position, and they went trotting and kicking into the center of the dance floor. Vlado felt like a puppet, with the syncopations jerking him this way and that while his feet shuffled to keep up with the tempo, but he bore down, got ahead of it, and soon was swinging Joe to and fro like they were a couple of high school kids. Meanwhile, Stefani and Martina pushed through and joined them in the middle, dancing up their own storm. Vlado dipped Joe and spun him twice, then looked over at the girls, where Martina was biting her lip and concentrating on the steps. Her eyes met Vlado's, and she gave him the *you're-a-bad-boy* look he knew so well, and her toothy smile broke out like a flash of sunlight.

He laughed as Moten's players kicked it up a notch and he redoubled his efforts with Joe, spinning in time with the mirror ball, the sound swirling around him and the faces flashing by, his head buzzing, and he waited for it all to vanish like a dream, for the song to end, for his heart to give out, for the river to swell and engulf them all. But the band kept playing, and the music went on and on.

Acknowledgements

Big thanks to my top advisor and co-conspirator Mike Magnuson, who, along with Kim Parsons and Kellie Wells, helped me shape this book into something three-dimensional, and to McKenzie Watson-Fore for her hawkeyed editing prowess. Appreciation also extends to my early readers: David Shaw, Susan Berardi, Victor Pollak, Erin Walters, Emilie Harting, Bob Hughes, Richard Krizman Sr., and Claire Krizman, and to the talented Garth Krizman for understanding the book and designing the perfect cover (We're #1). I also owe a debt of deep gratitude to my professors and cohort from the Pacific University MFA in Writing, especially Mary Helen Stefaniak, Claire Davis, and David Long, who taught me a thing or two about sentences and imaginary people. And a special shoutout to the crew at the Starbuck's at 26th and Wilshire for their camaraderie, and for the many hundreds of doppio macchiatos that fueled this book. And hold on, stop the playoff music! Most importantly, I have to thank my partner in love and life, Debra Young Krizman, for making everything possible.

And to my agent, . . . wait, I don't have one.

Finally, a special note of thanks to my grandfather, born Joseph Krizmanic in Lukovdol, Croatia, in 1896, whose bold move to escape WWI and create a life for himself and his family in Kansas City, Kansas, is the reason for this book and so much more. *Zivjeli*, and say hi to Grandma.

www.ingramcontent.com/pod-product-compliance
Lightning Source LLC
LaVergne TN
LVHW041752060526
838201LV00046B/977